The Unbinding the Gospel Series
by Martha Grace Reese, JD, MDiv

In more than 15,000 congregations, 50 states, 49 denominations, 8 countries…

"Evangelism" is anything you do to help someone move closer to a relationship with God, or into Christian community

MOTIVATION – *then* INVITATION

Enrich Spiritual Lives & Deepen Spiritual Relationships → Invite!

Evangelism books presume everyone *wants* to do evangelism, so they tell you *how* to do it. Nine years of national, Lilly Endowment-funded research in ten denominations have demonstrated conclusively that most people would rather get a root canal than think about evangelism! You can tell people to "go be missional" until the cows come home. You can give them great suggestions, brilliant lists of activities to invite friends into faith. How's that working for us?

Let's get real: none of us are going to do anything until we *want* to. Your church won't do statistically successful evangelism until a large percentage of people (1) pray, and (2) talk comfortably about their faith experiences, and (3) think about people beyond church walls. We need to know *why* to share our faith. Prayer & deepening spiritual relationships in small groups stir motivation. It's "*pre*-evangelism." Motivation moves us to action. Once we can answer "**WHY** share my faith?" we'll start wanting to know "**HOW** can God use me?" Now you're ready for evangelism—listening, sharing your faith and actual invitation. The *Unbinding the Gospel Series* helps your whole congregation address first the **Why** (motivation) *then* the **How** (faith sharing and invitation).

Start with *Unbinding the Gospel,* progress to an all-church saturation study with *Unbinding Your Heart.* This creates motivation—people will *want* to invite! *Unbinding Your Soul* will help with your small group stream of invitation and discipleship.

WHY Churches: A Year of Motivation ("*pre*-evangelism")

STEP ONE— *Church Leaders' Studies:*
Unbinding the GOSPEL (red ribbon). Start with a test study with 8-10 "quick adopter" leaders. Pastor leads. (DON'T preach or write newsletter articles – you'll create resistance! Remember: "Evangelism" = "Root Canal".) Pastor: read the introduction and chapters 1 & 4 of ***Unbinding Your Church*** now.

- Study ***GOSPEL*** in eight weekly sessions
- Do the exercises at the ends of the chapters
- Pray with 40-day prayer journal

Lead more small group studies of ***GOSPEL*** with your church leaders and teachers (20% of your worship attendance).

See www.GraceNet.info for *Best Practices* - step by step instructions to use the Unbinding Series

STEP TWO—*All-Church Saturation Study:*
Unbinding Your Heart (purple ribbon) is a six-week version of ***Unbinding the Gospel*** with a new individual prayer journal. We see significant changes in churches that bring the "unbinding" experience to at least 85% of worship attendance. Each week, for 40 days, people will:

- Pray each day's scripture and prayer exercise & work with a prayer partner
- Study a chapter with their small group
- Worship – sermon, music & prayers centered on the week's chapter

red ribbon

SUPPORT FOR STEPS ONE & TWO— *Pastor's and Leaders' Guide:*
Unbinding Your Church (green ribbon) offers research-based best practices for small group leaders, prayer teams, youth leaders, pastors. It provides comprehensive organizational aids, coordinated resources for children, youth & families, worship, full music plans in four styles & 7 sample sermons.

HOW Churches: A Year of Invitation
(Relational Faith Sharing)

purple ribbon

Unbinding Your Soul: Your Experiment in Prayer & Community (yellow ribbon) is for:

- Churches that have finished their all-church saturation study of ***HEART***
- New churches
- New members' classes
- Young adult / college groups

SOUL is the small group foundation for your year of invitation! Seekers would love to try a no-obligation experience of substantial spiritual discussion, prayer and community. ***Unbinding Your Soul*** prepares church members to invite their friends into a four-week small group experience with short study chapters, an individual prayer journal, prayer partner activities & group exercises. A second four-week small group process is included for groups that want to keep going. NEW! Sermons, liturgies & updated facilitators' guide available at www.GraceNet.info.

green ribbon

yellow ribbon

> **See www.GraceNet.info**
> **for videos, sermons, children's materials,**
> **free resources and info on a new**
> **Lilly Endowment study**

"Not even the grumps can kill it!"
"We never want to go back to normal."
"We're baptizing adults and we have an influx of young couples visiting."
"I haven't been so energized about ministry in 15 years!"

UNBINDING the GOSPEL

Real Life Evangelism

2nd edition

Martha Grace Reese

CHALICE
PRESS

ST. LOUIS, MISSOURI

Cover photograph: GettyImages
Photograph of author: David Bjerk
Cover and interior design: Elizabeth Wright

www.chalicepress.com

14   13   12   14   15   16

Library of Congress Cataloging–in–Publication Data

Reese, Martha Grace.
  Unbinding the Gospel : real life evangelism / by Martha Grace Reese.
     p. cm.
  ISBN 978-0-8272-3808-4
  1. Witness bearing (Christianity) 2. Evangelistic work. I. Title.

  BV4520.R42 2008
  269'.2—dc22

                                                              2008036068

Printed in the United States of America

Contents

Acknowledgments

How do you thank all the people involved in a book based on 1200 interviews? This book arises from a national four-year study, the Mainline Evangelism Project. Over 1200 people took time to talk and write about their faith, their ideas and feelings about God, the church and evangelism. Thank you to each of you. You welcomed us into your offices, homes, churches and inner thoughts. I hope this book reflects the best of what you told us. I pray that it will be helpful to you and to others who love God and want to help others move into deeper relationship with God and the church.

The heads of five mainline denominations have been supportive of the project since the very beginning. They read descriptions of the Mainline Evangelism Project, listened to ideas, responded generously with advice, access and support. Thank you, Wes Granberg-Michaelson, Dick Hamm, Cliff Kirkpatrick, Roy Medley, John Thomas and Sharon Watkins.

I can't articulate my gratitude to the people of the Religion Division of the Lilly Endowment, past and present. You have encouraged, counseled, nudged and trusted me since my beginning years in ministry. Your clarity, discernment and heart for the Gospel continue to help the Spirit change our churches. Bob Lynn, Craig Dykstra, Jeanne Knoerle, Jim Wind and Chris Coble: thank you each for your support and wise counsel.

Jacqueline Wenger helped design and oversee the sociological part of the Mainline Evangelism Project with scholarly insight, deep faith and humor. Our full report can be downloaded from www.GraceNet.info. J. Kristina Tenny-Brittian gave two years of her life to interviews, data collection, sorting and interpretation. She served as my conversation partner and prayer partner to make sense of years of stories and information. Thank you both!

Elizabeth Lang Harman and Sarah Emily Gauche are two brilliant Midwestern pastors' daughters who go to college on opposite coasts. They live in circumstances in which Christianity is viewed with deep suspicion. Each has a fresh perspective on evangelism that we, in the safe confines of middle age and established churches, almost can't imagine. They have done research, kept journals, mulled ideas for hours and read drafts of this book. A third amazing young woman, Sarah Montgomery White, has also shared her strong faith, her insights, her questions and love of serving others. My talks with each of you echoed in my soul as I thought about which things were really important and how to say them clearly. Thank you.

My understanding of congregations and ministry have been shaped by two tremendous experiences in leadership: seven years as senior pastor of Carmel Christian Church (Disciples of Christ) near Indianapolis, and the years as director of the Bethany Project, a Lilly Endowment project in congregational revitalization through spiritual leadership. I will always be grateful for those people and all they taught me.

Many dear friends have helped me think about faith, church and evangelism during these last years. Thank you each for your insights, your ability to spot the weak point in an argument, your appreciation of a glimmer of truth. You have prayed for this work and for me. Most of

Acknowledgments

you have poured over this manuscript and made wonderful suggestions. The mistakes are mine! Thank you all, more than I can say: Ann Azdell, Liz Bowman, Ellie Campbell, Laura Cuaz, Betsie Czeschin, Beth Dorton, Chuck Denison, Sue Dullard, Patricia and Barry Feld, Kim Gage Ryan, Nancy Lee Gauche, Jeff Gill, Jim Griffith, Dick Hamm, Bob Hill, Todd Hunter, Julie Ingstad, Tryna Loos, Jerri Lynn, Paul Scanlon, Dave Schoen, Nancy Stimson, Gary Straub, Joanne Thompson, Sharon Tutko, Maribeth Blackman Westerfield and Newell Williams.

I am grateful to the people at Chalice Press for all of their work on this book. Pam Brown, Wes Buchek, Trent Butler, Lynne Letchworth, Cindy Meilink, Lisa Scronce, Gail Stobaugh, and Elizabeth Wright—you have been kind, gracious and skillful. Thank you.

Don Schutt has been a partner in ministry for more than 15 years. Each part of this project and book has been shaped by his insights into people, life in Christ, the church, scripture and by his prayer. I have no words. Thank you, Don.

I used to think it was pro forma good manners that prompted authors to thank their spouses for their infinite patience and kindness, endurance of obsessive narcissism, skilled reading of drafts, sweetly worded advice, prayer, supportive critique, encouragement and enticement to long walks and the occasional meal away from the keyboard. I now see that fulsome gratitude falls short of the mark. Thank you, Russ White. You have been a saint—a patient, kind, insightful, brilliant saint, a sparker of creativity, and ballast.

MGR
Marcell, Minnesota
September, 2008

Note for Second Edition: I have had the joy of working with thousands of pastors and lay leaders who have studied **Unbinding the Gospel** *in the year and a half since it was published. People have stopped me in hallways, left voicemail messages and sent e-mails asking the same big question: "Our church LOVES this book—we can do evangelism if this is what it is! It's great that you emphasize prayer so much.* **But how do we pray the way you're talking about? How do we pray together?"** *This second edition of* **Unbinding the Gospel** *may help you answer these questions.*

I have written a 40-day individual prayer journal (Part Four) that you can use while your group studies **Unbinding the Gospel** *together. (***Unbinding Your Heart** *contains another set of 40 days of prayers for your whole church to use later, if these are helpful to you.) Pray on your own each day. Meet with a prayer partner once a week. Talk, argue, think, laugh and pray with a group of other church leaders from your congregation each week as you study this book together.* **MY** *prayer is that you will have a wonderful time with* **Unbinding the Gospel** *and with these prayers. May you and your group become even more faithful disciples of Jesus and faithful friends to each other. People who don't know about God are waiting to hear from us! Blessings, mgr*

Most of us, most of the time, feel left out—misfits. We don't belong...One of the ways we have of responding to this is to form our own club, or join one that will have us. Here is at least one place where we are "in" and others "out"....The terrible price we pay for keeping all those other people out so that we can savor the sweetness of being insiders is a reduction of reality, a shrinkage of life.

Nowhere is this price more terrible than when it is paid in the cause of religion. But religion has a long history of doing just that, of reducing the huge mysteries of God to the respectability of club rules, of shrinking the vast human community to a "membership." But with God there are no outsiders....

As Luke tells the story, all of us who have found ourselves on the outside looking in on life with no hope of gaining entrance (and who of us hasn't felt it?) now find the doors wide open, found and welcomed by God in Jesus.

Eugene Peterson, Introduction to the Gospel of Luke, *The Message*

PART ONE

- **PART ONE** looks at evangelism in churches today. What is evangelism? Why <u>do</u> it? How is the church doing?

- **PART TWO** shows examples of great churches sharing their faith. You can see and analyze what is possible.

- **PART THREE** will help you move into the possibilities God has in mind for you.

- **PART FOUR** is your 40-day personal prayer journal. Move closer to God through your individual prayer, then discuss it with your ***Unbinding the Gospel*** group.

Wake up, and strengthen what remains (Rev. 3:2)

CHAPTER 1

Breaking the Curse

October, 2004. The country watched as the curse was broken. On the night of a total eclipse, after 86 years of heart-wrenching defeat, Boston fans' cheers ricocheted off the walls of Busch Stadium and ascended into the firmament as the Boston Red Sox won their first World Series since trading Babe Ruth. Ballplayers can be superstitious folks. They believe in things like Lucky Game Underwear That Can't Be Washed or the Winning Streak Will Break. Trading Babe Ruth Was a Bad Thing for the Red Sox. As the results rolled in, year after year, the fans, the Red Sox Nation knew it. But 86 years later, the miracle happened in St. Louis, and the cheers echoed around the world.

About 86 years ago the mainline churches did something. Maybe we washed our lucky game underwear. Maybe we traded Babe Ruth. Lots of people have lots of ideas. But we have not been winning any evangelism series for one looong stretch of time. It's about time *that* curse gets broken. It can be done. It is time to see *our* players jumping and slapping each other's backs. It is time to hear the cheers of *our* fans echoing into the firmament again. It is time.

A Book about the E Word

That's what this book is about. It's about breaking the curse. It's about untying the knots that keep us from living exciting lives in the Spirit. It's about unbinding the good news that God adores us and everyone else, that God has shown this to us through Jesus Christ. This is a book that is unabashedly about evangelism: faith sharing. It's intended for members and pastors of churches that want to start living a more exciting life with God and with each other. It's intended

This book is about breaking the curse. It's about untying the knots that keep us from living exciting lives in the Spirit. It's about unbinding the Good News that God adores us and everyone else, that God has shown this to us through Jesus Christ. This is a book that is unabashedly about evangelism: faith sharing.

for members and pastors of churches that want to share that joy with people who don't know it.

This book is about *evangelism,* the "E" word. The E word seems to have replaced sex and money as That Which Must Not Be Named in our mainline churches! The most comprehensive survey ever made of American congregational pastors (the Duke Clergy Study),[1] revealed that most pastors love being in ministry. It also showed that these pastors' greatest discouragement is that they feel ineffective in sharing the Gospel.

A recent study of Christian Church (Disciples of Christ) laity shores up the findings of the Duke Clergy Study. Over 25,000 members of 262 Disciples congregations completed a 53-question survey covering the breadth of congregational life (Disciples Members' Survey).[2] They ranked statements about their churches according to how strongly they agreed with them. The statement ranked dead last was, "This church is effectively reaching unchurched persons." The second weakest score was in response to, "This congregation provides training in sharing Christ with others."

Most of us feel guilty about our losing streak. Sometimes we ignore it. Sometimes we rationalize it. Let's stop that. Instead, let's look at what's going on and make some changes in our focus, our training, our lineup and our game plan.

The book you hold in your hands can provide a starting point. It was born from the Mainline Evangelism Project, a four-year study of hundreds of mainline congregations.[3] We interviewed over 1200 church members, new Christians and pastors. We scoured statistics and visited churches. We met with pastors and laypeople, professors and seminarians, denominational officials and kids in the youth group. We conducted a statistical study of the beliefs, motivations and actions of 150 of the mainline churches that are doing the best job reaching people with no church background.[4]

The purpose of the study was to find churches that were doing effective evangelism and to discover their motivation. We also wanted to discover what made these congregations, their pastors and their members tick. How do they think? What are they doing? We found some exciting answers.

Our most important discovery is that a vivid relationship with God lies at the heart of real evangelism. People who share their faith love God and believe that other people's lives would be better if they were in a relationship with God, too. They know why they are doing evangelism: they want to share a driving force in their lives. These Christians are growing in their own faith. They

---

This book is about *evangelism,* the "E" word. The E word has replaced sex and money as "That Which Must Not Be Named" in our mainline churches!

The purpose of the Mainline Evangelism Project was to find churches that are doing effective evangelism. What motivates their faith sharing? What makes these congregations, their pastors and their members tick? What are they doing?

learn to talk about their faith. Their churches put a high priority on evangelism—faith sharing.

We will look into many aspects of faith sharing in this book. Here are three highlights:

1. Evangelism arises out of healthy relationships with God, within the church and beyond church walls.

2. Great evangelism exists in churches all along the theological spectrum. The Holy Spirit is the one who gives faith, but churches where evangelism flourishes cooperate with the Spirit. These churches focus on helping new people begin a life with God.

3. People who learn to share their faith say evangelism changes lives—theirs included!

Let's take a brief look at each of these three highlights:

1. Evangelism emerges from a trinity of relationships. Congregations that are doing evangelism best are held together with three inseparable yet distinct areas of honest, loving relationships:

- with God,
- within the congregation and
- with people outside the church whose lives are not centered in Christ.

The heart of evangelism emerges from the interaction of these three sets of relationships: our personal relationships with God, healthy congregational relationships, and caring about people who don't have a conscious connection with Christ. The heart of evangelism is being in love with God, being part of a church you love and caring about other people who do not know that faith. Faith sharing focuses on relationships, not "bringing in more young people," or "helping our church to grow again." Evangelism is motivated by growing love——not by all the lists, bread deliveries, mailings, parties for unchurched friends, small group curriculum decisions or new members classes. Details matter. Means of showing love are important, but the heart of evangelism is love—of God, of church, of others.

2. Key leaders in churches of every theological stripe are doing great evangelism. These leaders hold their churches to a laser-like focus on: (a) church members' growing relationships with Christ, and (b) sharing their faith with others.

People in evangelistic churches can tell you what difference being a Christian makes in their own lives. They believe passionately that having a relationship with God and being part of their church community will help both friends and people they've never met. Many

These Christians learned to articulate their faith and share it with others. Life felt different. They never want to go back to the old days of mute, and muted, faith.

other mainline Christians, along with many mainline pastors, have a hard time articulating how being a Christian matters—for themselves or for anyone else.

Evangelism has no theological bounds. It isn't about talking people into beliefs. It isn't about scaring them with horror stories of Hell. There are no quick fixes, no silver bullets. At its core, evangelism is people sharing with others their personal understandings that life is better, richer, truer if one has faith in Christ and lives in a faith community. These are some of the things that people in churches, many of them quite ordinary churches, are discovering as they begin to share their faith beyond church walls.

3. Faith sharing changes the lives of Christians who do it. Many Christians in evangelistic churches (and their pastors) volunteered striking experiences. When they started learning to articulate their own faith and to share it with others, they began to see "coincidences," "answers to prayer," "miracles." Life felt different. They were more aware of tiny promptings from the Spirit. They say this new life with the Spirit felt even richer when they started seeing changes in the lives of the people with whom they talked about their faith. They never want to go back to the old days of mute, and muted, faith.

> The heart of evangelism is having an alive relationship with God, being part of a church you love and caring that people outside the church find what you've discovered.

One pastor said, "I used to preach and run the church. After the accident, I started talking with people about what really matters in my own life. After I had experienced a tragedy and recovered a bit, I wanted to at least listen to other people about whatever situation they're in. This has given me a feeling of being more in touch with God and of being a more 'full-time' Christian instead of a maintenance pastor. Talking about faith one-on-one and working with the church on it has become completely addictive. As addictions go, it's a great one!"

How to Use This Book

You can read this book alone, but it will help you most if you do a small group study with other church leaders. Elders, evangelism teams, groups of key leaders can profit immensely from both the faith-sharing ideas and the faith-developing prayer journal you can do on your own and discuss with your group. See ***Unbinding Your Church,*** the Pastors' and Leaders' Guide for the ***Real Life Evangelism Series*** for my best advice. (The first two pages at the beginning of this book describe the ***Series***).

Here's my bottom line, best advice: (1) ***Do the exercises*** at the ends of chapters with your small group; and (2) The more people in your church that study the book and begin to pray seriously, the greater chance for real change in your church.

Part One of *Unbinding the Gospel* is a look at "what is." Chapters 1 through 3 deal with the questions, "What is evangelism? Why do it? How are mainline churches doing?"

Part Two shows examples of great churches doing powerful faith sharing. It should help you see what is possible. Chapter 4 deals with prayer in congregations. Chapter 5 discusses the three sets of healthy relationships we found in evangelistic churches. Chapter 6 looks at what new members say they need, and find, in their new churches.

Part Three will help you get started in your own congregation. Chapter 7 analyzes nine types of evangelism, barriers that fend new people off and ways of building bridges into the church for new members. Chapter 8 discusses "who does what" in healthily functioning congregations, with a special section for denominational ministers. Chapter 9 will help you see and deal with the growing pains, conflict, and distractions that can result from growth and change in churches. The final chapter, 10, suggests a year-long plan for several churches to help each other begin a year of evangelism.

Part Four is a 40-day (six-week) personal prayer journal. Underline, scribble thoughts, and dog-ear pages! Please don't try to share a copy with someone. ***Unbinding the Gospel*** works best as a group study, with each person doing these exercises each day. Then come together once a week to discuss what you're learning in the chapters and what God's showing you through your prayer time.

Length of Study. An eight-session study is best (weekly for a class or monthly for your elders or a church board). Combine the first two and the last two chapters. If you must collapse it to seven weeks (the very minimum), put chapters 3 and 4 together. Be sure to begin the prayer exercises (Part Four) so that you discuss the completed first week of prayers in the same session your group discusses chapter 4. Some groups schedule ten weeks and allow extra time for the chapters that spark most discussion.

Discussion Questions and Exercises. Use them! Thousands of congregations are using these books. Their feedback reveals a clear trend: The more you use the exercises, the greater the chance for change in people's lives and in your church. People report that they are talking for the first time about deep things in their lives with people they have known for years. They're praying together. Talking for real is scary, but it produces results. No matter how much benevolent arm-twisting it takes, ***do the exercises!***

Have Fun! One of the hallmarks of the great congregations I've been able to visit is that they have fun. I hope a glimmer of that joy is reflected in this book. I am praying that your reading and discussions

Highlight Findings of the Mainline Evangelism Project

1. If we know **why** to do evangelism, we'll figure out **how** to do it.

2. Faith sharing arises out of vibrant relationships with God.

3. It is important to learn to talk about our faith.

4. Where it flourishes, evangelism is a high priority for pastor, congregation and individuals.

feel light rather then weighty and that they will help you get started on whatever adventures God wants to bring you next.

A Big Thank You…Names…and Stories. Over 1200 people spoke honestly with us about deep feelings and understandings of their faith. Thank you to each of you. This book would never exist without you. I quote many people and describe many churches. The geographic and denominational descriptions are accurate. I have changed people's and congregations' names. Where a full name is given for a person, it is a real name. I have masked the few negative examples more heavily. The quotations are accurate, although I have simplified some sentences and clarified some grammar. A few of the long quotes are compilations of basic stories that we heard again and again. Each of the three stories in chapter 4 is accurate to a particular church—they are ***not*** compilations. If you would like more detail from the sociological portions of the Mainline Evangelism Project, an expanded bibliography or additional information, please download them from www.GraceNet.info.

Let's Get Started!

We have heard stories of inspiration, struggle, excitement, disappointment, spiritual learning and changes in lives and churches for four years. We studied hundreds of congregations and talked with over 1200 people about evangelism. It is clear. We found no rigid formula for success, no magic plan that will work for every church. Each individual must enter the great adventure by thinking, learning more, praying, and asking God a humble question: "Which small things can I do today to help more people know you?"

This adventure may take you on a trip you can't anticipate. You may have to pack a bag and go far. The Boston Red Sox won the Series in St. Louis—not before the home crowd at Fenway Park.

Are you ready to get going?

> We found no rigid formula for success, no quick fix, no silver bullet. Each one of us must enter the great adventure by thinking, learning more, praying and asking God a humble question: "Which small things can I do today to help more people know you?"

---

[1]See the *Survey of Clergy* at www.pulpitandpew.duke.edu/research.html.

[2]Homeland Ministries and Church Extension Faithful Planning Congregational Survey Results, 2001—2005.

[3]The Mainline Evangelism Project, made possible by a grant from the Lilly Endowment, Inc., studied congregations in seven denominations over a period of four years: American Baptist Churches USA, Christian Church (Disciples of Christ), Evangelical Lutheran Church in America, Presbyterian Church USA, Reformed Church in America, United Church of Christ and The United Methodist Church.

[4]See www.GraceNet.info for a formal sociological report on this survey.

CHAPTER 2

Why <u>Do</u> Evangelism?

WHY Do Evangelism?

Let's start at the pivot point. Why did you pick up this book? Why does evangelism matter? Right now, will you stop reading and write down the first thoughts that come to mind?

We made a surprising discovery during our four-year study of mainline evangelism. A huge number of mainline church members and pastors feel awkward, embarrassed, uncomfortable, defensive or angry when evangelism is mentioned. We believe that most mainline members, pastors and denominational ministers would rather not think too much about evangelism. Christian book publishers have said that a book with the word *evangelism* in the title is death at the box office! So you are in a special minority to be reading this book at all. What motivates *you*?

We found that most mainline Christians who are doing successful evangelism are motivated by two things: a love of their church and a living relationship with God. Now, *many* of us love our churches and have a living relationship with God. Why aren't we all doing significant evangelism? One reason is simple. We haven't focused on it for decades. Evangelism has drifted into a side stream of our attention, in denominations, in seminaries, and in most congregations' preaching and teaching. We now have generations of pastors who have little or no training in evangelism. Worse, many pastors have no positive, personal experience with evangelism.[1] And evangelism isn't cool. One pastor said, "Why don't I do evangelism? Do you want me to be really honest? Doing evangelism wouldn't help me get along with my pastoral peers. And I'd look like one of those naive, earnest, sort of scruffy guys to our bishop."

What Is Evangelism?

For this book, evangelism is anything you do to help another person move closer to a relationship with God, or into Christian community.

9

Lack of inspiring emphasis on evangelism in our pastors' backgrounds and training both reflects the mainline churches' feelings about evangelism and reinforces such feelings for the next generation. Lack of training and personal experience—in their churches growing up, in seminary, and in peer relationships as congregational pastors— contribute to ministerial frustrations related to evangelism. Remember? American pastors say their greatest frustration in ministry is their inability to convey the Gospel in this culture (Duke Study). If pastors aren't excited about evangelism, it is unlikely that their parishioners will be. I believe that our pastors' experiential vacuum explains why church members identify key pieces of evangelism as their congregations' two weakest links (Disciples Members' Survey; see chapter 1).

> Our churches are made up of the "evangelism lovers" and the "evangelism-cautious!" The majority hear the word *evangelism* and begin to feel queasy. They back quietly toward the door, trying not to attract attention as they slip silently from the room.

We did discover heartening new developments in the study, but decades of inattention to an inspiring evangelism that fits mainline theology have consequences we will live with for a long time. Evangelism in our churches is like a yellow Lego™ piece that skidded unseen under the refrigerator one hot July afternoon. By the time moving day rolls around four years later, that little Lego™ has collected more fuzzy dust and dog hair than **anyone** wants to look at!

So what dust has our Lego,™ evangelism, collected during these years of snoozing quietly under the church's refrigerator? To begin to understand this, let's look at three areas:

1. What do we think when we hear the word *evangelism*?
2. What difference does it make if people are Christians? and
3. What motivates us to share the Gospel?

What Do We Think When We Hear the Word *Evangelism*?

The biggest predicament we face in relation to evangelism involves our emotions! We talked with over 1200 laypeople and pastors about evangelism during the Mainline Evangelism Project. We asked both individuals and groups: "What do you think about when you hear the word *evangelism*?" Typical first-impression answers included:

- "No! I don't want to knock on strangers' doors and give them some pamphlet."
- "A televangelist is asking for money for the theme park."
- "Our pastor gives this boring, annual, muddled sermon (in a slooow, deep, stained-glass voice) that 'evangelism is pointing out the laden table to a hungry man,' whatever **that** means."

- "My college roommate kept hammering me about salvation and trying to talk me into giving my life to Christ."
- "I cringe at the memories from the years when *I* pummeled people with those embarrassing questions about salvation! I don't believe in Hell now. I think people should make up their own minds, without pressure."
- "I don't even want to *think* about evangelism. We're doing a bad job and we've tried."
- "I know we're *supposed* to talk with people about faith and invite them to church, but I don't want to lose friends. I feel guilty."
- "I don't think we *should* do evangelism—it implies other religions are wrong."

After this book was sent to the publisher, long after I had called evangelism "the E word," I discovered that the United Church of Christ's "God Is Still Speaking" campaign uses the phrase, "the e-word." Another confirmation! Those of us who are trying to do it in the mainline churches all figure out, sooner or later, that "evangelism" is not a good out-loud word! And then, after almost losing hope, the one person in ten will say:

- "I had this amazing experience last year with a friend at work who came to know Christ because of our friendship. It was *incredible!*"

> Many of the cartoonish evangelistic pictures in our heads are caricatures of bad practices.

Evangelism Lovers and the Evangelism-Cautious

Some mainline church people *don't* have strong feelings about evangelism, but they represent a small minority! The Mainline Evangelism Project uncovered a Great Divide in the way our church people, pastors and denominational ministers feel about evangelism. After years of conversations, in my mind's eye I see two groups of people, poised on opposite banks of a chasm that opens up in the middle of the living room when the "E" bomb is dropped into a conversation! Almost everyone is on one side of that great divide or the other. A minority of people in mainline churches are passionate about the importance of evangelism and love sharing their faith with others. The majority hear the word *evangelism* and begin to feel queasy as they back quietly toward the door, trying not to attract attention as they slip from the room.

The Evangelism Lovers

Theology, education, and financial status seem to matter little in determining on which side of this chasm you land. People who share the Gospel as a pattern in their lives, as a spiritual practice, love to think about it and talk about it. They remember specific conversations with people they care about. They call up pictures of time spent in prayer for friends. They have stories of lives that were changed because someone is now a Christian and has a deep sense of meaning and community.

They tell of a man who gave his life to Christ. He is now sober and cares for his family. They talk about a woman disillusioned by a hypocritical church. Now she loves being an elder in their congregation. They tell about a gay couple who have gained a church home. They think of high school kids, off drugs, who have something to work for and people to lean into as they face the challenges teenagers encounter. They have memories of a businesswoman who was isolated and bitter. Now she has organized a ministry to feed homeless people with extra food from restaurants and grocery stores. They tell of a 70-year-old who came to grips with questions about God that had haunted him since he was in high school and his father died. People who share their faith talk about Jesus (if they're theologically liberal, they tend to talk about Christ) and about their relationships with him. They talk about God teaching them more each day.

> Evangelism is no panacea. A conversion moment is a *moment,* and a life with Christ continues for years of ups and downs, of "little conversions."

The Evangelism-Cautious

Now, what does evangelism feel like for most pastors and people in mainline congregations? The very word can push buttons that carry a 220 current! We asked groups of church folks to call out words that the term "evangelism" brings to mind. The air was full of only half-laughing shouts like "pushy," "embarrassing," "uncomfortable," "going to Hell," "awkward," "tracts," "pressuring," "Tammy Faye Bakker," "Bible thumpers," and "Don't **talk** about it—I don't even want to **think** about this!"

After a while, interview discussions tended to center on questions and opinions like, "How can I do evangelism when I believe that many paths lead to God?" "Why do I think I know enough to tell someone what to believe?" "I love God, but I'm uncomfortable with the people who do evangelism. I don't think they're expressing authentic Lutheran (Presbyterian, Disciple, UCC, Methodist, Episcopalian, Reformed Church, American Baptist) theology." "What if someone asked a question I don't know the answer to?" "If a congregation really focuses on evangelism, it doesn't do much with justice issues or deal with the systemic effects of racism." And, "I don't want to alienate my friends."

The evangelism lovers and the evangelism-cautious paint vastly different pictures of evangelism. One is beautiful—it could be an idyllic painting of a mother and daughters by impressionist Mary Cassatt. The second painting is perhaps by Edvard Munch (he painted *The Scream,* which looks the way it sounds and raises the hairs on the back of your neck). These portraits by the evangelism lovers and the evangelism-cautious are both accurate to some degree, but neither captures the full faith landscape.

Evangelism lovers tend to concentrate on the glorious high spots of a life of sharing their faith. They talk about what motivates them. In their enthusiasm, they don't always tell about the teenagers who drift away, the dad who starts drinking again, the depressed 70-year-old's bad days. Evangelism is not a panacea. A conversion moment is a *moment,* and a life with Christ continues for years of ups and downs, of "little conversions."

On the other hand, the evangelism-cautious frequently are living with fears of coercive misuses of evangelism. These fears can stunt one's spiritual life. If our faith is real, if being a Christian makes a deep difference in our own lives, it matters that we be able to talk about that with the people we care about and the people that Christ cares about. Many of the cartoonish evangelistic pictures in our heads are caricatures of bad practices. Some of these ideas are slanted or simply wrong (for example, the thought that evangelism has to do with arguing people into believing they're going to Hell if they don't choose Christ, or the prejudice that evangelism doesn't go together with service to the poor or deep commitments to justice issues.)

Many of these emotions are unconscious. They are the fuzz and dust on the under-the-refrigerator Lego.™ Why should the fact that some people do a bad job of evangelism stop us from sharing our faith? It shouldn't! During the study discussions and conversations, we discovered an exciting thing. The emotional fuzz and dust can be washed off evangelism if we will:

- look at our feelings about evangelism,
- think about why it matters that *we* are Christian, and
- get a grasp of why it could matter that *other* people become Christians.

What Difference Does Being a Christian Make in Your Own Life?

If you ask most mainline church people why they are (or should be) doing evangelism, they answer, "So that people will join our church." Sometimes they say, "We need more people [young families,

People who have grown up in the church think of Christianity like breathing. You just *do* it, you just *are* it! This is the downside of growing up nurtured by the church. It's hard to have perspective on what a life *without* faith would feel like.

children] in our church." This is a secondary focus. I suspect this secondary focus contributes directly to the malaise in our beloved churches. Too often, we slip into treating church like a club. Then our faith slides into thinking first about **church**—about the building, the activities, the friends, the important life we've found there, the ministries we do. We know these ministries can lead to faith in God, a faith life, a prayer life. But we wait too long for the **church** part of a Christian life to lead up to the **God** part of faith. Both are important, but we emphasize the less crucial of the two.

God matters more than church. The purpose of evangelism is to help new men, women and children begin a life of relationship with God. Church supports that relationship. Going to church is not an end in itself. Our failure to focus on our relationship with God has mixed us up. We have let secondary church slide into God's primary place.

The idea for the Mainline Evangelism Project can probably be dated to one conversation I had with some of my favorite people. I was leading a retreat for eight smart, loving pastors of growing mainline churches. Off the cuff, I asked, "Hey, what difference does it make in your **own** life that you are a Christian?"

Silence. **Loud** silence stretched on. And on. I stared around the circle in disbelief. Finally one volunteered hesitantly, "Because it makes me a better person???"

That question hadn't been intended as a pop final. I was not raised in the church, so I have a very clear sense of having made a choice to become a Christian that went against the culture in which I had always lived. I have a good sense of what it is like to be Christian and what it is like **not** to be Christian. Most Christians and most pastors grew up in the church. They did not change cultures to get there.

That silent minute crystallized my understanding that people who have grown up in the church think of their Christianity like breathing. Being Christian is so natural you don't really think about it. You just **do** it, you just **are** it! This is the big downside of growing up nurtured by the church. You think the church **is** the culture. Unless you think about it hard, you assume everyone thinks the way church people do. It's hard to have much perspective on what a life without faith would feel like. So it's hard to help others see what faith would add to their lives.

Since that retreat, I have asked hundreds of pastors what difference being a Christian makes in their own lives. Most reacted

"You know, if we had any *idea* what being a Christian really was, we'd walk around every day feeling like Martians!"

to the question with surprise. Most had a hard time answering. The study revealed a clear difference between typical mainline pastors and pastors who are leading successful evangelistic churches. The "evangelistic pastors" have more complete, integrated, and faster answers to the question.

What Faith Can Be

One Ash Wednesday morning, my ash-crossed forehead prompted three comments at the supermarket (including "Oh, you've got some dirt on your forehead," from a clueless clerk). I mentioned this to one of my wonderful seminary professors, who replied, "You know, if we had any *idea* what being a Christian really was, we'd walk around every day feeling like Martians!"

Annie Dillard wrote, "Does anyone have the foggiest idea of what sort of power we so blithely invoke? Or, as I suspect, does no one believe a word of it? The churches are children playing on the floor with their chemistry sets, mixing up a batch of TNT to kill a Sunday morning. It is madness to wear ladies' straw hats and velvet hats to church; we should all be wearing crash helmets. Ushers should issue life preservers and signal flares; they should lash us to our pews."[2] With that perspective, here's the question: What difference does it make in your life that you are a Christian?

We only dabble our toes at the edges of the waters of faith. Few us have a clue how vivid and powerful life with Christ can be.

Say It in Words

Here's the next big step. If your faith is already vibrant and alive, can you talk about it? That's the challenge. I was at a friend's house when her toddler threatened to hurl himself out of his high chair. Stretching out a yard-long arm, he shrieked "uhh…Uhh, UHH, UUUHHHHHH," as he grabbed for the Cheerios™ in her hand. Sue murmured sweetly, "Say it in *words*, Mac."

Well, if we want evangelistic Cheerios,™ if we want to help people discover the joys of being a Christian, we're going to have to learn to say it in words! What's at the heart of life with God? A powerful relationship between each one of us and the Trinity. A powerful relationship between each one of us and other Christians, all of us together helping to bear Christ to those who don't know him. Now let's learn to say it in words. Knowing it and saying it —that's the heart of evangelism.

Faith Quiz

Do you say yes to any of the following statements?

1. I'm living a faith that doesn't make me buckle my seatbelt when I reach for my Bible in the mornings.

2. I'm living without Christ guiding me through the meetings, conversations and choices of my day.

3. I don't feel a deep sense of repentance or forgiveness.

4. I am seldom aware of leadings from the Spirit.

If you answer yes to any of these questions, please, *please* ask God to help you find a book, a group, a church, a friend who will help you take the next step in a richer faith life. There's more. You haven't yet seen some of the glorious horizons of faith.

Does It Matter That Other People Are Christians?
The Motivation to Share Your Faith

Great evangelism arises out of vivid faith lives. It occurs all along the theological spectrum. The reasons people articulate for why their own faith is important to them are powerful—and personal. But to do evangelism we must take the next step. We must go beyond ourselves and our faith lives. We must reach out to others. We must *speak* to others! Why does it matter that other people become Christians? When we know *why* it matters to be Christian, we will learn to talk about it. We're smart people. When we know *why* it matters to be Christian, we will figure out *how* to help others begin lives of faith.

The move from our own feelings and experience of faith to evangelism involves motivation, a sense of importance, of urgency. Barbara Tuchman, the popular historian, wrote, "With all its problems, Israel has one commanding advantage: a sense of purpose. Israelis may not have affluence…or the quiet life. But they have what affluence tends to smother: a motive."[3] One thing is certain. Like national existence for the Israelis, unless we have a clear motivation to hold the evangelism banners high, they will slip into the dust.

Motivation for sharing faith is the one area in which we found a significant difference between people with conservative and progressive theologies. People across the theological spectrum have deep, personal relationships with God. People across the theological spectrum have reverence for scripture and live in it as the life-giving Word it is. The difference lies in two related areas:

1. biblical belief that the decision to become a Christian is a decision that has eternal consequences (a literal Heaven or Hell upon death) and

2. education and peer support for doing evangelism.

Generally, the more toward the evangelical/conservative side of the spectrum, the greater one's motivation to do evangelism because of Heaven or Hell. Generally, the more evangelical the training, the greater education and peer support for doing evangelism.

One evangelistic mainline pastor spoke with me on the phone for well over an hour. Halfway through the conversation, he began to speak from the depths:

> Ok, so there I was, raised in a fundamentalist church, ordained at 21, served churches until I was 29, and my wife left me. Even though the divorce was not my "fault" according

God is more important than church. The purpose of evangelism is to help new men, women and children begin a life of relationship with God. Church supports that relationship. Going to church is not an end in itself. Our failure to focus on our relationship with God has mixed us up. We have let secondary church slide into God's primary place.

to church order, my denomination removed me from serving a congregation for a minimum of two years. My pastor friends and I had a really hard time staying connected. I didn't fit categories and I threatened them. I was ashamed and a wreck. A friend in my apartment complex was a mainline seminary student. He and his wife and their friends were so loving. They included me, prayed with me, listened to me for hours on end, and finally drew me into a part of the church I had always looked at with suspicion.

Long story short, I became part of a mainline denomination, and you don't find people much more progressive biblically than I am now. I haven't believed or preached that people are going to Hell for 30 years. I wouldn't change theologies at this point. The theological freedom and the grace of this church still amaze me. But I'll tell you, there is one thing that was really hard for me to adjust to. I couldn't believe—I STILL can't believe—how the liberal church that knows so much about God's grace doesn't understand the power of what it has to share. And they don't share it!

I grew up with sword drills and living in the Word,[4] praying every day and training to witness to people about God's offer of salvation. I have years of training that pushes me to care enough for people outside the church to lay my life down for them to help them know Christ. Now I live in this wonderful mainline church. I can't believe so many of my friends don't have the drive to share the Gospel. They've shown the Gospel to me, but they don't share it with strangers. It's Gospel constipation!

I know evangelism was drilled into me when I was young. I know most of my normal mainline colleagues haven't been trained in it. I know 30 years ago when I went to [my fairly typical mainline] seminary, there was a lot of talk about interfaith dialogue and liberation theology. When some new student brought up evangelism, people smiled patiently and sneaked looks to see where he'd parked his tractor. It didn't take us long to get quiet!

It isn't just the pastors. The other piece of it is that the typical laypeople in my congregations with mainline backgrounds are hesitant to talk about their faith. Most haven't had a lot of experience with prayer or scripture.

"I think most mainline pastors don't connect their great theology and biblical interpretation with a real experience of God. It's the converts like me—with my background, training and prayer disciplines—who appreciate the strengths of the mainline church the most. The old evangelicals like me are also the ones to look at the church and sound like the girls in our high school youth group, 'Like, wow, totally, can't you guys pull it together?'"
                —*mainline pastor raised in fundamentalist church*

Talking about God in any very personal way is foreign to them. Once they are exposed to some retreats and prayer groups, Bible studies with real sharing, they're fine. No, more than fine! A lot of them catch fire.

I think most mainline pastors don't connect their great theology and biblical interpretation with a real experience of God. It's the converts like me—with my background, training and prayer disciplines—who appreciate the strengths of the mainline church the most. The old evangelicals like me are also the ones to look at the church and sound like the girls in our high school youth group, "Like, wow, totally, can't you guys pull it together?"

When we know *why* it matters to be Christian, we'll figure out *how* to help other people enter the faith.

This pastor articulated the heart of our mainline churches' predicament. For decades, most of our seminaries and churches have radically downplayed Hell, the classic motivator for evangelism. Interfaith dialogue has increased the mainline church's sense that many paths lead to God and that we should not bombastically insist on Christianity, or on our particular version of Christianity as the only right faith life. It is interesting that frequently the people who know the most about other religions feel the most comfortable doing Christian evangelism.[5] At the same time, training pastors (and consequently laypeople in congregations) in evangelism has dwindled alarmingly in the last 50 years. No wonder mainline pastors don't know what to share!

The theology most mainline pastors preach is grace-filled. Where that grace is supported by a vivid sense of relationship with Christ, it is real and rich. THIS is what we share! It is important. The good news is that we can share our faith. God exists. We have hope. How do we start?

The Mainline Evangelism Project has demonstrated that churches of all theologies can do exciting, effective evangelism. What matters is having a living relationship with God, being able to talk about it, and church leadership that maintains a laser-like focus on evangelism. Here is a way that may be helpful to analyze your own motivation and your congregation's motivation to do evangelism:

The Gospel Overflowing: The Motivation to Share Your Faith with Others

All right, let's say you know why being a Christian makes a difference in your own life. ***How could being a Christian matter in someone else's life?*** If you care about other people, think about how it could help someone to become Christian, to have a much more conscious relationship with God, and to be a part of Christ's body, the church. There are MANY reasons that being a Christian could help someone. Before you read further, which ones come to mind first?

Traditional American evangelism, true to our national individualism, has put strong emphasis on choice and personal responsibility. Classic teaching stresses that each individual's choice—to be Christian or not to be Christian—decides whether the individual will spend eternity with Christ in Heaven or without Christ, in Hell. Do you believe this? Why or why not? Many people in mainline churches say that they "sort of" believe it, but haven't heard much about it in sermons, so they don't really know. Fair enough. (But not good enough! Don't stop there!) We in the mainline churches are supposed to be such clear, logical thinkers, but our thinking is fuzzy in this area. This fuzziness affects our evangelism. This is a critically important question that we should not gloss over. What do *you* believe? Why?

Evangelism is of massive importance if an eternity in Heaven or Hell is the consequence of the choice to become Christian. If you love people, it matters where they spend eternity. This is a huge motivator.

If you don't believe that becoming a Christian saves you from Hell, what reasons do you have to do evangelism? What else could motivate you to help other people become Christians? These are a few of the more typical reasons people name:

- "A relationship with Christ makes life make sense—it's true."
- "I love God so much I want people to know this joy."
- "Being in a church community gives you a way to serve others and keep growing."
- "Jesus told us to do evangelism in the Great Commission."
- "Life with the Spirit is exciting."
- "I used to be so afraid—with my church and with God, I'm learning to trust."
- "As a Christian, you're part of something important that lasts forever."
- "Children need to learn about God. Parents need help raising kids."
- "I used to feel so guilty about things I had done. Christ has forgiven me, and my church friends love me. I want to help others now."
- "God healed me with a miracle. I want other people to know it's possible."

The theology most mainline pastors preach is grace-filled. Where that grace is supported by a vivid sense of relationship with Christ, it is real and rich. *THIS* is what we have to share.

■ "Being with Christ has changed my life from addictions to learning acceptance and grace."

The more important your faith is to you, the more you want to share it. We have hundreds of reasons to share our faith. But the reasons have to be real enough to us that we actually say them out loud.

Imagine that you are like a pitcher. You'll only share your faith when you are filled up with reasons and motivations to help other people with their spiritual lives. If you believe that Hell or Heaven is a consequence of a decision to become or not become a Christian, that may fill your pitcher almost to the top! If you don't believe that, you have to have your pitcher filled with many other reasons to get it to the top. Here's a drawing of a pitcher. It has to be overflowing before we share our faith. What is filling your pitcher? Is it overflowing?

Churches across the theological spectrum can do exciting, effective evangelism. The crucial factors are living relationships with God, the ability to talk about our faith and church leadership that maintains a laser-like focus on evangelism.

Think about the level of your pitcher at other points in your life. Where was it when you first became a Christian? Where was it when you were 17? when you had a child? when you were going through a divorce? when you lost your job? when you attended the most wonderful church service you've ever been to? when someone you loved died? when you moved to a new town? when someone you cared about got the diagnosis?

What motivates you to share your faith?

Our "pitchers," this image of how motivated we are to share our faith, can be filled up by growing faith, by thinking about other people, by encouraging each other to learn how to talk about our faith, by talking about what we believe. But our pitchers can be drained! How?

- by feeling made fun of,
- by thoughts that it's wrong or strange to do evangelism,
- by ideas that you're supposed to know answers to any question that might come up,
- by fear of risking a friendship.

Just imagining these negative thoughts about sharing your faith can drain you of motivation!

What's at stake in evangelism is transformed lives, yours included! You and your church can begin to work together on something that matters tremendously. Here is how some people who are sharing their faith talk about it:

- "I love to see people's lives change."
- "I can't tell you what it felt like to see my sister baptized after all those years and all the tough things she had gone through. It was like a new start. I really understood in the Bible then about being 'born again.' That's what happened to [Mary]. She *was* reborn and her life has been a lot better since."
- "I started inviting people to church and they became Christians. Now nine of my friends who weren't attending a church before are in *my* church. I love these people! I can't tell you what it means to me to have had a part in helping them move into faith."
- "I believe so strongly in the church and the power of God to heal people's lives through this community."
- "I've been praying for prisoners. We have a prison ministry in our church. Four of these people now have a relationship with Jesus. It has changed my life, too."
- "I love the feeling of working with the Spirit that I get when I pray for someone. Sometimes later there's an opportunity to share with them about God. These openings feel miraculous. And if that person comes to faith in Christ from that conversation, it's the most amazing feeling. You know you've helped God change someone's life forever. And the thing is, it's really just being open to God. You pray and wait and then the Spirit does the work."

So, what motivates you?

What's at stake in evangelism is transformed lives, yours included!

DISCUSSION QUESTIONS _____

1. Did any Bible passage come to mind when you read this chapter? Does one occur to you now? Discuss how it connects with what you have read. (If no passages come to mind, you might want to look at: John 3:16–17; John 20:30–31; Isaiah 45:22–23; and Isaiah 55:1–3.)

2. How do **you** feel when you hear the word *evangelism*?

3. What difference does being a Christian make in your life?

4. Why does it matter that other people become Christians? Use the "motivational pitcher" to talk about what motivates you to do evangelism, and what drains you.

EXERCISE _____

Reading assignment for next week: Chapter 3 & Introduction to Prayer Journal (page 149)

Gather a small group of Christian friends. Sit quietly for a few minutes and ask God to bring to your mind the most important time in your life with God. Think about it. Recall details. Share this memory with the others. Let each person talk for four minutes without comment. Pray for the person who is speaking—that they will have exactly the right words and that you will hear them with Christ's ears. (Leaders—time each person's four minutes precisely and remind them when they have one minute to wrap up.) When all have had a chance to speak, discuss how these experiences have formed your life as a Christian. Have you ever discussed this time with God with anyone else? With someone who is **not** a Christian? Do your other group members' experiences with God feel important? How does it feel to be entrusted with these stories? Close with prayer for each other.

_____

[1]Today, only 10 out of 60 denominational seminaries in the mainline denominations we studied require even a half course in evangelism for graduation with a ministry degree. Most of them combine a half semester of evangelism with a half course in stewardship, the other "tough" area in a pastor's life! (How's that for a tasty meal of lima beans and liver? Most kids whose parents had enrolled them in the Clean Platers' Club would sit staring at **that** course until long after it had congealed on the plate.)

[2]Annie Dillard, *Teaching a Stone to Talk* (Toronto, Ontario: HarperCollins, 1988), 40.

[3]Barbara Tuchman, *Practicing History* (New York: Alfred A Knopf, 1981), 137.

[4]Sword drills are Bible verse memorization tests and Bible search contests for kids. "Living in the Word" is an evangelical expression for steeping your life in scripture—living into it and living your life increasingly framed and guided by the teachings the Spirit puts in your heart from the Bible.

[5]One Midwestern pastor serves an old church with high numbers of transfers and adult baptisms. He is as theologically progressive as anyone with whom I spoke. He is a former seminary professor (church history and world religions) and was a missionary in Asia for many years. He has a profound spiritual life. His conversation revealed a deep love of people. He loves Jesus. This ex-missionary, ex-professor with a Ph.D. in world religions was enthusiastic and absolutely non-apologetic about offering Christianity as an option in Asia, and in the American city in which he now lives.

CHAPTER 3

If You Don't Like Statistics, Skip This Chapter!

"There are three kinds of lies: lies, damned lies and statistics."

Mark Twain, in his autobiography,
quoting Benjamin Disraeli, who didn't really say it

This chapter contains statistics, key findings of the Mainline Evangelism Project and some signs of a turn in the church. If your eyes glaze over when you think of statistics, skim this chapter, read the sidebar quotes and move directly to chapter 4, which begins the more practical part of the book. If you are a fact and statistics hound, go to our Web site (www. GraceNet.info) for free downloads of a detailed sociological report based on our study of high adult baptism churches.

You may feel as if you have already been battered with bad news about the church. That is not the purpose of this chapter! Instead, I hope it will help you envision the new world within which we are doing evangelism. We need to know our context before we can act effectively. This chapter will start with that context, then examine a few important, specific findings of the Mainline Evangelism Project. Finally, we will look at some signs of hope.

We need to envision the new world within which we are doing evangelism. We need to know our context before we can act effectively. This chapter will start with that context, then examine a few important, specific findings of the Mainline Evangelism Project. Finally, we will look at some signs of hope.

How We Hear Bad News

I do not set out to bludgeon people or hurt feelings. Still, some of these statistics can hurt. The closer we feel to Christ and the more we love the church, Christ's body, the harder it is to see that body far from marathon conditioning. Like anyone dealing with a sick person they love, we church people have some typical ways of hearing bad news:

1. Shut down. Some of us go within ourselves. We "shut down" to deal with painful situations. Here's how the inner voices can sound:

- "I don't think I need to tell Betty about the marijuana I found in Tommy's car yesterday. She'd make a big deal about it and it would only stir things up."
- "I think I'm going to go to bed early (and sleep really late). I'll think about it tomorrow, at Tara."
- Hands-over-ears: "LA-LA-LA-LA-LA-LA-LA-LA-LA. (Have you stopped talking yet?)"

2. Go into hyper-overdrive. Another way of dealing with uncertainty is to get very active about _other_ stuff!

- "Let's create and ramp up a new sales campaign. I know it's early, but it feels like good timing for the market." (Could the "good timing" be that your wife just started exercising, bought that nasty little red sports car and has scheduled more business trips?)
- "Oh my gosh, I have to get all those Christmas presents wrapped, labeled and in the closet by August 12."

3. Nit-pick. A third way of holding off bad news is to clutch at straws or to get argumentative over picky details.

- "Look, we probably have a whole year's worth of oil in Alaska. OPEC will speed up production. It's ridiculous to think about pouring money into research and development for wind and solar energies."
- "Oh, no, no, no, my cholesterol isn't that high normally. I ate a cheese ball and a bunch of cashews that week. And I only fasted 11 hours before the blood test, not 12."

Many of us can do all three of these "this-isn't-happening-to-me" options simultaneously! Remember: shutting down, rocketing around or nitpicking details can be an unconscious attempt to make bad news Not True. We are built to buffer bad news. When her beloved, 93-year-old father was in the hospital with congestive heart failure, a doctor friend looked up at me as she polished the silver creamer from the sideboard. She had just finished scrubbing out those pesky edges of the kitchen floor with a toothbrush. "Hey," she said in her best clinical voice, "defense mechanisms are a gift from God." We cracked up!

Many older members remember wonderful days of citywide Fifth Sunday hymn sings. They remember when almost everyone from work went to the Billy Graham Crusades and when most of the neighbors turned out for the community Thanksgiving service. Things are smaller now. Many churches have fewer young families, fewer children and lower budgets. Furnaces are older, bathrooms antique.

She was right. But at some point it helps if we put down the silver polish, stop creating that master index for the CDs, and deal with the realities. With that in mind, let us examine some statistics about the state of the mainline church in the U.S. Beware! You may want to get up and go do the dishes or change the oil in your car. You may slam the book down and say, "Well, you shouldn't look at adult **baptisms**! What about all the people who were baptized as infants but drifted away? That's important, **too**!" But if you'll hang in there, by the time we get to the last part of the chapter, some of these statistics and indicators may give you the instinct to say, "Hey! This is interesting. I think God may be able to turn some things around **here**, if we cooperate!" Some of these statistics are **good** news.

What's the Big Picture?

You may be a member of a church that is smaller than it was in 1950 or 1960. Many older members remember wonderful days of citywide Fifth Sunday hymn sings. They remember when almost everyone from work went to the Billy Graham Crusades and when most of the neighbors turned out for the community Thanksgiving service. Things are smaller now. Many churches have fewer young families, fewer children, and lower budgets. Furnaces are older, bathrooms antique. People say, "You know, it's not just happening to our church [our denomination]; this is happening to everyone." Not all churches are shrinking, but that statement has a lot of truth to it. It's **not** just your church. Things have changed in the whole country. Let's take a look so we can see our situation clearly.

Have the Mainline Denominations Lost Members?

Yes. There were 179 million Americans in 1960.[1] Twenty-six million of them were members of the seven mainline denominations in the Mainline Evangelism Project. In 1960, 14.4% of the people in the United States were members of a mainline church.[2] Forty years later in 2000, these mainline churches had only 21 million members.[3] We have lost almost 20% of our members over 40 years. That's not good.

The picture dims when we learn that in those same 40 years the number of Americans grew by 100 million–from 179 million in 1960 to 280 million of us in the year 2000.[4] Remember, in 1960, mainline church members made up 14.4% of the American population. In 2000, mainline church members comprised only 7.4% of the American population. **Looked at as a percentage of the population, mainline church membership decreased almost 50% in 40 years.**

In percentage terms, in the year 2000 there were only half as many mainline Protestants as there were 40 years before.

In percentage terms, in the year 2000 there were only half as many mainline Protestants as there were 40 years before.

Is the Protestant Presence in the U.S. Declining?

Yes. Recent research from the University of Chicago shows that America's Protestant majority is fading rapidly and will be gone by the time you hold this book in your hands.[5] From 1972 until 1993, the percentage of Protestants in the U.S. remained fairly stable at about 63%. However, by 2002 the number had dropped to 52%. Protestants are in steady decline.

Aside from all questions of salvation and religious meaning-making, does it matter that this country no longer has a Protestant majority? In some ways possibly not, but Protestant preaching, teaching and thinking have affected American legislators, judges, philanthropists, social activists, parents, and teachers for hundreds of years. Protestant churches (in particular the mainline churches) and their members had massive impact on the abolition of slavery, community volunteerism and community service, business, prohibition, education, civil rights, child welfare, the arts. The list is substantial. Good and bad, right and wrong, Protestant understandings of what is real, right and important have shaped this nation.

We don't even think about the importance of community service. We just help out with the Kiwanis Club, the Boy Scout troop, the symphony. Who knows how many of the things we "just know" come from being people of faith? Who knows how many of the things we "just do" come from having been raised in a country that has been overwhelmingly Christian and Protestant? That is changing and no one knows the results to come. We may be feeling the leading edge of the change by seeing how much harder it is to do evangelism.

Is America Becoming a Less Religious Country?

Yes. The University of Chicago study also shows that more and more children are being raised with no faith at all. This increases the likelihood that they will be without a religious faith as adults. Only 3% of people who were born in the U.S. between 1910 and 1919 were raised without religion. Now, as 80- and 90-year-olds, only 4% of those people say "none" when asked for their religious preference. That's a tiny number. Only 4% of Baby Boomers, who grew up in the '50s with hula hoops and *Father Knows Best,* say they were raised without a religious faith. However, in their 40s and early 50s, a much larger 11% of the Baby Boomers say they have no religious preference.

Recent research from the University of Chicago shows that America's Protestant majority is fading rapidly and will be gone by the time you hold this book in your hands.

Now for the youngest adults: 13% of young people born between 1980 and 1984 were reared with no religion. Already, 27% of them say they have no religious preference. We don't know if they will return to church as they age. Some undoubtedly will, but the trend is discouraging. Each generation is less involved in religious life than the one that came before it.

What Do These Big Picture Statistics Mean?

What do these broad-sweeping statistics have to do with your local church or mine? Looking at statistics is a bit like going to the doctor. First the doctor makes a diagnosis, then together doctor and patient make decisions about treatment options. We shouldn't get the treatment cart before the diagnostic horse! We can't make accurate decisions about what evangelism looks like or how we should do it until we have a sense of what the people God may want us to reach are like, what their needs are, and what they may know about God. (Evangelistic treatment options begin in Part Two of this book.)

Our big picture diagnosis for the church is that the whole country is getting more complicated and, in many ways, more interesting! We have more types of people, with different racial, cultural and religious backgrounds, than we did 50 years ago. Children are being born to parents who have no faith tradition whatsoever. One hundred years ago you would have had to search hard to find someone who didn't know the Christmas story. Today all we have to do is walk into the local high school. No matter how we feel about it, gone are the days when it's rude to ask someone if they're Christian. It's a real question again. Asked in the right spirit, it's a respectful one.

In 1960, pews filled when a loving, well-run church opened its doors. Today, people who have never attended a church populate our neighborhoods and work places. The next decades will see millions more. They won't have memories of a Christian grandmother, father or next-door neighbor. The thought of "going back to church" when they're in trouble will never occur to them, because they have never been inside a church building in the first place. For them, a church is an alien, possibly intimidating place—not a cradle of comfort and hope.

We used to be able to share the faith easily because just being part of our country took care of some of the beginning parts of evangelism. That's happening less and less. Have you ever said, "I don't talk to people about religion because people need to make their own choices about what they believe?" Think about it. Right or wrong, we have relied on just being American to teach people about

One hundred years ago you would have had to search hard to find someone who didn't know the Christmas story. Today all we have to do is walk into the local high school.

Christianity. Those days of passive absorption are ending. We now have to do more of the beginning work of educating people about the faith, or we will rob millions of people of the option of being Christian. Is that a shocking thought?

We must make organized, conscious, coordinated efforts to change our reliance on "passive absorption" of the faith. If we want people to understand or enter a faith life, we have to figure out ways to share our faith. Now.

FINDINGS OF THE MAINLINE EVANGELISM PROJECT

How Well Are Mainline Churches Helping New People Become Christians?

We don't even think about the importance of community service. We just help out with the Kiwanis Club, the Boy Scout troop, the symphony. Who knows how many of the things we "just do" come from having been raised in a country that has been overwhelmingly Christian and Protestant? That is changing, and no one knows the results to come. We may be feeling the leading edge of the change by seeing how much harder it is to do evangelism.

Very Badly. The main focus of the Mainline Evangelism Project was to find examples of mainline churches that are doing effective jobs of evangelism, to try to figure out what makes them tick and to share what we learned with other churches interested in doing more effective evangelism. In the process of doing that, we discovered:

- New Christians are joining the faith in the mainline churches, but the vast majority are our own children or new spouses.
- 65% to 80% of the fastest-growing congregations in each denomination are in the South or are predominantly racial/ethnic. (Only the American Baptists, at 51%, have a large percentage of racial/ethnic churches. The other mainline denominations are 88% to 97% Caucasian.

These are overwhelming statistics. A huge portion of the evangelism and growth in our denominations comes from natural growth in Christian families, from the South (which is still a "churched" culture—where there is some expectation that people will have a church affiliation), and from vibrant racial/ethnic congregations. This minority of congregations is responsible for about three quarters of our best evangelism.

You could say that our Southern and racial/ethnic churches are "covering" for the primarily Caucasian churches. Statistically, the effect of looking at evangelism statistics averaged together is that primarily white churches are hiding behind better statistics that don't belong to them! In addition to not being fair, these "lumped together," undifferentiated statistics can give the mostly white, mainline churches a false sense of security that things are still pretty much the way they always were. Things are not the same.

Therefore, we decided that it would be most helpful to take an undiluted look, a look that might prove to be an uncomfortable unmasking, at our majority of primarily Caucasian congregations located outside the South. We could tell that the primarily Caucasian congregations outside the South were struggling with evangelism from the lists of the congregations with most new additions, most baptisms, and highest growth rates. We didn't know how bad it was. It is important to know the truth.

Evangelism of the Unchurched

So, we decided to take an unadulterated look at the hardest type of evangelism in the large part of the church that has the least success with evangelism. We decided to look at examples of great evangelism under these hardest conditions: evangelism (a) of people with no church background (the rarest type of evangelism), (b) in primarily Caucasian congregations located outside the South (the large part of the church that is not doing well).

Our purpose was twofold: (1) to see what is really going on in congregations that still form the numerical majority of the mainline church,[6] and (2) to find examples of flourishing evangelism under some of the hardest circumstances. We believe that these examples will help us understand the most important aspects of effective evangelism. We discovered a great deal, both scary and encouraging.

The rarest type of evangelism is reaching people with no church background. We took a deeper look at these churches doing "the rarest of the rare" type of evangelism. We discovered that these churches were also doing a beautiful job of other types of evangelism. (Chapter 7 analyzes all nine types of evangelism we identified during the study.)

The best statistical measure we had to find these churches was to look at the churches that recorded the most adult baptisms. Here's where the questions usually start! "Well, adult baptisms aren't the only important..." "What about people who were baptized as children but left?" "Why did you leave out the racial/ethnic congregations? Is this a racial bias?" We know the questions; we've grappled with them ourselves! Here are some thoughts I would share if I were speaking with your church group right now:

■ The adult baptism, statistical part of our study, was only about a third of everything we did. For the rest of the study, we looked at all kinds of churches and all kinds of evangelism.

No matter how we feel about it, gone are the days when it's rude to ask someone if they're Christian. It's a real question again. Asked in the right spirit, it's a respectful one.

Right or wrong, we have relied on just being American to teach people about Christianity. Those days of passive absorption are ending. We now have to do more of the beginning work of educating people about the faith, or we will rob millions of people of the option of being Christian.

- Absolutely right! Evangelism of unchurched people isn't the only kind of evangelism. We chose it because it is the rarest kind of evangelism, and the type that people who are doing evangelism say is hardest for them. They also say that if they are reaching some unchurched people, former Christians and transfer members flock to their church in larger numbers.

- Each denomination records statistics from its congregations. The categories are different, so making cross-denominational comparisons has something of the feel of sifting through bushel baskets of apples, eggplants, Irish setter puppies and old golf balls! Yes, adult baptisms are not anything like a perfect measure of new people coming to faith for many reasons, but it is the best we have from the statistics our churches keep.

- If you are tempted to object to racial/ethnic churches being left out of the study pool for this adult baptism portion of the evangelism study, remember that we were studying the part of the church that is doing the poorest job of evangelism. Actually, most of the African-American, Hispanic and Asian church leaders with whom I have spoken about this statistical part of the study are delighted that we were looking for the truth and not relying on their good statistics to bring up the average.

- If you need more reasons than this, remember what we said at the beginning of the chapter about how we as humans react to painful news!

So, we asked each denomination to give us a list of every primarily Caucasian, non-Southern congregation that had baptized an average of five or more adults a year (age 18 or over) for a three-year period.[7] The pool of churches contained about 30,000 congregations from six denominations. After months of research and phone call verification of statistics, we discovered harsh facts.

Our findings reveal that fewer than one half of 1% (.005) of these 30,000 primarily Caucasian, non-Southern congregations are baptizing a significant number of adults. We call a "significant number of baptisms" an average of five or more adults a year over a three-year period. All baptisms had to be first-time adult baptisms (not "re-baptisms"), and the number of baptisms in three years had to be at least 1% of the church's worship attendance.[8] Half of one percent is the percentage of congregations doing a good job of reaching unchurched adults. That translates in numerical terms to fewer than 150 congregations out of a possible 30,000 mainline churches.

We ignore this Good Friday news at our peril.

Signs of Hope

There is good news:

Great News! Old Congregations* Are *Reaching Unchurched People. Here is the first green leaf dropped by a dove into the office of the Mainline Evangelism Project. How long do you think the 150 congregations performing all those adult baptism have been in existence? The accepted wisdom is that new churches can reach unchurched people most effectively. That lets the rest of us in all our old churches off the hook, right? Wrong!

We found something wildly different. Our high adult baptism congregations ranged in age from 4 to 270 years! The median age of our high baptism congregations was 96 years old. The average age was 89 years. (Median age means that half of the congregations surveyed were younger than 96 and half were older.) It is now clear: a congregation may be too stuck in its ways to do evangelism, but it's not too old! That's an exciting thought.

A Change Coming: Three Signs

The purpose of this study in mainline evangelism was to search and describe "hot spots" of great evangelism, not to provide discouraging documentation of our lack of evangelism. We have been on the lookout for vivid examples of coherent, incisive, and effective evangelism. We found them. You will hear much more about them in Part Two of this book.

We found something else. Some evidence suggests we may be on the leading edge of a change. These indicators of shifts are not yet widespread, but they are clear.

1. Mainline pastors and laypeople are beginning to see and say out loud that they are not doing a good job with evangelism. It bothers them! Insight helps.

2. Some of the old liberal/conservative/charismatic polarizations are beginning to shift and melt. With that is coming a deeper spiritual/ prayer life and more attention to scripture for many mainline pastors. Spiritual disciplines often free up a desire to share their faith. In effective, small-scale ways, we are starting to learn things people in other parts of Christ's church already know.

3. After decades of lessened activity in new church planting and evangelism, some denominations, synods and churches are shifting their priorities. Let's look at these three signs of hope:

In 1960, pews filled when a loving, well-run church opened its doors. Today, people who have never attended a church populate our neighborhoods and workplaces. The next decades will see millions more. They won't have memories of a Christian grandmother, father or next-door neighbor. The thought of "going back to church" when they're in trouble will never occur to them, because they have never been inside a church building in the first place. For them, a church is an alien, possibly intimidating place—not a cradle of comfort and hope.

1. We Are Beginning to Talk about the Problem

The most dangerous way to face a serious threat or a dangerous situation is to ignore it, to be unconscious of it, to pretend it isn't there. This is the way many of us have dealt with evangelism. We haven't felt good about it, so we pushed the thought into the back of our minds, for later, or for someone else to think about! Many of us are still so overwhelmed with our churches' smaller numbers and lower funding that we trundle along concentrating on "business as usual." Ask any corporate executive, psychologist, doctor or spiritual director what the first step to change is. Chances are the answer will be, "first you have to recognize that there's a problem. *Then* you can do something about it."

Signs of a change are emerging. Evidence affirms that pastors are beginning to recognize that we face a predicament with evangelism. (Remember the Duke Clergy Study and the Disciples Members' Survey referred to in chapters 1 and 2?) We may not know what to do about it yet, but we are beginning to say it out loud. That's the first step toward asking people and God for help!

How is *your* congregation doing? If you can assess the reality of the situation, you can explore options and search for solutions that may really help.

2. Old Polarizations Are Beginning to Melt

Each part of Christ's church has specific strengths. Unfortunately, coordination in the body of Christ sometimes looks like a 15-year-old boy who has grown six inches in the previous year! We have ignored what other families of churches have learned about faith. Each part of the church has different strengths and different gaps. Some have a deep love of scripture; others have greater understandings of the workings of the Spirit. Some have tremendous insight into human beings and human society; others delve into prayer. Evangelism works best with a dovetailed understanding of scripture, the Spirit, people *and* prayer. We need them all.

Some other churches' insights have scared us at times and we have developed prejudices against them. Too much delving into scripture, too much talk of the Spirit (let alone the terrifying thought of the Spirit giving us the words), too much prayer, and we can be quietly viewed as disloyal to our team ("not Methodist," "not Lutheran," "not One of Us.") Remember what Eugene Peterson said about our tendency to turn the church into a club? (See page viii.)

Fewer than 150 out of 30,000 congregations are baptizing a significant number of adults. (We call a "significant number of baptisms" an average of five adults a year over a three-year period.) This represents one half of 1% of primarily Caucasian, non-Southern, mainline congregations.

Great news! Pastors and bishops, board chairs and small groups are starting to toss the disloyalty thinking into the trash. Live, responsive Christians from different traditions are crossing lines that were carved in stone 20 years ago. Progressive pastors in each one of the mainline denominations we studied told about "sneaking off" to go pray with the Pentecostal or Southern Baptist ministers in town! American Baptist, Presbyterian, Disciples and Reformed Church pastors confessed to having a lot of disagreements with Catholic theology and church structure, but having somehow gotten hooked up with Catholic spiritual directors or Catholic priest friends who have taught them life-changing things about prayer, spirituality, and a bigger picture of the church. Categories are scrambling.

One Reformed Church pastor described his pastors' prayer group: "We just started getting together a couple of years ago for someone to really talk to, and now we're praying for all the churches and the businesses in town, and for the county and for the kids. We're praying for each other and for spiritual protection and for conversions to Christ. You wouldn't **believe** this mix of pastors! And after 15 years of decline, things are starting to happen in our churches that I sure can't explain. Go figure!"

These mixes are crucial. No part of the church has a full understanding of the faith: we all have gaps. We each have much to teach the others. We each have much to learn. The more we can exhibit the humility that John Calvin called a "teachable spirit,"[9] the richer our faith, the fuller our understanding, the more joyous the news we will have to share with others.

3. Denominational Support of Evangelism

The shift in spirit seems to have invaded larger groups than individuals, single congregations and small groups of pastors.

- Under the leadership of Bishop Claude Payne, now retired, the Episcopal Diocese of Texas (the Houston area) coordinated a huge drive to do evangelism and start new churches.[10] They started five new congregations during a ten-year period and the diocese grew by 5% a year for a period of four or five years. True growth is possible, with great emphasis on evangelism by leaders.
- The 745,000 member Christian Church (Disciples of Christ) has a national goal to establish 1000 new congregations between 2000 and 2020. Although many of the new congregations are

The accepted wisdom is that new churches can reach unchurched people best. We found something wildly different. The median age of our high adult baptism congregations was 96! A congregation may be too stuck in its ways to do evangelism, but it's not too old.

Signs of Hope

1. Mainline pastors and laypeople are beginning to see and say out loud that they are not doing a good job with evangelism. It bothers them! Insight helps.

2. Some of the old liberal/conservative/ charismatic polarizations are beginning to shift and melt. With that is coming a deeper spiritual/prayer life and more attention to scripture for many mainline pastors.

3. After decades of lessened activity in new church planting and evangelism, some denominations, synods and churches are shifting their priorities.

"adopted" rather than begun by the denomination, the Disciples are on track to meet the goal of 1000 new Disciples congregations by the halfway mark in 2010.

■ The Presbyterian Church USA made a conscious decision in 1965 to stop their denominational emphasis on new church establishment. In 1972, the denomination dissolved its Board of National Missions. Today is a different story. During the decade of 1992–2002, the PC(USA) planted 284 churches.

■ The Reformed Church in America and the Evangelical Lutheran Church in America are putting significant resources into training leaders in a highly effective process for congregational health and renewal called Natural Church Development.[11] Denominational officials and pastors of the churches using NCD are enthusiastic about both the process and the results in their congregations.

■ Moderate and liberal Presbyterian presbyteries in Utah and California have hired open-spirited evangelical consultants to help churches improve hospitality and evangelism. A liberal United Church of Christ conference in the Midwest has hired an evangelical new church consultant to work with pastors and congregations. In a way that the assistant conference minister describes as being mediated by the Spirit, people are open and receptive. They are beginning to see significant signs of growth.

■ Lay movements are flourishing. The Walk to Emmaus/Great Banquet/Cursillo movement is helping church leaders and high school youth to move more deeply into relationship with Christ. They pray for friends and for the church. They hold each other accountable in their relationships with Jesus and in their commitment to share the Gospel. Congregations are delving into year-long Bible studies. Many churches are offering Alpha courses, which focus on the role of the Spirit in evangelistic growth.

■ For the first time in decades, the United Methodist Church is requiring a seminary course in evangelism as a requirement for ordination. Pray that others will follow the Methodist lead.

■ The 8.2 million member United Methodist Church cut its rate of decline in membership in about half between 1995 and 2000. Although the membership loss has increased again in the last couple of years, they have had an increase in worship attendance, a critical indicator of church revitalization.[12]

■ The American Baptist Church has grown 3% a year for several years in a row.[13]

The Spirit Seems to Be Doing Something

Let's say this right out loud. The Spirit of God seems to be doing something in the mainline churches. I am rarely accused of wearing rose-colored contacts. However, after years of working with pastors and denominational leaders, I recognize a pattern of movement toward life and health and an overflowing of the Gospel in the mainline church. We can choose to focus on the same old treadmill of church maintenance. We can choose to be paralyzed by the grief of institutional decline. We can get angry about a lack of vision and power that many experienced during the Civil Rights movement of the '60s and in social justice work in the '70s. But these may not be the threads to follow out of this particular labyrinth.

The scale is small, but new things are happening! Recently I spoke with a United Church of Christ pastor about what he perceived as "one of those crazy reversals only God can do." In 2004, the United Church of Christ began a national focus on hospitality and evangelism entitled "God Is Still Speaking." Conference ministers (the UCC middle judicatory—comparable to a presbytery, a region, a diocese, a synod, or a classis) offered training in hospitality and evangelism that was to lead up to a national ad campaign just before Christmas. Two television stations refused to air their ads, calling them controversial. The ads emphasized that the UCC was open to all people and that no one would be excluded. The refusals triggered an avalanche of free advertising, with coverage on Good Morning America, C-SPAN and other national media.

James Dobson, outspoken leader of Focus on the Family Ministries, entered the mix with a denunciation of SpongeBob SquarePants. Within a week, a huge spongy SpongeBob was shown (in newspapers and on-line) sitting in a chair discussing the situation with Dr. John Thomas, General Minister and President of the UCC. John assured SpongeBob that he is welcome in UCC churches!

The pastor with whom I spoke laughed about this, yet he was deeply serious about the amazing thing he was seeing. "Look, I'm an East Coast *UCC!* We're the social action people. We're knee-jerk liberals. It's ludicrous to think of us doing evangelism. But here we are, doing it! I have friends I met in protest marches talking with people about *Jesus*. This [TV commercial] thing generated about

There are mainline church leaders open to unbinding the knots with which we've trussed the Gospel. Significant numbers of us appear willing to change and learn new things. We are putting ourselves on the line and putting resources—time, energy, money, prayer and focus—behind these efforts. "It almost doesn't matter where you start to do evangelism. God has blessed some pretty halting, stumbling efforts we've made. Maybe when it comes to sharing the Gospel we just need to jump in from whatever point on the shore we're standing and start paddling around."

—*from the pastor of an Ohio congregation*

30,000 hits a week on the UCC 'find a church in your area' Web site link. I think this whole situation is so off the wall only God could be arranging it."

This is the good news. Large numbers of pastors, church members, elders, deacons, heads of church councils and evangelism committees, synods, regions and entire denominations stand ready to open their minds and hearts to the idea of unbinding the knots with which we've trussed the Gospel. Significant numbers of us appear willing to change and learn new things. We are putting ourselves on the line and putting resources—time, energy, money, prayer and focus—behind the efforts. Our efforts are bearing some fruit.

As the pastor of a now rapidly growing Ohio church said, "You know, it almost doesn't matter where you start with evangelism. God has blessed some pretty halting, stumbling efforts we've made. Maybe when it comes to sharing the Gospel we just need to jump in from whatever point on the shore we're standing and start paddling around."

Lots of different things are being tried to help new people move into a deeper relationship with Christ, into an experience of powerful Christian community. Almost everyone we have seen doing effective evangelism—pastors, laypersons, regional ministers—stresses the joy and personal renewal of moving into a ministry where sharing Christ is at the center.

Each of us has a choice: Will I decide to let go of one or two of my old opinions and fears and join in these new things God is doing?

DISCUSSION QUESTIONS _____

1. *How is your individual prayer going? Spend the first 15-20 minutes of your group time talking about the highlights: What was the most wonderful prayer day? What happened? What did you learn? What challenged you? What are you wondering about? Go around the circle and everyone say something!*

2. Do statistics generally fascinate or frustrate you? Which statistics in this chapter do you find most disturbing? Most hopeful?

3. If you could change one statistic you have read, what would it be? How would you change it?

4. How has reading this chapter changed your ideas about the importance of faith sharing?

5. Did any Bible passage come to mind when you read this chapter? Does one occur to you now? Discuss how it connects with what you have read. (If no passages come to mind, you might want to look at: Isaiah 43:18–19; Habakkuk 1:5; and Psalm 46:1–2.)

EXERCISE

Most churches keep careful records of worship attendance, membership, new members, baptisms, people who have transferred to another church or become inactive, and deaths of members. Retrieve the records for these areas of your church life for the last five years. Do you remember the people who joined? Who was baptized? Who were the people who moved away? Who passed on? Write down as many names as you can remember and describe these people to anyone who didn't know them. Tell a short story about the people you loved who died, the people who became Christians, the babies baptized.

Gather in a circle and pray for each of these people. Ask God to bless them. Thank God for their part in your life and in your church. Then pray for the people who God can bring into faith and into your congregation in the next few years. Imagine who they might be, what they might look like. Pray for the ones you can't imagine. If any specific people come to mind that you think God may be able to reach through you or your church, name them in prayer. Write those names down and commit with each other to pray for them in the coming days and weeks.

Start your prayer journal tomorrow.

---

[1]In some ways, 1960 is an unrealistic "high water" mark of church attendance. However, it is extremely difficult to get accurate denominational figures much older, and 1960 is a year many mainline Christians remember.

[2]The number of people in church on a given Sunday usually ranges from half to a quarter of official membership numbers.

[3]All calculations for these figures are as conservative, simple and realistic as we could make them. Four of the denominations have had mergers between 1960 and 2000, so we added together the denominational figures for the merging churches at the beginning. In two cases, a sizeable number of churches left the denomination. We have taken those churches (the Lutheran Church Missouri Synod and the Independent Christian Churches and Churches of Christ) out of the numbers from the beginning, so they never show up in these tables. So, for example, the Evangelical and Reformed churches are counted as part of the UCC numbers in 1960, even though the merger between the E & R and the Congregational Christian Churches hadn't yet occurred. The Missouri Synod Lutherans and the Independent Christian Churches are **not** listed in 1960 figures for the ELCA and the DOC even though they were counted in denominational numbers at the time. Our intent is to show only true decline, since no one would make the case that Missouri Synod Lutherans or Independent Christians are lost to the Kingdom! Our figures are compiled from the American Religion Data Archive at www.thearda.com/Denoms/Family.

[4]Population figures are from the U.S. Census, 1960 and 2000, http://www.census.gov/prod/2002pubs/censr-4.pdf.

[5]The University of Chicago's National Opinion Research Center (NORC) published a study in July 2004 called "The Vanishing Protestant Majority." The principal author of the study is Tom W. Smith, who is also Director of NORC's General Social Survey, one of the most scientifically reliable gauges of public trends. For details or full text of the study, see www.norc.uchicago.edu., Tom W. Smith and Seokho Kim, "The Vanishing Protestant Majority," *GSS Social Change Report No. 49* (NORC/University of Chicago, July 2004), 21 (http://www.norc.uchicago.edu/issues/PROTSG08.pdf).

[6]We could not include the United Methodist congregations in the final adult baptism numbers because they do not keep separate adult baptism statistics, but we

made random phone calls and interviews with pastors from the list of the top UMC baptism congregations. Our unofficial conclusions are that the UMC can rely on the data that we have gathered for the rest of the mainline churches—they are not very different, in one direction or the other.

[7]We found significant denominational record-keeping differences, mistakes in record-keeping and data entry, and theological differences between infant and believers' baptisms and "re-baptisms." We made the lists as comparable as possible and verified congregational statistics with hundreds of phone calls to congregational record keepers and pastors. Although United Methodist congregations were called, interviewed and participated in the survey, they are not included in the pool of 30,000 congregations because they do not keep distinct adult baptism records. For a more complete report of the survey results and our judgment calls to correlate and verify data, please see the Mainline Evangelism Project report by Jacqueline E. Wenger with Martha Grace Reese and J. Kristina Tenny-Brittian at http://www.GraceNet.info.

[8]To be included, the congregation's average number of baptisms over the three-year period had to represent at least 1% of average worship attendance. We excluded churches like a great congregation that grew more than 350% in worship attendance in a decade. It now has 10,000 members with 4000 people in worship each week. This church performed exactly 15 adult baptisms over a three-year period (the per capita equivalent of a church with 80 in worship baptizing one adult a decade!) We studied these large congregations for other purposes, but did not include them in the group to which we sent surveys.

[9]See Richard Robert Osmer, *A Teachable Spirit* (Louisville: Westminster/John Knox Press, 1990), 52–58. See also pp. 84–138 for a beautiful analysis of Martin Luther's understanding of the teaching office in comparison to Calvin's.

[10]For the story of the Diocese of Texas's effective efforts, see Bishop Claude Payne and Hamilton Beazley, *Reclaiming the Great Commission: A Practical Model for Transforming Denominations and Congregations* (New York: Jossey-Bass, 2000).

[11]For more information on Natural Church Development, see the Web site at http://www.ncd-international.org or read Christian A. Schwartz's *Natural Church Development: A Guide to Eight Essential Qualities of Healthy Churches* (Carol Stream, Ill.: Church Smart Resources, 1996).

[12]See the "2004 Statistical Review," copyright 2005, by the General Council on Finance and Administration, The United Methodist Church (http://www.gcfa.org/StatRev.pdf).

[13]"New Life 2010 Report Card Mid-course Gatherings 2004," published by the American Baptist Churches USA at http://www.nationalministries.org/newlife/docs/report_card.pdf.

Unbinding the Gospel

PART TWO

- **PART ONE** of this book focused on "what is," both in the church and in our individual lives and thinking.

- **PART TWO** should focus your sights on new possibilities for what could be.

- **PART THREE** will help you start moving toward that goal.

- **PART FOUR** is your 40-day personal prayer journal. Move closer to God through your individual prayer, then discuss it with your *Unbinding the Gospel* group.

Hear my voice and open the door
(Rev. 3:20)

CHAPTER 4

Unbinding the Gospel

Three Stories of Victory

In an *Anne of Green Gables* book I read as a girl, Miss Cornelia, staunch pillar of the Presbyterian church, asked one of her friends about another woman's health. "Oh," Susan said, "I'm afraid she's going to have to rely on the Lord now." "Oh, no!" Miss Cornelia responded, "Surely it isn't as bad as all that?"[1]

If you read the beginning of the last chapter, you might have suspected that Miss Cornelia was inquiring about the health of the mainline Church. "I'm afraid we're going to have to rely on the Lord now! Oh, no! Surely it isn't as bad as all that?" Well, you know, it *is* as bad as that. People, families, churches, denominations and the aircraft carrier USS Nimitz don't make radical shifts in trajectory easily. Our denominations and many of our congregations have been on a downward pathway for decades. It would take a miracle to turn things around.

It will take a miracle to turn things around.

Isn't that what God has promised to do through us? Doesn't Jesus tell the disciples that they will do greater things than John the Baptist? (Lk. 7:28). Doesn't Jesus tell the disciples that after he left and the Spirit came, that they could do greater things than *he* could do? (Jn. 14:12). Doesn't Jesus tell the disciples that what they agreed on together in prayer God would do for them? (Mt. 18:19). We're the disciples. The decline of the mainline church is not merely serious. In Søren Kierkegaard's words, it is a "sickness unto death." We must not ignore this fact.

> It would take a miracle to turn things around.
>
> Isn't that what God has promised to do through us?

41

We must do the only realistic thing. We need to look the facts in the face, to pray that God lets us continue to love and honor God, and to see the state of the churches with as much clarity as each one of us is able to bear. Then we can ask God to guide us, step by step, to do whatever things we're each supposed to be doing. If we really believe in crucifixion and resurrection, in a life of worshiping God and surrendering self, what real option do we have but to let God guide us through thought, study and open-spirited prayer?

A regional minister (bishop, synod executive) confessed at the beginning of a first long prayer retreat, "Well, you know I've been doing this ministry for 24 years now. We've strategized and prioritized and done mission statements that have kicked around the backs of closets. We've never prayed together except to say, 'God, bless this fight.' We've tried everything else; we might as well try prayer. What have we got to lose?"

> We each touch the heart of the faith through our individual interactions with God. This relationship is nurtured in community. It is expressed through community. But at its center stands each of us, individually, being given glimpses of God's face.

How's it going under your own steam? Is it time to try to hand this church to God? Things change when people surrender time, choices and decisions to God. Are you ready to try it? Whatever you try won't be perfect. Yes, some congregations are too far in decline to turn around. Yes, many of us will have such needs for security that we will continue doing the same old things even though they haven't worked. Yes, not everyone will join in. Many dear, hardworking, faithful Christians—for one reason or another—will waste more energy and time, opportunities, life and money.

But there really *is* a God. And we each need to decide if we're going to let God work through us and do miracles that accomplish amazing, unexpected things among us. There really *is* a God, and that God will nudge us into the most curious places—into conversations that are impossible to anticipate, in directions that we couldn't have thought out for ourselves.

After years of talking with pastors and laypeople in churches that are thriving, and in churches that are failing, I am clear that the only way to do ministry successfully, to lead a church or to live a life in today's United States is to pray deeply. We must hand ourselves over to God in clear-headed, accountable, non-naive prayer. We need to rely as much on God for pragmatic guidance as we can stand! Without God vividly in the mix, we drift, life declines.

What does trusting in the Lord look like? After all those statistics and hard facts in chapter 3, it seems wrong to have some formulaic chapter on "How to Do Evangelism in Your Church." Instead, let's do what we might do if Jesus were here. Sit down and listen to some stories. Curl up on the sofa and hear what the Spirit might be saying through three stories of different churches. See what you think. The names are changed; denominations and locations are accurate.

Story One: What Do You *Mean,* "Sit and Pray"?

Benton Street Christian Church (Disciples of Christ) is a solid, healthy congregation. The staff is beloved. They have been together for 15 years. The church is administered efficiently and with grace. It has been growing smoothly and steadily for 15 years. People respect and like each other. The congregation is typically Midwestern, moderate to fairly progressive in theology, with deep biblical roots. The associate minister, Connie, has great relational gifts and a rich spiritual life. The church formed a new evangelism team a year and a half ago. I met them for lunch as they started. The four women's energy and excitement impressed me immediately. They kept asking me what to do. For once in my life, I didn't tell them. I felt they were up to a challenge, so instead I said, "Will you all trust me?"

> We work so *hard,* but the joy, the "first love," the "in love" feelings with God fade to dusty duty, good works, more work.

"Sure, Gay, anything you say."

"Would you spend three months praying together and not do anything else, not make any decisions for three whole months?"

"WHHHAAAAAATTTTTT?????"

"Yes," I murmured sadistically. "You three pray. Meet every week for at least an hour. Pray for the church, for the members, for discernment and for the people you don't even *know* that God would love to be able to bring to Benton Street. Pray that you'll be open. Pray for each other and what's going on in your lives. Pray that God will show you what you're to do and that God will nudge the right people to help you. But promise me that you won't make any decisions or do any "work" for three months. You can read a few books, but mainly pray, okay? What do you think?"

"Can Connie lead our meetings?" (In grief theory, this is known as "bargaining.")

"Why don't you pray about whether she should lead the meetings?"

"Oh. Hmmm. Okay."

So began an Agony and Ecstasy three months. The evangelism team prayed together frequently (**with** Connie present, **without** Connie leading). Every morning at 7:30, wherever they were, they prayed. They read books and searched the Internet. They went to board meetings every month and reported what they were doing. Everyone asked, "Ok, so what is your committee doing now?" They gave their report: "We're still praying. We're not allowed to make any decisions yet, but we are praying for you all and the church and the new people." This was no typical committee report, but the board laughed and loved it. The evangelism team received some gentle ribbing. Then they started getting prayer requests.

Exactly four months after our lunch, Connie told me that at the end of their three-month sentence, the team of three women had leapt out of the starting gate like Preakness winners. Now almost 50 people were helping with evangelism. I blurted,

"Wwwwwhhhhhaaaaattttttt?????"

"Yea, they're welcoming people in worship and talking about the Spirit. Right after the worship service, we encourage visitors to pick up a small gift at our new welcome center. People bake bread, and "Loafers" deliver it to first-time visitors. We have other gifts for first-time visitors at a welcome center outside the sanctuary. There's a computer analyst keeping lists of visitors and we're praying for them. They've decided that we may be situated by God to have a ministry to the apartment complex near the church."

Later on, the evangelism team had 65 members, including intercessors and thank-you gift teams, designers of little feedback and prayer cards. A schizophrenic person visited one Sunday. A social worker pitched in to do follow-up. Visitors were increasing, return visitors were increasing, baptisms were increasing, baby dedications were increasing. I met with the team ten months into the experiment. They were thrilled. They were starting to get a little tired. I asked if they were praying as much. "Oh, oops. I guess we've sort of let that slip. It has been feeling dry and sort of like work. I guess we pick up the prayers again, right?" "Sounds like a plan," I agreed.

Connie wrote to me, "It was incredibly difficult for these four 'can-do' women to *wait* in prayer. All four of us have highly motivated, extremely organized, get-it-done personalities. A year and a half later, all four of us would say our prayer lives have been permanently impacted by this experiment. Two of us have moved into leadership in other areas of the church's ministry and are continuing to emphasize the importance and priority of prayer. The entire church is still being impacted by this willingness to risk praying first."

Exactly a year after our lunch, Benton Street held a board meeting at which the evangelism team presented their report. Instead of the traditional 6 or 7 infant dedications, they had 16, 15 of which were of children of new members or visitors. New members and visitors were involved in small groups. There were 80 new members. That

We must do the only realistic thing. We need to look the facts in the face, to pray that God lets us see the state of the churches with as much clarity as each one of us is able to bear. Then we can ask God to guide us, step-by-step to do whatever things we're each supposed to be doing.

was wonderful. But possibly as extraordinary was the fact that 65 long-term members of that church had a hand in praying and helping to reach out to people they didn't know. Many of those lifelong Christians had experienced intercessory prayer and nudges from the Spirit for the first time in their lives. They felt it individually, they saw it together, and they heard those new voices in worship saying, "Yes, I accept Jesus Christ as my Lord and Savior." Benton Street members listened with lumps in their throats to the tight voices of parents vowing to raise their children in Christian homes. They are living in answered prayer; they are living *into* answered prayer.

Story Two: The Gift from Honduras

I placed hundreds of phone calls to pastors whose churches had the highest rates of adult baptisms in their denominations. These conversations transported me into the worlds of extraordinary congregations led by some wonderful men and women. One call I won't forget soon was with Don, the lead pastor of a 42-year-old Reformed Church in America (RCA) congregation in California. I explained about the evangelism study and told Don that his congregation was among a handful of mainline churches across the country that were doing lots of adult baptisms. I asked him to tell me what made the church tick, what motivated the members, what he believes, and how he leads.

So he started. He loves the church. Like most of the pastors who are doing lots of adult baptisms, he was surprised that they were doing relatively well (his church is in the top hundred in that pool of 30,000 mainline congregations). He talked for a solid 40 minutes about the church. He's been there for 12 years. He told me about worship decisions, what types of services they have (two contemporary and one traditional so they don't have to be too blended, which helps both their longer-term parishioners and the new people they're trying to reach). They've grown from 500 to about 960 adults in worship, not counting the 300 kids.

He told me about "life stage ministry" for the 20- and 30-year-olds and the gifted minister they have working with these younger folks. I heard about small groups, about Celebrate Recovery (a model for expressly Christian 12 step groups). Don told me about education classes they offer, ways they're working consciously to teach and integrate the new members they're attracting.

He was born and raised in the Reformed Church in America in the Midwest. He had his "fires lit" about evangelism as a young

"For 24 years... we've strategized and prioritized and done mission statements that have kicked around the backs of closets. We've never prayed together except to say, 'God, bless this fight.' We've tried everything else: we might as well try prayer. What have we got to lose?"

—from a regional minister

man—he's in his 40s now. The minute he started talking about evangelism and sharing the Gospel with new people, his voice gained energy. Then he told me more about what they're doing with the 25-40 age group (contemporary praise music). He referred me to "this guy in San Jose who's doing amazing stuff with postmoderns—it's an RCA church plant specifically aimed at postmoderns and it's much edgier than anything we're doing." He talked about how important music is for younger people. He said they invite these younger adults to come forward and kneel for prayer and communion. These practices helps young adults worship in a way that feels real to them. Small groups foster intimacy, connection and peer relationships.

> Prayer is the way to stay in love with God. Prayer is the way individuals, small groups and congregations grow and become vivid. It is a habit, a discipline, but not discipline with a clenched jaw.

After at least 40 minutes, I asked a question. "You've been telling me amazing things about what God's doing in the church and in people's lives. You haven't mentioned prayer. Does prayer enter into your ministry in any special way?"

.......Silence......

"Oh, my gosh. Wow, don't let Beth, my wife, know I didn't say anything about prayer sooner." (He later told me it was okay to tell you this story. So did Beth.)

"Oh, listen." *(Trust me, I was listening.)* "Prayer is a HUGE thing here. We have a prayer action team that's a group committed to fasting and prayer. They undergird every thing we do. You almost can't talk about it as a separate thing because the prayer is right there all the time. It has changed everything. Prayer makes openings, and we see possibilities and shifts and openings happening all the time. Now that I think about it, we really assume the Spirit's going to be leading."

"When did the praying start?" I asked him. "What does it look like? I take it Beth's very involved?"

"Six or seven years ago, Beth and I went to Community Church of Joy[2] for a week-long training event. It was great to be together and to get away for a new perspective. At the conference, you picked different sessions to attend. I went to the worship, administration and leadership sessions. Beth started going to sessions on prayer."

The prayer training affected Beth powerfully. On their return, she began to train a group of people to do intercession—to pray for others. In 2000, their classis (the Reformed Church version of a region, conference or synod) sponsored a joint workshop on prayer with the Moravian Church. A small group of Moravian Indian lay brothers from a tiny mountain town in Honduras were visiting. Beth and a couple of people from the church went. The brothers told about their ministry of intercession and fasting. Beth described the brothers to me in a later phone call. She was stunned by the men's simplicity, depth and integrity. During a later prayer retreat, the lay brothers taught 30 people from Beth and Don's congregation about prayer and fasting. Beth said that the most important thing the brothers taught them was to trust in the Spirit and to listen to God. Not talking. *Listening.*

"That was the beginning of another stage in the long journey," Don said. For two years, a changing group of 75 people participated in worship, praise, fasting and intercession for the first weekend of each month. "Now we have a group of four to six people praying for every single worship service. We have a group of intercessors for every minister in the church and a PIT team [Prayer and Intercession Team] for each ministry in the church."

Beth is a woman with a deep faith life. She is both wife and daughter of RCA ministers. She is a born teacher. As she explained prayer in the congregation, she had a clear grasp of ways people could begin to understand prayer and how they could move into deeper layers of experience. Her combination of deep sensitivity to the Spirit's promptings and her gift mix to teach, inspire and maintain relationships is clearly a major reason that prayer has taken such a deep hold in the congregation.

I asked what these nine years of learning and leading the prayer ministry had been like for her. Beth replied, "The best way I can describe it is as a journey. What I understand is changing; what we're led to do changes; we keep learning. I used to pray with lists: every Monday I prayed for the children's schools and their teachers and all the students. The next day I moved to my Tuesday list. Now I listen to God more and God gives me the people and the situations to pray for.

I asked her, "Can you articulate any differences the prayer makes in the congregation?"

"It's hard to say," she said. "Prayer is so subtle and so hidden. Sometimes it's hard to be part of the prayer ministry in the church because it never gets the big splash announcements in worship. We depend on word of mouth. Seeing results has a lag time. I'm starting to give workshops and teach in other churches. Often they're discouraged because maybe only three people will show up for a prayer event. I tell them that those must be the three God wants there that day.

Many of those lifelong Christians experienced intercessory prayer and nudges from the Spirit for the first time in their lives. They felt it individually, they saw it together, and they heard those new voices in worship saying, "Yes, I accept Jesus Christ as my Lord and Savior." Benton Street members listened with lumps in their throats to the tight voices of parents vowing to raise their children in Christian homes.

—Story 1

You have to let go of the idea that numbers matter or that it's visible results that count. That's very difficult for Americans in our culture to understand. It's hard not to have immediate results.

"But if we can leave the results of our prayer to God, if we can just praise God and listen to God rather than giving him a list of what we want, things do happen. On Friday this week, we're having a Halloween party for the children of the community. We're expecting about 2000 people from the community to visit our church. There will be "Prayer Walkers" moving through the crowd the entire time they are here. The Prayer Walkers are praying all the time, that specific children and parents will see Christ in something that happens, that some of the families will be moved to come to worship.

"We started using Prayer Walkers during our Vacation Bible School, praying that the children would learn, that this would change their lives. The number of children who made some kind of commitment to Christ has gone way up. We began having intercessors pray together [in a different room] during the entire four hours of our adult new members' class. There's a part in this first-level, introductory class where Don asks if anyone who has not become a Christian will make that decision and commitment. The number of those commitments has skyrocketed since we have been interceding for them."

I asked Don if he could articulate how all of the prayer had changed things in the church. He said, "The spirit of the church is different. There are 'coincidences' that I know are answered prayer. We are more flexible. We have fewer disagreements. When we plan things, every once in a while someone will say, 'Wait a minute, what if we did this, instead?' Everyone will think about it for a minute, and many times we change direction. We can turn on a dime in this church. People are less attached to their own ideas and presuppositions. I haven't seen that happen, especially to this degree, anywhere else. You can't define it. You just get to know how different things are."

Story Three: Tuesday Mornings with the Guys

Andy is a thoughtful, gentle pastor with a quiet sense of humor. He has a humble spirit and has faithfully served First Presbyterian for over 20 years. He has done beautiful ministry, because the church hasn't shrunk. They have 125 people in worship (200 members). Their entire Midwestern county has only 4,500 people. The county has lost population every census since 1900, when it claimed 13,500

How's it going on your own steam? Is it time to try to hand this church to God?

residents. The county has the same number of churches today as in 1900. This includes two small Methodist churches and an Assemblies of God new church start. Jobs disappear quietly. Many of the younger people and families have to move away to get better work. The town is not only shrinking, but the population is aging. So is the church. But, in a quiet voice, Andy talked about what it's like to serve these people and how hard they try.

About two years ago, a new Methodist minister came to town. The four pastors began to pray together every Tuesday morning for two hours. Andy said, "At first I thought, 'How in the *world* could I give two hours a week to pray with these guys?' Now I really miss it if we don't meet one week. It's really a support group as well as a praycr tcam. Thc competition between us is gone. That's a big thing, because we have four churches and only 1,700 people in the whole town. We've realized we're going after the people in town who aren't doing anything."

"How do you spend the two hours together?"

"Well, we talk a little bit about how each of us is doing and about where our churches are. We pray for each other, and for our churches, but then we're also praying for the people who don't attend any church. We have started praying for a revival."

"What's happening since you started praying? Has anything changed? Are you seeing any signs of a revival?"

"We're sort of shy people here. You have to be pretty brave to even ask people in church to break into small groups. And this thing with the pastors is not like any group I've ever been involved in. Things are happening, but it's hard to talk about. Pope John XXIII said to 'keep a window open for the Spirit.' That's one of the images I'm really working with—to keep a window open for the Spirit to do something. Things are changing. There's a real concern among the pastors for evangelism. That's different. The competition is gone. We're in this together. I think the Spirit's doing that.

"New people are coming to church —many of them are related to oldcr, activc mcmbcrs, but had never attended much. New things are happening. It's sort of a springtime season around here right now. Ministries are growing out of nowhere. People are starting to say, 'I think I need to do this,' and 'is that okay?' We just say, 'go to it, and blessings.'"

When one of the new members heard, "Go to it, and blessings," he went to it. Blessings followed. Greg is in construction. His new wife Sue is a lifelong member of the church. The Presbytery has a

"Prayer is subtle and so hidden...You have to let go of the idea that numbers matter or that it's visible results that count. That's very difficult for Americans in our culture to understand...But if we can leave the results of our prayer to God, if we can just praise God and listen to God rather than giving him a list of what we want, things do happen."

—*Beth, leader of a prayer ministry, Story 2*

connection with a Catholic ministry to little villages in El Salvador. Greg and Sue were soon headed out on a "first-timers" mission. They loved the people. They loved helping. They caught on fire doing this kind of ministry!

Half of the children in the villages they visited die before they are five years old because of the poor quality of the drinking water. When they got home, Greg called a friend in the construction business who had developed a drinking water purification system. They improved it to the point that the system operated with regular table salt, a car battery, and a hand crank.

Then Greg started to raise money because he thought it would be great to go back to El Salvador, taking three water pumps. Here's where a change came in. Andy, the pastor described it: "Greg started raising money, but it was different than any way we've ever done anything related to money. I'm pretty methodical. I've always done decision-making in the church through the session. The session is cautious about decisions. We're Presbyterians. We do things decently and in order!"

Greg didn't know a lot about either Presbyterians *or* their decent order. He stood up in worship and asked if people wanted to help with the water ministry. He and Sue sold bottles of water and said, "You'd pay $2.50 for this water at the ball game. How much would you pay for it if you didn't *have* any water?" They raised $4,500. The session dedicated $3,000 to the project. It was an accountable ministry with long-term ties to the presbytery. It wasn't a fly-by-night scheme. But a lightness entered into the church's traditional, responsible, dutiful ministry. People were having fun. Entire villages now have clean water.

Andy says they have introduced a few bits of new music in worship. Some of the older folks say, "Well, it's been okay so far, but you know if you take this to its logical conclusion, it could really get out of hand!"

Greg just got back from Africa, where he helped assemble ten prefabricated buildings for congregations that didn't have buildings yet. He and Sue are heading to Mexico at Christmas. "Everybody just watches them go, helps and cheers them on. And we're encouraged. Other people are doing new things, too." Andy tried to describe this new life in an old congregation with its veteran ministry. "Stuff just happens that you've been trying so hard to get going for *years.* All of a sudden something is blooming. You didn't even plant it and it's unfolding like a rose."

Prayer is more about receiving from God than it is about asking God for things or working hard at intercession. Prayer involves effort, habit, and focus; but it results in lightness and energy and excitement.

Windows Open for the Spirit

I don't want to tame these stories by analyzing them. I will make a few observations about prayer in alive and inspired congregations. Remember, we each touch into the heart of the faith through our individual interactions with God. This relationship is nurtured in community. It is expressed through community. But at its center stands each of us, individually, being given glimpses of God's face.

Many pastors and church leaders said essentially the same thing when I asked them if they had one piece of advice for people who want to do evangelism: "Tell them that you can't give what you don't have." "So much that can happen in the church is led or stopped by how healthy my relationship with Christ is." "It's consistent openness to God that really matters." The heart of faith sharing is one person giving another a vision of what it's like to be in love with God.

Remember the Spirit's word to the church at Ephesus? "I know your works, your toil and your patient endurance…I also know that you are enduring patiently and bearing up for the sake of my name and that you have not grown weary. But I have this against you, that you have abandoned the love you had at first" (Rev. 2:2–4). We work so **hard**, but the joy, the "first love," the "in love" feelings with God fade to dusty duty, good works, more work.

Prayer is the way to stay in love with God. Prayer is the way individuals, small groups and congregations grow and become vivid. It is a habit, a discipline, but not discipline with a clenched jaw. Prayer is more about receiving from God than it is about asking God for things or working hard at intercession. As you may have felt in these stories, prayer involves effort, habit and focus; but it results in lightness and energy and excitement.

My life has been characterized by hard work and fairly grueling discipline. I'm trying (really hard) to add a bit more lightness. This spring, I started voice lessons with a great teacher, Kate. I'm having fun! Last week I was gutting my way through a beautiful old Italian song and Kate said, "It's charming, but do you need to sound like a vacuum cleaner at the end of phrases?" I told her I thought I probably **did** need to suck air in like a vacuum because otherwise I would asphyxiate and crumple in a heap right there on her floor. "Look," she intoned majestically, "if you'll open up your ribs, the air just falls in."

That's what prayer does. If we will open our time to scripture, prayer, adoring God and listening to God, the inspiration of the Spirit just falls in. If we pray, we won't have to suck in inspiration

"Pope John XXIII said to 'keep a window open for the Spirit.' That's one of the images I'm really working with—to keep a window open for the Spirit to do something. Things are changing. There's a real concern among the pastors for evangelism. That's different. The competition is gone. We're in this together. I think the Spirit's doing that."

—Pastor, Story 3

like a shop vac. The whispers of the Spirit will nudge around the edges of our minds and surface in subtle ways. If we will open our ribs in prayer, inspiration will fall in. Many of our early Protestant forebears called this a "prepared heart." If we study scripture, pray and prepare ourselves to be used, God will direct us, lead us, use us for things God wants to do. It's as simple as that. The people in the stories in this chapter have discovered these small-step truths. Christ stands at the door knocking. Open your heart and Christ will enter in. We have the choice.

About Prayer

If you feel called to begin prayer like the people in this chapter, here are a few ideas and suggestions for you and your church:

1. A prayer life has two aspects—individual prayer and prayer with other people. These facets of prayer are inseparable. Don't try to go it alone. Don't freeload on the efforts of the rest of your prayer group. We must learn both to be alone with God and to pray in agreement with others. Try a daily prayer time. Spend time with God by yourself. Read scripture. Journal or pray for others. Sit silently and listen to God. Then pray with others. Pray alone. Pray with others. Both are crucial aspects of the rhythm of prayer.

2. Trusting God for guidance is counter-intuitive. It is particularly tough for self-reliant Americans. American culture has rarely held up surrender and yieldedness, the heart of a spiritual life, as heroic values. (Remember the thunderous prayer George C. Scott made as Patton after the 5th Army was taken away from him? "An entire *world* at war and me left out of it? This will not be *permitted* to happen! I will be allowed to *fulfill* my destiny. His will be done.")[3] All right, most of us aren't Patton; but we do tend to set out to pray and hand Christ our lives to be used, then yank the control back. ("Gosh, God, thanks for the tip! That was *amazing*! Okay, so, I can take it from here.") Be aware of the tendency to trust God, then to snatch the reins from the Spirit's fingers.

3. Prayer is a lifelong practice. Praying feels miraculous at first. If we can get past the "I'll take it from here" impulses and get to the point where solitary prayer and praying with others become a normal part of our lives, the rhythms of trust in God and God's providence become as natural as driving a car. Remember that Don, the California pastor, didn't think to mention prayer in a congregation steeped in intercession? When I asked him after 40 minutes of conversation whether they prayed in any specific way, he was stunned. I suspect this

"New things are happening. Ministries are growing out of nowhere. People are starting to say, 'I think I need to do this,' and, 'Is that okay?' We just say, 'Go to it, and blessings.'"

—*Pastor, Story 3*

is because prayer has become so ingrained a part of life that in one way it didn't feel like an activity they **do**. He didn't mention prayer. He didn't mention tooth brushing. He never told me that people in their church exhale.

4. We need someone to help us learn prayer. Although our Protestant heritage is rich in prayer resources, the memory and training have thinned and faded in the last century. Our images of people who pray are more weighted toward cartoons of pious little people (who in reality may be spiritual heavyweights) than toward images of Martin Luther King praying before the Mall speech. Prayer isn't a sweet, nice, safe, naive little activity to do in your flowery hat. It is crash helmet action for people who flip kayaks in raging spring rivers. If you want to begin to pray seriously, please find a guide who knows the spiritual currents before your kayak sideswipes boulders under the water's surface. Chapter 9 offers more discussion of the realities of a congregation's prayer life.

Ask God to bring someone into your life or church who has prayed seriously for years. People like Beth (Story 2, *A Gift from Honduras*) teach prayer. I have heard mainline people who now pray in earnest mention beginning to pray with a Benedictine sister spiritual director, an Orthodox Church in America theology professor, a Southern Baptist evangelical friend, a Catholic priest from Botswana, an American Baptist pastor who's also a Jungian analyst, or a new neighbor who goes to the Vineyard Church. Please get help from people from different backgrounds.

You do not need to subscribe wholeheartedly to someone's theology to ask them to pray with you and for your ministry. If you get advice that feels strange, remember that learning about new areas of the faith is like eating fish. Eat what is good and spit out the bones. Ask God to show you the parts you need, and don't worry about the rest of it.

5. We need discernment and accountability. Can things get out of control when churches begin to pray? How can you tell an idea is from God and not spun out of your own fevered imagination? These are issues of spiritual maturity.

Look at the synergy between joy, excitement and accountability in the story of the Presbyterian church in the dwindling Midwestern town (*Tuesday Mornings with the Guys*). People were jazzed up with inspiration and hot ideas, but they talked them over with the church. The session (council) didn't stop the momentum, but after thoughtful discernment, joined in supporting a long-term Presbytery ministry. A

> Prayer isn't some sweet, nice, safe, naive little activity to do in your flowery hat. It is crash helmet action for people who flip kayaks in raging spring rivers. If you want to begin to pray seriously, please find a guide who knows the spiritual currents before your kayak sideswipes boulders under the water's surface.

life steeped in prayer is exciting and filled with change. It is not a life of froth or unconscious acting out. We need practice, accountability to a group of Christians, and wise counselors to help us discern which ideas are nudges from God and how they should be acted upon.

Think about scriptures like Galatians 2:2, in which Paul felt strongly about what he was to do, but went to Jerusalem to consult with the leaders of the Jerusalem church to make certain that they were in agreement.[4] Be open to the Spirit. Remember you don't have all the answers. You need the wisdom of others to navigate the currents. Be open to the Spirit. Don't be naive.

Unbinding the Gospel

Predrag

Matthew 18:15–20

In Matthew 18, Jesus tells the disciples, "Whatever you bind on earth will be bound in heaven, and whatever you loose on earth will be loosed in heaven" (Mt. 18:18). *We* are also given the power to untie or unbind things. As disciples of Christ, we have the power to affect great things. In the scripture, Jesus then says, "If two of you agree on earth about anything you ask, it will be done for you by my Father in heaven" (Mt. 18:19).

My friend Don Schutt is certain Jesus could make this promise because it's so hard to get two or three people to agree about *anything*! Don says, more seriously, that this mysterious passage means that if we try to discern the deep realities of a situation so that we can pray about it together, in sync with God's will, that it enables God to use our prayer to accomplish God's desires. If we will think about a situation, pray to understand it, talk together and pray in the agreement of the understanding the Spirit has given us, our prayer will be Christ's prayer. This is the kind of spiritual power the churches in the three stories in this chapter have experienced.

Many of the dear churches we love are inflexible. Many churches are tied into knots of self-involvement or old habit. Most of us are fairly knotted up as people. We're anxious, worried, stewing, angry or afraid. The Gospel is about freedom in Christ. Think of all the strands that tie us up—death, sin, fear, anger, addictions, nasty gossiping, fussy tediousness, age-old resentments, self-involvement! The Gospel, the Good News, is about freedom in Christ. It is about knots being untied, ropes loosened, ties unbound.

Every one of us is too narrow in our understanding. We don't want upsets in our lives, or changes in our habits, or threats to our

Prayer

1. A prayer life has two parts—individual prayer and prayer with others.

2. Trusting God for guidance is counter-intuitive.

3. Prayer is a lifelong practice.

4. We need someone to help us learn prayer.

5. We need discernment and accountability.

opinions. Shifting from Shredded Wheat™ to oatmeal exhausts me on a bad day! Telling God it's okay to change an institution I lean into for my stability (like my church) is really scary. But we need to do it. Many churches are slowing down because they are running on our human steam. I'm afraid we're going to have to rely on the Lord now. ("Oh, no! Surely it isn't as bad as all that?")

Do you dare risk agreeing with some others in your church to pray together and see what God can do? Do you dare **not** risk it?

DISCUSSION QUESTIONS _____

1. *How is your individual prayer going? Spend the first 15-20 minutes of your group time talking about the highlights: What was the most wonderful prayer day? What happened? What did you learn? What challenged you? What are you wondering about? Go around the circle and everyone say something!*

2. Which of these stories of prayer is most exciting or attractive to you? Do they seem real? Possible? Impossible in your context? Why? Did anything stir up resistance in you? Repel you?

3. What experience with prayer or intercession have you had? How is your experience similar to these stories? How do you think your congregation might react to prayer of this type? Who do you know who might be interested in praying like this? Are you one of them?

4. What prevents you from risking to agree with some others in your church to pray together and see what God can do? Do you dare **not** risk it?

5. What Bible passages came to mind when you read this chapter, or occur to you now? Discuss how it connects with what you have read. (If you don't think of any passages, you might want to look at: Matthew 18:18–20; Mark 4:1–9; Galatians 2:1–2; Revelation 2:1–7.)

> A life steeped in prayer is exciting and filled with change. It is not a life of froth or unconscious acting out. We need practice, accountability to a group of Christians, and wise counselors to help us discern which ideas are nudges from God and how they should be acted upon.

EXERCISE, PRAYER TRIADS _____

Divide into small groups of three. Choose two other people you know least well. The leader will keep time. First, sit in silent prayer for two minutes. As you breathe deeply and get quiet inside, ask God to let you know one thing you will ask these two people to pray about for you. It may be forgiveness, strength to go through each day without satisfying an addiction. The Spirit may prompt you to ask for prayer for healing, for a healing of anger, for boundaries, for a growth in patience or love, or for discernment.

There's only one rule: the prayer must be for *you* — not your mother-in-law, your child, or people at work. Ask God what *you* need prayer for. After the leader rings the bell to signal the end of silence, tell the others how they can focus their prayer for you in one short, timed minute. (Your leader will ring a bell at the end of each person's "This is how you can focus your prayer for me" minute.)

As soon as you have each taken your minute to share your prayer requests, pray for each other. You may use spoken or silent prayer. You may wish to lay a hand gently on the arm or shoulder of the person for whom you are praying. Take no longer than 6 minutes total to pray for all three of you.

---

[1]Lucy M. Montgomery, *Anne's House of Dreams* (New York: Grosset and Dunlap, 1917).

[2]A huge, 30-year-old Lutheran (ELCA) church just north of Phoenix. They are on the high adult baptism list. They also host educational events that have shaped the ministries of quite a few of the pastors and lay leaders with whom we spoke during this study. See the bibliography at www.GraceNet.info for books by their pastor Walt Kallestad. Visit Community Church of Joy's Web site at www.joyonline.org.

[3]*Patton,* 20th Century Fox, 1970.

[4]"I went up [to Jerusalem] in response to a revelation. Then I laid before [the leaders of the church]…the gospel that I proclaim among the Gentiles, in order to make sure that I was not running, or had not run, in vain" (Gal. 2:2).

CHAPTER 5

Real Life

By the end of college, my friends and I sounded like accomplished jazz musicians when we set off into our polished riffs on the theme, "It's time to get out of this ivory tower and get on to Real Life." Flies on the wall must have giggled a couple of years later to see us spiffed up as if in our mommies' dresses, lipstick and high heels. There we were in crisp suits (with stapled hems and paper clip buttons), carrying our unscarred briefcases, blackboard chalk, shiny stethoscopes and efficient stacks of files with desperate casualness. Real jobs, real paychecks—this is *great*!

The real deadlines, real car payments, real mortgages, real 2 a.m. feedings came next. Then the real car pool schedules, real shopping lists, real tax returns, real office politics, real layoffs, real marriage problems, real affairs began to exert deadly gravity.

At our tenth reunion we ditched the suits, slung on jeans and hiking boots, and stayed up talking till 4 a.m. to find out what was really going on in each other's lives. The talking, the reconnections, reimmersed us in the reality of being with people who would love us no matter what. We remembered what it was like to be with the ones who knew every secret, every screw-up, every foible in the past—the ones who cared. After spilling out everything, one woman looked up through tear-filled eyes and said, "Oh, my gosh, it's such a relief to get back with you guys—I've needed so badly to be able to be *real*."

That's what being a Christian ought to feel like.

Being a Christian should be the most real *real* there is. It should feel like coming home to a place where you are exposed to so many new ideas you can't integrate them quickly enough; of cheering for

> A Christian is a powerful individual on a powerful team. It's a life with no posturing, no pretending. That's the *real* real life!

57

your team, surrounded by your friends; of beginning to take risks and make adult choices alone for the first time in your life; of being able to say anything that pops into your mind because you're hanging out with the people you can trust with your life, of going back each September and meeting the new kids and showing them the ropes. That's what being a Christian ought to feel like, a powerful individual on a powerful team: a life with no posturing, no pretending. That's the *real* real life!

At its best, Christian life has two aspects that are inseparable. It must be real (honest, transparent), and it must be relational (be lived in relationships that are real/honest/transparent). Most churches don't come close because they're too involved in the quasi-real lives of briefcases, car pools, and covering your back from office politics. But God can create, redeem and sustain churches that are real.

A Trinity of Real Life

This real Christian life is a bit like the Trinity that God is. The Trinity is an enormous mystery. God is one God, indivisible, and at the same time three: Father, Son and Holy Spirit; or, as some say, Creator, Redeemer and Sustainer. The Trinity is a concept worked out in the earliest days of the church. It is embodied in our creeds. It is hard to understand. Somehow the impossibility of the idea of One *and* Three flips our minds into a little understanding of something very important. A vivid relationship lives in God's heart.

Think about the Trinity, God as One and Three, at the same time you consider another primary understanding of Christianity. We, as individuals, are made in God's image. So the doctrine of the Trinity must say something about who we can be as people and how Christ's Church (Christ's body) can be. The doctrine of the Trinity, the idea that God is made up of relationships, shows us something important about the nature of people and church.

I have seen many powerful, faithful churches during this study. The ones that have seemed most "real" have felt creative and complex. They support members' actions, growth and initiatives, while leaving space for each individual. No matter how clear they are about a few essentials, the best of these churches don't force rigid conformity on less crucial issues.

The great churches aren't mushily, sentimentally, smotheringly "caring." They aren't "damn the torpedoes, full speed ahead." They aren't all Venus; they aren't all Mars. They're messy. They allow intuition, action and spontaneity, while providing teaching, support,

Great churches aren't mushily, sentimentally, smotheringly "caring." They aren't "damn the torpedoes, full speed ahead." They aren't all Venus; they aren't all Mars. They're messy. They allow intuition, action and spontaneity while providing teaching, support, correction and accountability. They feel alive. They're in touch with joy. God is all over them. The Spirit is palpable.

correction and accountability. They feel alive and almost always are in touch with joy. These churches are real. God is all over them. The Spirit is palpable.

I want to use the Trinity that is God as a metaphor for the way these churches live, operate and do evangelism. These churches all have three sets of relationships that are distinct yet which constantly interact and affect each other. These three sets of relationships are:

1. with God,

2. between church members and

3. with people outside church.

A Trinity of Relationships

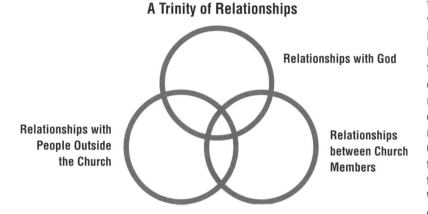

Relationships with God

Relationships with People Outside the Church

Relationships between Church Members

If we pastors don't talk about our lives with God, if we don't have substantial prayer lives, it is not likely that members of our churches will develop much of a spiritual life, either. If members are not afire with love for God, it is inconceivable that they will do much to share their faith. Why would we *think* evangelism would happen?

God works powerfully through these three sets of relationships in healthy churches. These great churches, large and small, have a spider-web wholeness about them. Touch one area of the web, and ripples shimmer across its entire surface. As individual relationships with God grow, people are able to be more real with each other within the church. As relationships within the church get richer, members of the church somehow know how to be better friends at work, in the neighborhood, coaching Little League. But if relationships with people outside the church—with neighbors, friends and far away family— begin to deteriorate, prayer time may falter. Then, the congregation may edge into isolation. Everything affects everything!

Positively or negatively, these sets of relationships affect each other. If one area grows and gets healthier, the other areas will change. Congregational leaders must pay attention to all three areas if the church is to thrive and do healthy ministry/evangelism. A congregation that is out of balance, with strength in only one or two areas, is merely limping along. Let's try to get a healthier balance by examining each of these three areas.

Individuals' Relationships with God

We had a great idea in the Mainline Evangelism Project. We asked almost all 1200 people interviewed, and over 400 people who filled in written surveys, for the best piece of advice they could give someone who is trying to help people become Christians. One of the most frequent answers advised that our relationships with God are the foundation stone of who we are as Christians. Pastors often say, "As pastor, I can't teach what I don't know." Leaders of evangelism teams talk about praying for others and keeping in touch with God themselves. Doesn't it make sense that if doing evangelism is about helping others connect with God's love, then the more connected we are with God ourselves, the better we'll be able to do our parts?

Let's hear directly from some of the people whose churches are doing wonderful evangelism with unchurched people. Here are exact responses to the question: "What one sentence of advice would you give to someone in your position who is trying to reach unchurched people?"

> Churches where people snap, snipe, pull power plays over the budget, then go home to fried preacher for Sunday supper don't do good evangelism over the long haul!

Advice from senior pastors:

- "Be a living example, pray."
- "Some of the most important things I have been able to teach are the things God just taught me. I'll go through some big struggle with God who will teach me something in my own life. Two days later one of my elders will call me to have lunch and what I just learned will be *exactly* what she needed to hear. I can't see it as coincidental after all these years. It's a God rhythm."
- "You can't give what you don't got—your relationship with God must be hot!"

Advice from laypeople highly involved in evangelism:

- "Keep in prayer for opportunities to witness about your faith, or answer questions someone has."
- "First pray, then accept training and discipline and then practice with more prayer!"
- "Demonstrate the power of Jesus by showing kindness, love, compassion, understanding, humility. Be honest and sincere and show them the love of God within you."

Advice from a new Christian:

- "[Our UCC church] is growing very rapidly due to the pastor and his closeness to God that he shares with all of us."

Having just listed all these quotes, I feel some discomfort. Those of you in churches with a healthy "relationship with God" emphasis will read the advice to attend to your spiritual life and will be nodding along, thinking, "Well, of **course**." But most of us are in mainline churches with a very light emphasis on relationship with God. And if we don't know what having a healthy spiritual life looks or smells or feels like, if we're good members of our churches, if we're faithful pastors who are working hard, we think we understand. We'll read this advice, nod, and think, "Well, of **course**." But we won't get it.

Churches that emphasize a growing relationship with God for its members, board and pastors are different than "normal" churches. I don't want to sound critical, but visiting one of these vibrant churches makes attending many of our mainline congregations feel like going to a Lions Club meeting—a good thing, certainly, but not the real thing.

Do you remember the three stories in chapter 4 about congregations that started praying? In two of them, the prayer (and the experiences that the Spirit led the people into) felt very new to most of the people involved. That is a typical mainline response to beginning to pray. We have not had much training. I loved my seminary. I will always be grateful for the people and for what I learned during my years there. But when I attended, in the 1980s, no prayer class was offered. Except for a bit in hospital chaplaincy training, the only discussion or training in prayer I had in my three-year seminary studies was a half an hour during the worship class on how to compose and lead the pastoral prayer in the Sunday worship service.

I had a fairly rich spiritual life personally, because I grew up outside the church and became a Christian in Spain as a college student. Brilliant evangelical college kids nurtured me through my first year as a Christian, so I had a year of learning fasting and prayer, of devouring devotional Bible reading and theology, and of intense Bible study and prayer for each other in a small group. After my seminary training, as a 35-year-old, self-confident ex-lawyer, I began serving my first congregation. I made my first hospital call on a founding member of the church who died the next day. I did not know how to pray with her, or with her family. I thought it might offend them, or be invasive. I knew people expected a chaplain to pray in the ICU. I knew how evangelicals prayed, but that had somehow been dismantled in me and nothing rebuilt in its place. So I listened and empathized, counseled and left. I think of that day now and cringe. I failed that woman and her family.

The more each of us looks to Christ and asks for forgiveness for our gaffs, foibles and mess-ups, the more likely we are to hear other people's ideas, to forgive and to get along. The more the Spirit is leading, the more energy is freed to go into gear. We will experience fewer power struggles and more joy.

If faith and church have changed your life, you'll want others to understand that there is no sin, no resentment, no bitterness, no wound, no fear, no illness, no loneliness that Christ cannot forgive, dissolve, heal, cure, fill. You'll want everyone to know that the God of infinity is there to lead them by the hand into forever. Nothing is more real than this good news.

I wish I could look back on that hospital visit as the normal fumbling of an inexperienced pastor. It **was** that, but I think my discomfort, my ignorance, revealed a blank spot in the mainline experience. I think this blank spot, this gap, is helping cause the declines in our churches you read about at the beginning of chapter 3. I have spent the last ten years working with hundreds of mainline pastors. Many of them know that they "aren't evangelical," (meaning "not biblical literalists"), but there's nothing rebuilt in that spot. What do we believe *positively*?

Many, many mainline pastors do not have a regular personal prayer life. Many are surprised by an offer to close a phone conversation with prayer. I have asked many pastors as we end a phone call, "Is there any specific way I can focus my prayer for you?" A typical response is, "Wow, I never had anyone ask me that. Let me think a minute." The response is usually a heartfelt request.

We in the mainline, even pastors, can be shy people when it comes to our faith. If we pastors don't talk about our lives with God, if we don't have a substantial prayer life, it is not likely that the members of our churches will be developing much of a spiritual life, either. If members are not afire with love for God, from a vivid sense of what God is doing every day, it is inconceivable that they will do much to share their faith with others. **Why** would we think evangelism would happen?

The good news is that mainline pastors and mainline church members *can* learn to pray and can develop spiritual disciplines. It's like getting into the habit of an exercise program. Of **course** it would have been easier if you'd been exercising since your high school track star days. But do something for 21 days, and it becomes a habit! Try asking God to give you a subtle nudge (or a smack upside the head) within the next couple of days with an opportunity to do something to make God more real and personal in your life.

More good news is that there are several movements within the mainline churches that are helping reignite interest in the spiritual disciplines. We can learn from Christians from all backgrounds—evangelical, charismatic, catholic, orthodox. Be brave. Make some phone calls! Go to lunch. Ask questions. Ask Christ.

If you and your congregation do not have a primary focus on having a relationship with God, please ask the Spirit to help you change that. Everything depends on it.

Relationships within the Church

The second part of the "Relationships' Trinity" is the relationships within the church. Congregations that are doing great faith teaching/ faith sharing over the long haul are healthy from the inside out. If individuals are devoted to staying alive in Christ and have a spiritual life that is sustained over time, if the congregation puts a long-term focus on helping people be in primary contact with God, then healthy relationships have a much better chance of developing. Churches where people snap, snipe, pull power plays over the budget, then go home to fried preacher for Sunday supper don't do good evangelism for the long haul![1]

Members of growing churches usually love going to church! Why would this surprise us? If you love your church, if being part of it is adding good things to your life, if you're learning, if your kids love youth group, you probably think your friends would get something out of church, too!

More hardworking, smart, kind Christians than I can count have said to me, "Well, I just can't invite people to our church. Our friends are here. We've been here forever, so we're committed; but I just don't want other people to have to get into it." You and other people in your church reading this book together may feel this way yourselves. Could you be brave enough to say it out loud?

I asked an elder and former board chair who had sat in the front row of the choir of her church every Sunday for 30 years, "Why do you go to church? What do you get out of it?" Her husband of 35 years had just died slowly and painfully. Horror stories pocked her memories of her marriage and raising the children. She answered, "Church has always meant a lot to me because I knew that if things got really bad, I could tell someone about it." I asked if she ever *had* talked with anyone about anything really bad. "No, but I always knew that I *could* have."

That is not the type of church that warms people's hearts and draws them to Christ's love by way of their deepest yearnings. Yet when people were asked to describe this congregation, the two most frequent responses were that it was "friendly" and "it's like family here." Here's the question: Do you tell people in your church what's really going on in your life? (Not *could* you, but *do* you?)

Churches with healthy relationships don't experience a lot of ego-wrangling. People in these churches (individually, in small groups

> Do you tell people in your church what's really going on in your life? (Not *could* you, but *do* you?)

and all together in worship) are trying to yield their lives to Christ to be shaped and used. The more each one of us looks to Christ each day and asks for forgiveness for our gaffs, foibles and mess-ups, the more likely we are to be able to hear other people's ideas, to forgive and to get along. The more each of us is looking to Christ every day, the more likely we will be to share what's really going on in our lives, to help each other, and to pray for each other.

The more the Spirit is leading each person and each group, the more conflict recedes. The more the Spirit is leading, the more creativity, energy, and outward focus are freed to go into gear. People in love with God and serving each other live with joy. Life is less power struggle, and more fun.

So what does an alive, relationally healthy church look like? Decades ago, the United States Supreme Court was asked to consider a case involving obscenity laws. Many people wanted the court to define obscenity for the whole country. The court declared that a definition wouldn't work because communities are different. (For example, it's probable that more people in rural Minnesota would think a film or an advertisement obscene than the same number of people in certain sections of San Francisco or New Orleans.) Justice Potter Stewart wrote in a concurring opinion that he wasn't going to attempt to define obscenity, "but I know it when I see it."[2]

It's like that with a great church. People ask me to define them. I wouldn't **attempt** to find some ultimate definition of a church with healthy internal relationships. It can look totally different, depending on whether it's in piney Louisiana or in the Bronx. One thing is certain, though: people know it when they see it. Visitors can feel it when they step across that threshold.

Listen to some descriptions from people talking about healthy, loving churches:

from new Christians:

- ■ "I am very blessed to be a member of First Congregational Church. It is rich in its 100-plus–year history and it is rich in love for family and community, and for mission. The church members always have a warmth that would make any new visitor feel welcome and right at home. That was one of the many reasons that I felt so good about becoming a member of this church and this family."
- ■ "The members here support each other."

Healthy Relationships in Churches

1. People are real. They are honest. They share their lives with each other in significant ways rather than putting on a "perfection show."

2. People see each other for who they are, and show respect by telling the truth lovingly.

3. Relationships are not sentimental. People acknowledge their own frailties and sinfulness. They may have disagreements, but they find ways of resolving them without undue conflict or long resentments.

4. Visitors can feel it when they walk in the door!

■ "My church is a very loving, supportive, and caring church. My church always makes sure newcomers feel welcomed. I felt so loved and that I mattered to everyone when my children and I first attended. My pastor is such an amazing man. His love for Jesus shines all over his face. He is a very important part of my children and I choosing to become members here. When you walk into our church, you can feel the Holy Spirit with the worship and love all around you. It feels like Jesus is with us clapping and singing. I know He is very pleased how much He is loved."

from a new member

■ "With regard to my church: it is very real, very relevant, very comfortable for everyone to be who they are and where they are in their spiritual journey. There is an abundance of love and support and caring, which radiates outward from the pastors through everyone in their wake. Anyone in proximity to these guys gets a real 'Jesus Glow.' How cool is that?"

Evangelistic churches live out real life, real relationships—with God and with each other. And, contrary to what happens in other places, what happens in church doesn't ***stay*** in church. Lives are transformed in the congregation. Those changes move out into everyone's lives and all their other relationships. The power of the loving church can't stop at the door, or it will turn inward and fade. Let's take a look at the third part of this trinity of relationships.

Real Relationships Christians Carry into the Rest of Their Lives

Vibrant congregations contain people who are attending to spiritual disciplines and alive in Christ. Live congregations, where relationships within the church are nurtured and where the congregation tries to work together in the Spirit, change people's lives. Church is no longer a "place to go." It isn't just for Sunday morning. It isn't the ticket you punch to get new clients and make useful contacts. Church isn't the place you go weekly for "a little encouragement to get you through the rest of the week." Church is an igniter of faith, an instigator of growth that affects your whole life. Thinking extraordinary new ideas about surrender of self, healing of bodies, addictions, marriages, wounded souls, and serving others—these thoughts come to mind when members of great congregations hear the word *church*.[3]

Church is an igniter of faith that affects your whole life. Members of great congregations think of spiritual growth; surrender of self; healing of bodies, addictions, marriages, wounded souls; and serving others when they hear the word *church*.

Once you have a rich faith life and a healthy church, your questions shift from, "Why would I do *evangelism*?" to, "Oh, Lord, *how* can I help people see your face? Show me today, lead me to the ones you can reach through me. Let me be part of what you want to do next."

Church merges with real life. If faith and church have changed your life, you'll want to share that discovery with your friends. You want everyone to know that Christ lives. You want everyone to know that God loves us extravagantly. You want everyone to know that God will overwhelm their souls with grace and wash away sins. You want everyone to understand to the soles of their feet that there is no sin, no resentment, no bitterness, no wound, no fear, no illness, no loneliness that Christ cannot forgive, dissolve, heal, cure, fill. You want everyone to know that God, the Great I Am, the God who says, "before Abraham *was*, I *AM*," the God of infinity is there to lead them by the hand into forever, into an eternity of powerful love. Nothing is more beautiful than this good news.

Understanding these things unbinds the Gospel. Understanding these things frees captives, including us. Understanding these things gives people the ability to choose real freedom. Once we understand this, the only question is how to help people hear it clearly. Our questions shift from, "Why would I do *evangelism*?" to, "Oh, Lord, *how* can I help people see your face? Who do you want me to pray for? Show me today, lead me to the ones you can reach through me. Please show us how our church can serve you, how we can better organize ourselves to help you. Let us be a part of what you want to do next."

Hundreds of new and old Christians, members and pastors of great congregations, have told us of their desire to share their faith. One person responded to the question, "What advice would you give to someone like you who is trying to reach unchurched people?" by writing, "Be loving and let God set the opportunity to tell them about Jesus. It might be of interest to know that I came to the Lord after I was married at age 23 through my neighbor who had been a Christian for one day. She had no knowledge or strategy."

The new Christian wants to hand on the excitement within 24 hours. This Gospel can't be contained! Is it just new Christians who are excited about sharing faith? Not on your life. A 60-year-old, lifelong Christian described a new type of Bible study for teenagers: "It was amazing! This new way of working with the kids entranced them. I couldn't get them out the door (not that I was trying too hard)! Computerized Bible scavenger hunt put together with acting, and kids were moved to prayer and commitment. I can never anticipate what God is going to do next or how people will respond. Sharing Him is the adventure of my life."

A female pastor from the East Coast went to a Midwestern Presbyterian congregation as an interim minister, but is going to be able to stay as the permanent pastor. She's a happy woman and a smart one. She loves the congregation and kept saying, "We're having so much *fun* here. These people are wonderful." In two short years, she has helped begin Bible studies, create a neighborhood food pantry, send kids on mission trips, establish Great Banquet participation (the Presbyterian Cursillo/Walk to Emmaus movement), and perform six or eight adult baptisms a year. She loves reaching out to people. The congregation is loving it, too.

First Reformed Church is seeing an influx of Hispanic migrant workers into their traditional city. Demographics are changing dramatically. The reserved, Dutch descendants of First Church decided that they needed to help the new people. They want to preach the Gospel to people, but as their pastor says, "We need to earn the right to speak." So they help. They call on people and ask if they can do anything. They are tutoring and helping with educational and food needs. And the joy of serving is changing First Church members. They now see the need for a more solid relationship with God as they face new situations in their outreach to the migrant workers. Church members have had occasional disagreements over all the changes. They are learning to pray more about that and to talk with each other honestly and kindly. It's a steep learning curve, but they're learning!

"You can't give what you don't got—your relationship with God must be hot!"

A Real Life, Non-Vicious Cycle

Do you see how these three sets of relationships work a bit like the Trinity? They are separate, but they are a unity. An individual's relationship with God affects the way s/he works in the church. If many people are praying and becoming more yielded to the Spirit, relationships within the congregation can shift. Then the church feels lighter, more joyful, more real. People want to invite their friends. So friends and new Christians add their own excitement and growth to the mix. Things change again. The changes create a bit of dissonance in the church, so members move into more prayer and work on their relationships. (Chapter 9 deals with some of these issues.)

Growth can start from any one of the three parts of this trinity. A new member with a Pentecostal background can be happy and excited and get some mission projects started. Then people's focus turns outward. They don't obsess over the budget quite as much.

Prayer can begin in the session/council/pastor-parish/board/ committee meetings, and who knows where Christ can lead from there? The addition of some critical number of new members who are different than the "old" church members usually drives pastors and board members to their knees! Changes are tough. Real church relationships, like a real marriage or a real family, come about through prayer, honesty and attention. Because relationships involve people who are always changing, they *force* you to prayer so you don't smack somebody! As Woody Allen said in *Annie Hall,* "Relationships are like sharks. They have to keep moving, or they die."[4] Growing people are dynamic. Growing churches, comprised of growing people, help transform lives.

DISCUSSION QUESTIONS _____

1. *How is your individual prayer going? Spend the first 15-20 minutes of your group time talking about the highlights: What was the most wonderful prayer day? What happened? What did you learn? What challenged you? What are you wondering about? Go around the circle and everyone say something!*

2. With which person of the Trinity do you relate the most? How much of your focus is on this relationship? How highly does your congregation prioritize a relationship with God?

3. How are relationships in your congregation? With whom in your congregation (besides the pastor) do you talk about what is really going on in your life? How Christlike is the process of decision making in your church? What do you feel best about in the relationships in your church? What could be improved?

4. How strongly do you live out of your faith into your relationships outside church? How many times in the last three months have you had a conversation with an unchurched person about faith?

5. How do these three sets of relationships (with God, within the church, reaching out to others) interact in your church?

6. Does any Bible passage come to mind when you read this chapter? Does one occur to you now? Discuss how it connects with what you have read. (If no passages come to mind, you might want to look at: Mark 12:28–31; Ephesians 4:13–16; Philippians 3:12–16.)

EXERCISE _____

Will you try something new in your spiritual life this week for your "homework?" Let's try to scramble your patterns! Change something in your way of interacting with God. Do you talk to God a lot? Try sitting for ten minutes a day, thinking of Christ and listening.

Do you spend your prayer time mainly praying for others? Try something different. Sit quietly and ask the Spirit to show you anything you're using to block God in your life, or an old hurt buried in you that God could heal. Do you journal? If not, try it.

You could pray the Jesus prayer. This is an Eastern Orthodox prayer that is repeated over and over to still our spirits and to open our souls to Christ. Get a bead necklace, a set of Eastern Orthodox prayer beads, a string of pearls, or a string of Mardi Gras beads! Sit quietly, holding the beads. Hold one bead and say the Jesus Prayer once, breathing slowly in and out as you think the words, "Lord Jesus Christ, Son of God, have mercy on me."[5] Move to the next bead and think the prayer again, slowly, in time with your breathing. Pray the prayer with your beads for 5 or 10 or 15 minutes each day for a week.

Have you been reading one Bible translation for the last 30 years? Change it. Get a copy of Eugene Peterson's paraphrase *The Message*. Better yet, get a recorded version, and listen in the car or while you do the dishes. If you listen to Christian Rock on the radio, get a CD of African-American spirituals. The point is, ask God to scramble your circuitry and show you something new.

At the end of the week, discuss (or write) what God has shown you.

Note: Next week's exercise involves homework! Be sure to look ahead tonight while you're together, then do your assignment on page 83 during the week. You'll discuss it when you come back together next week.

_____

[1]My hero, Fred Craddock, New Testament and preaching professor, used the phrase "eating fried preacher for Sunday supper." It was in some sermon one time. He also said "carry the freight of the Gospel," which slips out of me in chapter 8. There are probably more Craddockisms here. We Disciples pastors compete in sword drills on the Craddock canon. We don't *try* to plagiarize. It's just that his phrases are integrated into our cells at a submolecular level. Go ahead. Listen to Craddock sermons. Read a collection of his stories. You'll start talking like this, too, and your life will be better. Read *Craddock Stories*, ed. Mike Graves and Richard F. Ward (St. Louis: Chalice Press, 2001).

[2]*Jacobellis v. Ohio,* 878 U.S. 184 (1964).

[3]Please do not hear "unattainable megachurch" when I say "great congregations." Some of these churches have 100 members and are located in tiny towns.

[4]*Annie Hall,* MGM, 1977.

[5]Another version of the prayer is, "Lord Jesus Christ, Son of God, have mercy on me, a sinner." Use whichever version you feel drawn to.

CHAPTER 6

What New Members Want— Transformed Lives

Mel Gibson starred in a movie called *What Women Want.*[1] Gibson was a ladies' man who could suddenly read women's minds. He knew what women, his natural prey, wanted. He knew when to give flowers, when to lean close, when to retreat, ***exactly*** what to say to get the reaction he wanted. He knew what women were thinking! This was going to be great!

The problems started when he learned what women were thinking. He could hear them think about what a jerk he was, about their loneliness. When he actually started listening, he changed. He didn't have to go to crazy extremes like talking about feelings during the Super Bowl, but it got close.

Mel Gibson is to women as churches are to church visitors. Perhaps not consciously, but under the smooth surface, a lot of us secretly look at new members as prey. Think of all the times you've heard, or said, "We need new members with children." "If we had more new members, we could meet this budget." "We have taught Sunday School all these years. It's time for some young women to take their turns." No matter that many of those young women have never been in Sunday School themselves. We need…we need…Ouch. That's new members as prey.

It is so easy to slip into the mind-set of a "church leader." We church leaders carry crucial responsibilities for the institution that is the church. Church financial secretaries and treasurers don't take money or budgets lightly. Nor should they! As council members,

He found the key, the secret combination, the hidden core of the heart of ministry. *"All I had to do was get people whose life Jesus had changed to get up and tell people about it."* Once we understand that the faith is about transformed lives, once we let the people talk about it in their own words, hearts will be touched and lives will be changed, including ours.

elders, trustees, members of committees, we are called to support the health of our churches. Inevitably, we focus on those jobs.

But our focus can get like a camera that's zoomed in too far. We miss the big picture. We forget that the larger purpose of the church is to take the Gospel out beyond the walls. We begin to see new members as fresh hands, energy and wallets to help keep the church going. We're not mean-spirited. We all do it. We just laser in on an important job and lose sight of that big picture…

Through the Eyes of Two Pastors

Pastor 1: The other day I received a letter from a brilliant young pastor. Jim has just moved from his first call as an associate pastor to his first senior pastor position. He is thrilled. His description was as sweet-spirited as it could be, "I can't believe what it feels like to look into the faces of these children and think that I'll be able to help teach them about Jesus and then baptize them. And the adults are wonderful. They've been so welcoming to Sarah and me. I see these old ones and want to know their stories. I wonder if I will be part of their final transition into a full life with God. The thought of summing up their lives in a celebration of life sermon overwhelms me. I know I am to be here, and I am so grateful to God for leading us here."

Jim could not have been clearer about his love (Christ's love!) for these people. But do you hear what is missing? Read his letter again. Do you see what is *not* there? *He goes through every age group, but never mentions anyone outside the church.* He shows no consciousness of those beyond the walls. He displays no sense of mission.

Jim is already concentrating on his job, his call, his church. This narrowing of focus is a huge risk for every one of us. This insider-focus is chaplaincy. It is not the vibrant ministry of the Gospel. The danger of that mind-set, sweet-spirited as it may be, is that it focuses on the church as an end in itself. This inward-focused perception leads to thinking of new members as cogs to fill slots, to do jobs. This perception lets us forget that visitors are precious souls who may or may not know God.

Pastor 2: At the beginning of the study, I spoke with a great Methodist pastor who had spent years thinking like Jim. Luke grew up a Methodist boy, became a Methodist college student, a Methodist man, a Methodist pastor. He is brilliant, funny and loving. The churches he served grew rapidly. Parishioners loved him. He was

> We found little difference between the opinions and perceptions of old and of young people who had been raised in the church. The real differences appeared between people who were raised in the church and those who weren't.

completely charged about ministry. This is the kind of guy we would *all* love to have as our pastor.

Then his bishop asked if Luke would start a new church in a quickly growing suburban area. He said, "Sure, why not?" And he started. Several months into church planting, he looked around and wondered, "Where are all the *Methodists*? All my life there have been Methodists. They're the ones who know what to do and who do all the work. Where *are* they? What am I going to *do*?"

He described the pain of this moment. "I realized that I had unconsciously presumed that there were only two ways to become a Methodist. You either were born one, or you married one."

It took three more months for Luke to figure out what to do. "It's so embarrassing that it took this long, but I spent three months drifting, trying harder. Then it all fell into place. It's completely simple. All I had to do was get someone whose life Jesus had changed to get up and tell people about it. Then I just sat back and clipped coupons. I supported them when they got great ideas."

Over 800 people were worshiping in that new church eight or nine years later, when the bishop asked him to do something else. His associate minister and many church members told stories that suggest he was doing a lot more than clipping coupons and eating bonbons on the divan. This guy worked hard. He preached great sermons, trained teams, encouraged and supported people who felt prompted by the Spirit to start ministries. Several high school kids got this computer/Internet idea. He encouraged them to develop their idea to huge results.

However, Luke was right. He found the key, the secret combination, the hidden core of the heart of ministry. *"All I had to do was get people whose life Jesus had changed to get up and tell people about it."* Once we understand that the faith is about transformed lives, and let the people talk about it in their own words, hearts will be touched, lives will be changed, including ours. Then ministry doesn't feel like pushing rocks up hill. It's standing on the top and letting the rocks roll down. When we finally see that the faith is about our lives being changed by Jesus, we no longer think of new members as prey. We think of their stories.

Generally, the newer the Christian, the more important the relationships with people as they discover it's God they're looking for. Whether children or adults, most of us first learn about God's love through other people.

Through the Eyes of the Unchurched

This chapter is about those stories. Let's hear from the people whose lives Jesus has changed. What do they think? What do they want? What do they see? What needs do they have? Let's not try to anticipate. Let's listen!

Have you ever talked with people who joined their church recently, or who have just become a Christian? We discovered that when new members, particularly new Christians, talk about their new churches, their answers cluster into two areas:

1. they feel loved, accepted and comfortable in the church, and

2. they are learning about God (Jesus, Spirit) and growing spiritually.

Same "Trinity of Relationships," from a Different Perspective

Do those new members' answers sound familiar? They should. Remember the three main characteristics of health we found in churches that are doing the best jobs of evangelism? These churches have a healthy "trinity of relationships" (individual relationships with God, healthy relationships between church members and a love for people outside the church, see chapter 5). The church members understand what it's like for God to transform their lives. They tell people outside the church walls. New members in these churches understand two things best: that God loves them and the church loves them. That's effective evangelism! Understand the Gospel, live it out, convey it accurately to new people. The new people understand it. That's as good as it gets!

The important thing to remember for us as insiders is that we see these three aspects of a healthy church from a "churched" perspective. New members see a loving church and learn about God through a different lens. The newer the Christian, the more differently they talk about church than do long-time members.

A big surprise came out of the statistical part of the Mainline Evangelism Project. We found little difference between the opinions and perceptions of old and of young people who had been raised in the church. The real differences appeared between people who were raised in the church and those who weren't.

If you grew up in the church, no matter how cool and young you are, don't assume you know what people outside the church are thinking or what they want! Early in your life, you absorbed Christian theology, behaviors, values, and understandings. These unconscious influences shape the way you think about life and what's real. If you want to know what nonchurch people think or what they expect, you have to ask them. Don't presume that you know.

"I was living a sinful, no meaning life with no real direction. I had just ended a ten-year relationship that I was trying to get over. As I struggled through depression, anxiety, and bad thoughts, God kept calling out to me. I would often have religious thoughts even though I did not understand what true religion was. I knew my life was a mess and I was ready or in the process of giving up. My friend who cuts my hair knew of my unhappiness but not the details. She invited me to [the UCC church I joined], and from that moment I knew I had been given a second chance with my life. I now live a simple, wholesome life and love every minute of it."

Think of it this way: Church is like comfort food. What's comfort food for you? Is it the tuna noodle casserole with peas in it and potato chips on top? Burritos? Could it be that green bean casserole with cream of mushroom soup and Durkee's™ onion rings? French's™ yellow mustard on that hotdog or Dijon?™ Miracle Whip™ or Hellman's™ mayonnaise on your Thanksgiving Friday turkey sandwich? Hershey's,™ M&M's™ or Godiva?™ The one thing we all know is that you don't mess with comfort food! You don't substitute or it's Wrong. We formed our rigid opinions about comfort food in childhood, at the same time our Christian ideas solidified.

Like it or not, the survey found that the opinions of 40-year-olds raised in the church are a lot more like the preferences of 80-year-olds raised in church than they are like 40-year-olds who were *not* raised in the church. If you grew up with liturgy and hymns, you probably feel comfortable with them. You experienced God early in connection with the smells of Easter lilies and the colors of Christmas pageants, with the doxology, hanging banners and the songs you loved from camp.

I don't feel as comfortable in a contemporary worship setting as I do with liturgy. Because of my upbringing and education I'm wired for liturgy. I love Hellman's,™ and I think Miracle Whip™ tastes nasty. A switch from Hellman's™ *worship* to either Miracle Whip™ worship *or* gourmet French mayonnaise worship is a bad thing for me on a grumpy day! I can feel put out by *any* kind of worship that doesn't feel like Hellman's.™ Then I remember: "Oh, phooey. It doesn't always have to be about me! It matters that I'm comfortable, but my comfort isn't as important as that 23-year-old over there whom the kids have been inviting to worship for three months. Pretty amazing he's here."

So, let's try to listen to what some new members of churches are saying. Don't change a thing you're doing. Your worship, your classes may be exactly right for the people God is calling you to reach. For now, let's simply try to *hear* what a few new members are saying.

What Do New Members Say about Churches and Faith?

Here are areas we investigated in our study. You can find more detail on the study at www.GraceNet.info under the section labeled "Survey Report." During the Mainline Evangelism Project, we asked all sorts of new members these questions. Their answers may help you understand how unchurched or non-Christian people think. We asked:

"I grew up never attending church or knowing Jesus. My family started attending after my husband lost his job and we felt something missing in our lives. We wanted our children to be exposed to Sunday School lessons. After attending over a year, I believed that if I just asked God to forgive my sins, I would meet my Savior in heaven."

1. Why do people first visit the church they join?

2. What gets visitors back for a second visit?

3. Why do new members join?

4. At what points in their lives are people most open to becoming involved or re-involved in church?

5. What does conversion/recommitment look like?

6. What aspects of being a Christian are most important to you?

New members' answers to these questions mesh with the "real relationships" discussion in chapter 5. People who join churches want a real relationship with God. They want a real relationship with loving people. Many new Christians discover that they wanted a relationship with God and loving people even before they knew they wanted it. One new Christian told me, "The church helped me see that I was built for God. I didn't know that, because I didn't know much about God and I was so busy being so busy. But [my friends in the church] helped me see what I'd been looking for off and on since I was a kid. Now that I've turned my life over to Christ, I feel like my life makes sense for the first time in 20 years." Generally, the newer the Christian, the more important the relationships with people as they discover it's God they're looking for. Whether children or adults, most of us first learn about God's love through other people.

1. Why Do People First Visit the Church They Join?

Almost 60% of new members of evangelistic churches get there first because a person invited them, or because they know someone in the church. This was one of the clearest findings of our study. Percentages are identical for both new Christians and Christians with a church background. The second place reasons for attending reflect a difference between new Christians and new members who have a church background. New Christians point to an event—a wedding or a funeral. Members with a church background place denominational affiliation in second place. But this second reason weighed in at only 9% in each case.

Both new Christians and new members with a church background said that the biggest barrier to attending the church was not knowing anyone.

Put these two findings together and you will see that the one most effective thing you can do to get evangelism going in your church is to invite people to church!

"Both my wife and myself must have felt the Spirit at the same time. When my sister-in-law invited us to an Easter Service, we both had a feeling it was something we wanted to try. I think David's greeting and words touched something in us. We felt compelled to come back. Each service left us feeling better and opened a new door for me. I think it was the first time I ever felt the Lord's presence."

One woman told us that she had been looking for a church during a tough transition time in her life. She talked with friends about what was going on in her life. After a while she decided to try a church. One Sunday morning, she walked into a congregation close to her house. She was shocked to find that five of her friends and coworkers were sitting in the sanctuary. She had discussed her problems with most of these people! Not one of them suggested that church might help. Even worse, she had no idea that any of them were even *members* of a church. She didn't know they were Christians.

2. What Gets Visitors Back?

What gets visitors back for second, third, fourth visits to a church? The people are the factor cited by 38% of new Christians and 30% of new members with a church background who say they return repeatedly because of the warmth, the love, the "realness" of the church members. *The pastor* is the second most frequently mentioned reason for returning to the church after initial visits (28% for new Christians, 23% for people with a church background). Also, 14% of new members say they returned because of worship.

Doctrine, theology and denominational affiliation matter to only 5% of the people with a church background and were not mentioned at all by the new Christians. It is interesting to note a seeming paradox. While 60% of new members say they visited the first time because of an invitation or because of knowing someone in the church, knowing someone in the church is only mentioned by 4% of new members as the reason for coming *back* to the church.

So, an invitation seems to get these visitors there in the first place, but the welcome, warmth and authenticity of people; the personality, teaching and preaching of the pastor and worship bring visitors *back* to experience church life again.

3. Why Do New Members Join a Church?

By the time people get to a point of making a firm commitment to Christ and the church, they have moved more deeply into faith issues. The following are the top reasons mentioned (in percentages of total responses) by new members of the highly evangelistic churches. We asked them to fill in the blank for the question, "What made you ready to join *this* church?"[2]

At the point of joining a new church, the reasons are much more about what's going on in lives, and less about the first issues of being comfortable and feeling welcomed. First-time visitors need

"God is so great. There is so much to learn and receive from him. The church is a very important part in growing your faith with God. My church is full of loving and caring people. I feel welcome every time I walk through the door by the smiles and the beautiful cross in the front of the sanctuary."

an invitation to get in the door. Visitors come back because of the warmth of members, the pastor and what they are learning.

MOTIVATION	New Christians	Church Background
Something was missing in my life	36%	27%
I'd been thinking religious things for a long time	16%	12%
Family/children motivations	17%	19%
Growth of relationship with God or Jesus	10%	18%
A birth or death	15%	2%
Want to be part of church (includes be part of church family, to serve, need to belong, support)	6%	14%

"It's been a long and arduous journey so far. I would say it started with the death of my brother when I was 15. That left me in a deep void and started my search for the unanswered questions and feelings I had."

At the point of joining, however, look how even the human relationships drop to the bottom of the list. New members are particularly thinking about questions about the meaning of their lives, like "What is missing in my life?" In the written comments, new Christians usually point to missing a relationship with God, but also describe some aspects of a maturing faith. New members with church backgrounds usually don't say that something was missing from their lives. That is not surprising. They already have some sort of faith life. The established Christians point instead to growth of their relationship with God or Jesus.

4. When Are People Most Open to Start Coming to Church?

The typical story from new Christians and from new members who have not been involved in church for a while starts with a transition. *People are most open to becoming involved with Christ and a church during seasons of change in their lives.* It can be good change (marriage, birth of a child, a physical move) or a painful change (illness, death of someone dear, divorce, loss of a job), but disruption in our lives seems to be a natural point at which people are open to a life change.

A church treasurer, a normal, quiet CPA named Brian, told me, "It's hard for me to be outgoing or really friendly like some people, so what I do is to pray that God will show me people to pray for who might be open to Christ now. When I ask, God brings people to my mind, or into my life, whose kids left for college a couple months before. Sometimes it's someone who just retired, or a lady whose husband just died, or someone who lost his job. When their names come into my mind, I call them for lunch or golf and then I ask them if they want to come to church. I don't talk about a lot of stuff, but I invite them."

I asked Brian what has happened with the people he has invited to church. He said, "Well, a lot of them have come to church, and a large percentage of them have joined. I really never have been able to tell them about the Lord or lead them to Christ or through the steps of salvation or all that, I just tell them church means a lot to me and helps me. I guess my job's just the praying and the inviting."

5. What Are the Most Important Parts of Being a Christian?

We asked new members of the high baptism churches, "Which of the following aspects of being a Christian are most significant in your own life?" New Christians and new members with church backgrounds gave almost identical answers when we asked them to identify the most important aspects of being a Christian:

A. "My sins are forgiven."

B. "It gives meaning and purpose to my life."

C. "It gives me a relationship with God/Jesus."

D. "I have eternal life."[3]

The least significant answer out of 11 possibilities for both groups was, "It saves me from Hell."

New faith or renewed faith is personal. It's deep. These new church members pointed out the four deepest elements of faith from a list of 11 options. These four aspects of faith the new members chose are some of the most profound issues of existence with which the faith has grappled over the ages. Faith is affecting the depths of these new members' lives.

Occasionally you hear Christians say that the churches that are doing evangelism are "shallow" or "selling out the Gospel" or "catering to what people want, not what they need." Our study showed something very different. We saw that the people who are pouring themselves into evangelism are thinking deeply about the heart of the faith and doing everything they can to convey those realities to people who do not know God.

New Christians usually don't sound like theology professors. But we have seen many new Christians gravitating to deep faith realities— love for God and yieldedness to God. Interviews and surveys reveal that the new members are learning to talk about their faith clearly, biblically, theologically. They are feeling their faith and are living it.

"My becoming a Christian was more of a journey than an event. I prayed for and received guidance and strength along the way. This journey has continued to my current church and my continued development as a Christian who spreads the word."

Eternal life with God matters to new Christians. Hell isn't mentioned, but the thought of Hell motivates many Christians who share their faith. One thousand interviews, congregational visits and the written surveys point to the same thing. Effective evangelistic people and churches have deep faith and comfort in their understanding of eternal life with God. They do not stress Hell in preaching or teaching, but many of them have a classical biblical understanding of Hell and therefore are motivated by it.

New Christians usually come to churches as theological clean slates. Our culture does a great job of conveying vivid images of Hell on Earth, but Americans may be shakier on the eternal kind! I suspect that most unchurched Americans don't think much about Hell. Once exposed to Christian preaching, teaching and biblical understandings, new Christians can learn about Hell and think more about eternity. But scaring people about Hell is not helpful for most Americans. Ruined lives, uncertainty, exhaustion, addictions, a treadmill existence or concern for their children seem to be more important entry points for the Gospel today.

Most unchurched Americans don't think much about Hell. Ruined lives, uncertainty, exhaustion, addictions, a treadmill existence or concern for their children seem to be more important entry points for the Gospel today.

6. What Does Conversion/Recommitment Look Like?

We will have more to say about this (see "Bandwidths of Evangelism" in chapter 7). Here is the highlight: people who were not raised in the church are different. They may not know the story of baby Jesus in the manger. Words like *grace, redemption, original sin*—or the books of the Bible—may be completely unknown. Unchurched Baby Boomers may think that *Amazing Grace* is a Judy Collins song and that Cat Stevens wrote *Morning Has Broken.* I have heard three different people say that they only know one hymn, "that one about walking in the garden with Jesus, because they sang it at my grandmother's funeral."

The great news about this is that the mysterious words of faith have not been worn slick by use. Reading the Bible is like reading Shakespeare for the first time, "Whoa! Is *that* where this comes from?" The hard news for us is that we can't communicate well through the theological words or concepts that we've worked so hard to learn and now take for granted! We need to know how to talk about Jesus from our own lives, out of our real feelings of faith and doubt, and in real-life words.

What do conversions look like? It's hard for most church people to imagine. It's not about church, it's about Jesus. It's about one human being, at a crucial point in his or her life, learning about God being love and about Jesus being God. Then s/he decides to live life with God leading. Some people come to Christ through their feelings—in response to a change, a crisis, a loss, a new joy like the birth of a baby. Others have important or complex intellectual questions answered.

One man with a church background transferred membership. Two years later, he responded to the question, "Why did you join **this** church?" this way:

> It is an outward-looking church. It is very involved in the community. It is not moralistic or legalistic but rather invites me to a personal struggle towards God and Jesus while supporting me in the midst of a community of believers. It's not a homogenous church in terms of belief, but the disagreements I've seen or heard of seemed to serve to enrich the faith of all rather than demoralize them. My faith is sustained and defined by social justice in the name of Christ and this church is actively engaged in the same struggle.

Do you hear his appreciation of the church? He is growing spiritually. The fit between his well-formed faith and the church is clear. You probably know people who have joined your church who sound like this. They have chosen your church. They probably bring fresh life to the congregation. And they are happy to continue their Christian growth there.

Now, listen to new Christians talk about becoming Christians and joining their churches. Hear the freshness in their tones of voice. Sometimes they sound theologically naive. Sometimes they show tremendous sophistication. They almost always sound grateful, in love with Christ and their church. I am usually awed by the power of new Christians' grasp of the supernatural and of the center of the faith—their love of God. How do you respond to these statements from new Christians?

- ◼ "I am too new to active Christianity to be able to add meaningful comment. However, for me, I believe that the only way to God is through my Lord Jesus Christ. In believing in the Christ as my Lord, it becomes important to me to try to change my life to become more like Him."
- ◼ "I became involved in church again for the first time since childhood. My life was so fun and so full. I was taking care of the twins, running them around to their activities, doing my job, keeping house. I went along like that for years. Then Ed had

"I was an alcoholic and drug addict. I went to order a pizza one night and misdialed the number. The person at the other end of the phone was a pastor from [the church I ended up joining]. I received Christ the next day. Since then I have known the joy and love of Christ. Later, I went on a short missionary trip to Cuba that made me realize how much God wants us to share his message."

this affair that broke my heart. No, not just my heart. It broke my life. And my neighbor Sandy was incredible. She listened and listened. She helped me pay bills and cook when I couldn't even function. She prayed for me. I'd prayed before, but this was different. I felt as if there really was a Jesus and he was standing right there with his arm around my shoulders. I mean it was really Sandy's arm, but it felt like Jesus'. That was the start."

■ "I never knew intellectual Christians. Actually, in the last two years since I began attending [my church], I realize I probably **have** known intelligent, liberal Christians, but I didn't know they **were** Christians. This congregation is amazing. The people are thoughtful. They have a variety of ways set up to serve people in our city. We have a reading program and a food bank. A group of us monitor legislation during the state legislative session. Different beliefs are represented in this church, but they have ability to discuss issues openly. I find no dogmatic, simplistic, theological strictures. I am beginning to develop an interest in the spiritual disciplines, which is completely new for me."

■ "I grew up in Indiana. After marriage I went to Iran. I was in an abusive marriage, and my husband would not allow me to see my children for two years. That is legal in Iran, and the courts would not allow me to see them. My husband accused me of crimes for which I was scared I might be stoned to death. I fled the country. After coming here, I felt drawn to Christ from my childhood Catholic schools in Indiana. I tried many churches here and ended up at First Christian. Here the Bible study taught me about God and the church helped me get political asylum." (Her children, ages 8 and 12 as I write this, are still in Iran.)

■ "Being frustrated by the other churches I tried, I thought about Mr. Rogers and the qualities he stood for. I found them here."[4]

New Christians have fresh faith. They appreciate their new church homes as much as new members with a church background. But these new Christians help us see a fresh faith, a new faith. Did you ever have a time in your life of first love for Christ? How did you feel about your first church? How do those early feelings compare to your faith today? Have you grown in love and in understanding?

DISCUSSION QUESTIONS _____

1. How is your individual prayer going? Spend the first 15-20 minutes of your group time talking about the highlights: What was the most wonderful prayer day? What happened? What did you learn? What

Almost 60% of new members of evangelistic churches get there first because a person invited them, or because they know someone in the church.

challenged you? What are you wondering about? Go around the circle and everyone say something!

2. Did you ever have a time of first being in love with God? How does that time compare with your feelings and understandings today? Have you lost anything? What have you gained in your faith?

3. Have you participated in helping Christ transform someone else's life? Who have you invited to church? When was the last time you welcomed a visitor? Helped organize a dinner for visitors? Talked with someone about your relationship with God or about asking God to lead your life? Prayed for someone to come to know Jesus? What happened?

We need to know how to talk about Jesus from our own lives, out of our real feelings of faith and doubt and in real life words.

4. What are your church's stories about people whose lives God has transformed as a result of your church's ministry, or because of the actions of Christians in your church?

5. Did any Bible passage come to mind as you read this chapter? Does one occur to you now? Discuss how it connects with what you have read. (If no passages come to mind, you might want to look at: Luke 15; Acts 10:9–16; Ephesians 2:11–22; Philippians 2:3–4.)

EXERCISE

During this week, will you each interview *either* a person who used to go to church, but doesn't attend now *OR* someone with no church background at all? You may have to hunt for these people, but look among coworkers, neighbors, your grandchildren's high school friends, a nurse friend, the clerk at the hardware store. Keep in mind that you're doing an interview to find out their opinions, so they'll probably be flattered to be asked and listened to, not threatened!

Explain that you and some of your friends in your church are trying to figure out ways to help your church be even more open to new people. Tell them that you have been a Christian for so long and love your church so much, you don't have a good perspective on it anymore. Let them know that you have decided to do interviews with people who aren't in the middle of things at church so that you can get a better perspective.

Over lunch or coffee, ask the following questions. *LISTEN* until they stop talking!! Take notes. Ask follow-up questions if it seems appropriate. ***Don't give advice or give answers. Just get their*** *opinions.* Try to hear not only what they say, but how they say it. Listen for what they ***don't*** say.

1. What pops into your mind when you hear the word *church*?

2. Has anyone ever invited you to their church? What did you think when they asked you? Did you go? How did it feel? If you didn't go, why not?

3. Have you ever had a sense of God or Jesus communicating with you? What was it like?

4. If you had one question you could ask God and knew you'd get an answer, what would it be?

5. Would you like prayer for anything? (You may pray there, if it's private and they're comfortable with that, or tell them you'll be praying for them during your prayer times. If they have asked for prayer, call them back in a week or so. Ask how the situation's going and if there's any different way you could focus your prayer for them. You may be the only person praying for them.)

Come back and share what you discovered with the people in your group. Were there similarities? Did the age or experience of the people interviewed make a difference? Did anyone in your group interview anyone with a tattoo? ...anyone over 80? ...someone with a different racial, economic or educational background than the majority of your church members? Did you end up inviting them to your church? If not, why not? While you are together, pray for each of these people you interviewed.

What do conversions look like? It's hard for most church people to imagine. It's not about church, it's about Jesus.

---

[1] *What Women Want,* Paramount, 2000.

[2] These percentages do not add up to 100% because many people gave more than one reason for joining when they wrote why they joined the church. These are the percentages of the total number of times people described something that fit in these top categories.

[3] Reasons C and D are in different order for new and "established" Christians. New Christians list eternal life as the third reason and empowerment by the Holy Spirit and connection with the Divine as almost equal in fourth place. For details, see full report at www.GraceNet.info.

[4] Fred Rogers, a quiet, cardigan-wearing Presbyterian minister, was the central figure of PBS's longest-running show, *Mister Rogers' Neighborhood.* Generations of children, from the mid-1960s through today, loved our gentle, kindly neighbor.

Unbinding the Gospel

PART THREE

■ **PART ONE** looked at what evangelism is, what motivates us to do it and some statistics that show how our churches are doing.

■ **PART TWO** centered on the heart of the Gospel—what the message is that we can share with others, and a look at who those others are.

■ **PART THREE** focuses on how your individual congregation is doing, and where you can go from here.

■ **PART FOUR** is your 40-day personal prayer journal. Move closer to God through your individual prayer, then discuss it with your *Unbinding the Gospel* group.

Pray…that God will open to us a door for the word, that we may declare the mystery of Christ, for which I am in prison, so that I may reveal it clearly, as I should. (Col. 4:3–4)

Look, I have set before you an open door, which no one is able to shut. (Rev. 3:8)

CHAPTER 7

How's Your Church Doing?

Bandwidths, Barriers and Bridges

Four years of talking with over 1200 people about evangelism brought several surprises. One of the biggest is the amount of guilt people feel about not doing much evangelism. The worst problem with guilt is that it can shut down clear thinking. It can also stop action. Most congregations ARE doing at least some evangelism, in many cases, good evangelism! So let's focus on what we are doing, then open up more bridges to the unchurched.

This chapter focuses on three things:

1. "Bandwidths of Evangelism"—nine different kinds of people to reach

2. "Barriers to Evangelism"—things that block us from sharing the Gospel

3. "Bridges into Your Church"—passageways to build for new members

Bandwidths of Evangelism

Remember your fourth-grade science teacher explaining how radios are tuned? Radio stations broadcast on different frequencies, different "bandwidths" of the airwaves. Let's think about evangelism as one big broadcasting of the Great Commission. Remember Jesus' final meeting with the disciples just before he ascended into heaven? Matthew's gospel reports Jesus' last words to the disciples:

Many Christians feel guilty about not doing much evangelism. The worst problem with guilt is that it can shut down clear thinking. It can also stop action.

Now the eleven disciples went to Galilee, to the mountain to which Jesus had directed them. When they saw him, they worshiped him; but some doubted. And Jesus came and said to them, "All authority in heaven and on earth has been given to me. Go therefore and make disciples of all nations, baptizing them in the name of the Father and of the Son and of the Holy Spirit, and teaching them to obey everything that I have commanded you. And remember, I am with you always, to the end of the age. (Mt. 28:16–20)

All nations! All authority! Everything I have commanded you! To the end of the Age! *That's* daunting. This is part of the problem. We see the big picture, get scared, and the guilt takes control. We decide if we're not converting Africa single-handedly that we're not doing evangelism. (Actually, Africa is sending us missionaries now, and thank God for it!) We feel guilt and we forget to invite our next-door neighbor to church on Sunday. Surely we can find some middle ground in between those two extremes.

For this book, let's agree on the vital importance of our connections with the entire world. Let's agree to go on mission trips in the U.S. and abroad and send money to missions in other countries. But for the purposes of this chapter, we will think of evangelism in terms of the people on your doorsteps with whom you and your congregation can share your excitement about your faith. The purpose of rethinking evangelism isn't to water down some definition. It's to help us be sensitive to opportunities that surround us.

You probably don't think of working with some of these people as evangelism. For this "bandwidths of evangelism" idea, ask two questions:

1. Are we helping this person move into relationship with God?

2. Are we helping this person move into Christian community?

If the answer to either question is yes, we are going to call it evangelism, the sharing of the Gospel. Here are some bandwidths on which your church may already be broadcasting its message of the love of God:

Bandwidth 101.1–Children and Youth of the Congregation. Who is closest to you, to your church, who doesn't fully know God through Christ? The children of your congregation. Think of every Sunday School class, every youth group meeting as a way to help our children know Jesus and learn the power of being part of the

Is It Evangelism?

1. Are we helping this person move into relationship with God?

2. Are we helping this person move into Christian community?

If the answer to either question is yes, we are going to call it evangelism, the sharing of the Gospel.

church. When they get old enough to make decisions for their own lives, they will be able to make choices, knowing the options. Most of the people who join churches as adults were raised in the church. Working with our own children is evangelism.

Bandwidth 101.2–Children and Youth's Friends. Our children have friends at school and in their neighborhoods. Inviting them and helping them get to church activities is evangelism. Many current church members and pastors did not grow up in the church with their families. A grandparent, a family friend, a neighbor, a godparent, a Sunday School teacher brought them to church.

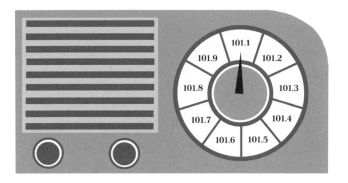

Bandwidths of Evangelism

101.1
  our children

101.2
  our children's friends

101.3
  attenders, not
  committed

101.4
  transfers, similar
  theology

101.5
  transfers, different
  theology

101.6
  far from church,
  drifted

101.7
  far from church, hurt

101.8
  not Christian, similar

101.9
  not Christian,
  different

Bandwidth 101.3–People Attached to Your Church Who Never Joined. Look closely at your congregation. You will discover people who attend church (steady visitors, relatives of a committed member, people with mental or physical disabilities) but who have never joined it or never offered their lives to Christ. Some of them have been connected with the congregation and served in various capacities for decades! When invited to be baptized or to join the church, they are often grateful and enthusiastic. Making a decision to be baptized or join a congregation can provide a life-changing boost in spiritual growth and involvement in the church. It's also life-giving for the person who extends the invitation!

Bandwidth 101.4–Committed Christians from <u>Similar</u> Church Backgrounds. Devoted Christians move to your town from other cities. They tend to start visiting neighborhood churches in their denomination, but denominational loyalty is not as strong a force as it once was (chapter 6). The younger they are, the more Christians are willing to move to a church of similar theology and cultural feel. New transfer members point to something that "felt right" about the new church they ended up joining. They are often drawn to what they loved most about their old church: commitment to Habitat and outreach, strong Bible teaching, a social justice focus, a specific type of worship, or speaking in tongues. These are some of the easiest people to help move into your church's life. They show up and if it feels like a good fit to them, if you're friendly and structured to assimilate new members easily, they join!

Bandwidth 101.5–Committed Christians from <u>Different</u> Church Backgrounds. Bandwidth 101.5 evangelism involves bigger jumps than the church changes in Bandwidth 101.4. These people must make a theological, and usually a denominational, shift. Do you know UCC members who have moved from a congregation with progressive theology to a Nazarene church? Has a family from a noninstrumental Church of Christ church joined your liberal Lutheran congregation? These are cases of Bandwidth 101.5 evangelism. This bandwidth more often contains a conversion element because the theological underlayment of the two churches is different.

> For this chapter, think of evangelism in terms of the people on your doorsteps with whom you and your congregation can share your excitement about your faith. The purpose of rethinking evangelism isn't to water down some definition. It's to help us be sensitive to opportunities that surround us.

Bandwidth 101.6–People Raised in the Church Who Drifted Away. We all know people who have church backgrounds, believe in God, but who are not committed to a congregation. No big rupture happened. They just drifted away. Often these disassociations from church happened during a time of change: going to college, a move, a job change, a divorce or other crisis, the children moving out and leaving the nest empty. Bandwidth 101.6 people may feel urges to visit a church again during life changes, when a friend talks about loving his church, or if they are invited to a church event. These people's biggest resistance to the idea of church is inertia.

Bandwidth 101.7–People Raised in the Church Who Were Hurt. Think of all the people you know who have had a bad experience with a church or a disillusionment in their faith. The list of types of people the church has wounded is impressive:

a. ex-church leaders burned out by congregational conflict

b. adults who were sexually molested by a church leader as a child

c. women who experienced fundamentalist theology as oppressive

d. people who lived through a traumatic death or tragedy that triggered a faith crisis (Frequently phrased as, "If God could let something like this happen, I don't want to have anything to do with God!")

e. people who felt "shunned" by churches that judged them

f. let's admit it—some people so bored by church that they gave up on it!

Many mainline congregations excel at working with people who have been hurt.

Bandwidth 101.8–Unchurched People <u>Like</u> *Current Church Members.* A growing number of people have had little or no exposure to Christianity or to churches. They were not raised in the church. They have not been baptized. They are not Christians. They may actually *think* of themselves as Christians, because they live in America and think of all Americans as Christians, so long as they aren't Jewish or Muslim. Millions of people are like this. They may have TV or movie images of Christianity. They may have hostility against the church even though they know little about it. They are like the members of your congregation in terms of jobs, schooling and ethnicity. Most mainline churches are doing very little to reach these people.

Bandwidth 101.9–Unchurched People <u>Different</u> *from Current Church Members.* Everything said about the last bandwidth (101.8) applies to this last group of people, but they are different than most of your congregation's members. Imagine a church of primarily upper-middle-class African-Americans evangelizing recent Chinese immigrants who have moved into the neighborhood. Envision a predominantly blue-collar Caucasian congregation working with Hispanic attorneys and professors. This is bandwidth 101.9 evangelism.

Review these bandwidths of evangelism. Do you suspect intuitively that they get more difficult as they progress from 101.1 to 101.9? Does your instinct tell you that it would probably be harder to evangelize a man angry at his old church than to help a happy 10-year-old in your Sunday School class grow in her faith? If so, your intuitions are right on target! In one way, the radio dial drawing at the beginning of this section is misleading. A more accurate way of picturing the bandwidths of evangelism is to stack them on top of each other in a pyramid. This "evangelism pyramid" gives us a better way to see the relative size and difficulty of the bandwidths:

As the pyramid gets skinnier nearer the top, helping the people connect with a church or become Christian gets harder and harder. In addition, the numbers of people added to the church in each of these ways also gets smaller as the pyramid gets up to its point.[1]

> Do you see that most churches are doing some kind of evangelism, some type of sharing of the Good News?

Your Church and the Evangelism Bandwidths

All right, how can you think about your congregation's evangelism using the bandwidth pyramid? Start at the bottom of that pyramid and see how many of these kinds of evangelism you're doing, or are

Sometimes these evangelistic movements start with a great idea and careful planning. Sometimes events or relationships percolate and evangelism begins to happen spontaneously. Prayerful people see God's hand in it and figure out next steps to keep participating in what God has started.

on the verge of doing. Why think you have to leap to the top of the pyramid to be doing any evangelism? You don't start playing the violin by launching into the Tchaikovsky concerto. You begin with *Twinkle, Twinkle, Little Star*. Little League kids learn to pitch the ball, to catch the ball, to hit the ball. We start where we are, then add a new challenge.

Do you see that most churches are doing *some* kind of evangelism, *some* type of sharing of the Good News? Do you really believe that God is crazy about us and wants a relationship with us? Almost any congregation is working with its own children—to teach them to love Jesus, who loves them! Almost all of our congregations are doing something to help their children know that the church loves them and to help their children and youth enter into a relationship with Christ that will last forever. That's the start. Where do you go from there? Take two steps:

1. Do what you're doing well a little better

2. Pray to see one new area of evangelism the Spirit would like you to try next

Look at the bandwidths in the pyramid. A logical starting place to focus the congregation's energies may leap out at you. Do the children in your youth group go to the grade school next door to the church? You may be ready for Bandwidth 101.2. Do you have adults with gifts and a call to work with a tutoring program for children?

Old basketball players? Ballroom dancing maniacs? A nursing home nearby? Quilters? Ties to the business community?
Think about:

- deep needs of people in your neighborhood
- logical opportunities to meet new people
- the gifts and passions of people in your congregations.

If you think about these three: needs, opportunities and gifts, you may find yourself zeroing in on a bandwidth that's logical and feels right.

A Mennonite congregation began teaching Hispanic migrant workers and new Hispanic residents to read. These quiet, intellectual Mennonites found themselves telling their new neighbors stories about Jesus loving them. Many of the tutoring students have been baptized and joined the church. A Disciples of Christ congregation in Oklahoma started a ministry to mentally handicapped people because a brother and sister from a residential home in the neighborhood showed up at church one day. They were baptized and joined the church. They brought their friends. They invited their social workers. A second service started; an ex-prisoner ministry began.

Sometimes these evangelistic movements start with a great idea and careful planning. Sometimes events or relationships percolate and evangelism begins to happen spontaneously. Prayerful people see God's hand in it and figure out next steps to keep participating in what God has started. The pastor of the Oklahoma Disciples church later shook her head, grinned and described the beginnings of the new ministry: "I try to be an organized person. I wish telling all this sounded better! There was something about trying to follow what the Spirit was doing that always felt as if we didn't quite have a plan and I was just punting." In California, pastors say following the Spirit feels like surfing—you catch the next wave God's bringing along. It takes a Sooner to express the follow-the-Spirit feel for many of the rest of us. We who don't live on a coast feel like we're punting!

Another congregation was full of golfers—imagine! They decided to invite unchurched friends to play golf. Conversations began. So did conversions to Christianity.

What is your ministry setting? Who are your church members? What are their interests and gifts? What is already happening with outreach in your church? Pray. Ask God to give you ideas. Discuss them. Keep praying. When it's time, do something. Just keep God in the loop!

There *is* great news: God is in the business of healing us and our churches; Christ will stand at our elbow and point out our entrenched positions, our towering battlements and those legions of yeomen who are always retipping arrows and heating oil. The Spirit can lead us to drain moats, open drawbridges, and build wheelchair-accessible bridges! We slam the door shut on the Gospel, but Christ opens windows in lives and in churches.

Barriers to Evangelism, Bridges into the Church

Can you see the Lincoln Memorial in your mind's eye? Can you picture that long, shallow flight of steps in front? The building is wide, beautiful and inviting. Picnickers sit on the steps, laughing together or thinking as they gaze into the reflecting pool. You look at that building, glimpse the statue of Lincoln from afar and want to glide up into it.

Now envision a medieval castle. See high walls rising out of that smelly moat. Look up at the crenelations, the bumps on top. Archers shoot arrows or pour hot oil on intruders from between them. The drawbridge is up. The huge wooden door, studded with metal spikes, is closed.

Some of us, as individuals, are as warm, open and welcoming as the Lincoln Memorial. Others of us are like a medieval fortress, bristling with defenses. The same goes for our churches. Some welcome and assimilate new members easily, joyously. Others are surrounded with barbed wire.

There *is* great news: God is in the business of healing us and our churches, Christ will stand at our elbow and point out our entrenched positions, our towering battlements and those legions of yeomen who are always re-tipping arrows and heating oil. The Spirit can lead us to drain moats, open drawbridges, and build wheelchair-accessible bridges!

We slam the door shut on the Gospel, but Christ opens windows in individual lives and in churches. A pastor named Sally said that she was overwhelmed one morning by St. Paul's explanation of a passage of Isaiah. Paul wrote to the Christians in Rome, "Thus I make it my ambition to proclaim the good news, not where Christ has already been named, so that I do not build on someone else's foundation, but as it is written, 'Those who have never been told of him shall see, / and those who have never heard of him shall understand'" (Rom. 15:20–21).

Sally lived with Paul's words for weeks. She said the Spirit started showing her tiny ways she blocked God from helping her reach out to people who were not yet Christians. "I kept having to ask God's forgiveness every time He showed me another little habit of never thinking to share my faith, or of deflecting faith discussions when I was away from church people. I was mortified. I wasn't talking about Christ unless I was being paid to do it! Finally I went to our elders and told them about it. We prayed together and they had the same sense of conviction I had. We realized we never talked about our

> Two types of barriers prevent us from doing effective evangelism: barriers inside our heads, and barriers in the church. Both can block people out.

faith except to each other, in church. It started us on a long journey. We had to rethink almost everything we were doing. We weren't talking about our faith. We realized we were discouraging visitors who hadn't been raised Lutheran. We had never thought of all the little ways our worship and our educational classes made unchurched people feel awkward or ignorant. Why had we assumed that being nice was enough?

"The evangelism minister on our bishop's staff helped us take a fresh look at our hospitality, our worship and our ways of discipling new members. He was great. He kept telling us to *try* things, to experiment. He said loads of our ideas wouldn't work, but just to try a whole lot of different things. We did. Some things flopped. The two big changes we've kept are the contemporary worship service and a coffee shop ministry for teens we're doing with two other churches."

Several years after the Spirit prompted Sally with Romans 15, she said, "The new members have helped, the new Christians especially. We can ask them to help us see how we can be more sensitive to 'seekers.' We've given up some parts of our old worship service, added screens, projectors, a sound system and a band. But the biggest change has been in our priorities, We 'old timers' are trying to think first of ways we can show Christ's face to people who are intimidated by the idea of church, or who were burned by the church. We used to think first about ourselves and what we liked. God is changing us as much as any of the people he is sending us."

As you sense from Sally's description, two main types of barriers to prevent us from doing evangelism: barriers inside people's heads, and barriers in the church. Both can block people out. Let's look at the personal issues first.

Individuals' Barriers and Bridges

Almost every one of us has blocks about sharing our faith. We have internal medieval castles, complete with moats! Many of us are embarrassed or feel as if we don't know how to talk about our spiritual lives or our churches. Obviously, ideas and feelings affect our priorities and our actions. If we don't feel comfortable talking about our faith, we're not likely to do it!

We discovered three primary personal barriers to doing evangelism:

1. The most solid barrier to evangelism, the anti-evangelistic bedrock upon which we build our churches, is that most pastors and laypeople in mainline churches are not clear *why* to do

Where to start? Think:

1. needs of neighbors
2. opportunities to meet them
3. your gifts and passions

evangelism. If we don't know ___why___ to do evangelism, we'll never get to the question of ___how___ to do it (chapter 2).

2. Once people recognize the importance of evangelism, we discovered that a typical fear about faith sharing kicks in, even among pastors who are leading great evangelistic congregations! It's usually expressed as, "I don't want to risk a friendship," or, "I don't want to pressure people."[2]

3. A third common barrier, and a fairly easy one to deal with, is, "I don't know **how** to talk about my faith."[3]

Dismantling the barriers: The great news is that the act of identifying barriers helps us build bridges. If we know why to do evangelism, we'll start being motivated to share our faith. We'll begin seeing opportunities. If we identify our fears about sharing our faith, our fears of risking friendships, our fears of not knowing what to say, then we can talk with other Christians about it. At that point, we usually realize that every one of us has bits of hesitation. Then we can learn and practice helpful ways of talking about our faith. Now we are not blocking the Spirit from using us. See the process? If we will be brave enough to see and dismantle our barriers, the process of talking about our fears and practicing with our friends becomes the means of developing new skills and confidence. We have used the stone and concrete our barriers were made of for bridge construction!

The typical barrier for people raised in mainline congregations is that we are foggy on why it matters that anyone be Christian. Most mainline Christians have little fear of Hell, but a horror of being embarrassed or looking obnoxious! Dismantling the barriers for most mainline Christians involves serious thinking, talking and praying about our relationships with Christ. If we are going to share faith, we need to know why we think it matters that we, or anyone else, are Christian.

Many people whose faith was formed in more traditional evangelical or charismatic churches have trouble with evangelism because they felt pressured to do it. The thought of evangelism feels negative to them. A 50-year-old evangelical woman lawyer articulated this barrier beautifully, "I always felt I wasn't really a Christian if I didn't do evangelism—door knocking, inviting people to church activities. I was in a campus ministry…Your ministry success was unofficially based on how many baptisms you performed each year. Less than 100 was clearly not successful. It never occurred to me that evangelism was sharing something you enjoy with someone you like (like quilting or

---

Individual Barriers to Faith Sharing

1. I don't know why to do evangelism.

2. I don't want to risk a friendship.

3. I don't know how to talk about my faith.

dog shows). It was something all Christians had to do to go to Heaven. So, as you can guess, it's a touchy subject for me."

The grace-filled idea that "evangelism [could be] sharing something you enjoy with someone you like" was barrier-dismantling for her. Our barriers often dissolve if we identify them, look at them, discuss them, and pray to see old situations with new eyes.

Un-muting the Mute Button

We discovered one big difference between successful evangelistic congregations and "typical" churches. Evangelistic churches, like many good churches, concentrate on helping people grow in their faith lives through spiritual practices. But the evangelistic churches also hone in, with laser-like focus, on helping their members articulate and share their growing faith. This focus on faith and on faith sharing is evident in sermons, in small groups and in congregational financial priorities.

We're smart people. If we know *why* to share our faith (for example, that Christianity is true, or that being a Christian makes our life better in specific ways), we will be able to talk about it. Congregations with evangelistic faith encourage members to invite friends to church. They train people to recognize and articulate their faith. Training to share faith can happen from any theological perspective, but it always involves helping people identify (a) the pathway of their individual walks with Christ, (b) how God is active in their lives, (c) the power of the church community and (d) how to talk about these things in normal words.

People who share their faith say that it's hard because it is so personal. Practice with church friends first helps. Trying little steps like inviting someone to worship or to an event at church helps. And yet, with support of others from church as we saw in chapter 5, once you try talking about the depths of faith with others, it is exciting. Talking about God and what you are learning spiritually is actually one of the ways your own faith will grow and deepen.

"If you are interested in going further to learn more about faith sharing—and more importantly, to pray and practice it—you may want to look at the rest of the *Unbinding the Gospel Series.* (See first two pages of this book for a Series Guide). *Unbinding Your Heart*[4] is a six-week version of *Unbinding the Gospel.* It includes a different 40-day prayer journal. *Heart* can help you bring the experience of this study to your whole church. If your group would like to move right into faith sharing with some of your friends who don't go to church, *Unbinding Your Soul*[5] may be the best next step.

> The grace-filled idea that evangelism could be "sharing something you enjoy with someone you like" was barrier-dismantling for her.

Evalgelistic churches concentrate on helping people grow in their faith lives through spiritual practices. These churches hone in, with laser-like focus, on helping their members articulate and share their growing faith.

Did you ever help a friend who didn't understand a class study for the exam? The first time I did it, I remember feeling frustrated because I was sure being nice to a friend was going to waste my precious study time. The exact opposite happened. When I struggled to explain hard material, simply and clearly, to my clueless friend, I understood it better myself. The structure of what I was learning, the most important points, fell into place in my own head. This is probably why teachers love teaching. You understand anything better when you try to put it into words. Could that be one reason why Christ asks us to help spread the Gospel to the ends of the earth? Did he want us to begin to get it ourselves by explaining it to others?

There's a great line in the movie *Jerry Maguire*.[6] Tom Cruise was a sports agent trying to help a frustrating, pig-headed, egotistical football player (whom Cruise really liked). In one scene, Tom Cruise said one line about 15 different ways to try to get it into the tight end's head, "Help *me* help you." "Help me help *you*!" "*HELP* me *HELP* you!" Maybe that's why Jesus asks us to help with evangelism. It's a cosmic "Help me help *you*" from God!

Okay, so we *can* learn to talk about our faith, if for no other reason than to help God help us! The important thing about our personal barriers to faith sharing is to: (1) identify them, (2) talk about them, (3) do something to dismantle them. Now let's think about the barriers and bridges we find in churches.

Your Church's Barriers and Bridges

Think! What does your church feel like to first-time visitors and new members? The Lincoln Memorial or the medieval fortress? Something in between? What's your best guess? *A church's biggest barrier is that long-term members can't see their churches with fresh eyes.* When you ask church members to describe their congregation, the two most common descriptions are: "Our church is so *friendly*." and "We're like a family." These statements couldn't be more true. The problem is that we forget what families are like!

Church is like family. Have you been a stranger at someone else's family reunion? Have you ever been the brand new son-in-law? There's everybody, laughing and joking, grabbing the good kind of baked beans and knowing to avoid Aunt Letty's sponge cake. They all know who's nice, who's fun and who's a big pain. They know the jokes. They know Uncle Larry drinks too much and that then, if you're a woman, you'd better give him Wide Berth. They all know not to pay attention to Aunt Edna, who manages to say something nasty to anyone within earshot. We all know *our* families; *they're* normal. It's *other* people's families that are nuts! But some families work hard to help new people fit in and to feel welcome. Other families make you earn your place at the table!

Churches are the same way. Once you're inside and have your group of friends and your round of activities, you forget about the first impressions and the initiation rites. You don't even **see** the nasty sponge cake or Uncle Larry's encroachments upon ladies' nether limbs. Aunt Edna's mouth may move, but you don't hear sound coming out any more. Once you're in the family and have your allies and buddies, once you've spent a couple of Thanksgivings and Christmases together, it's friendly. It's family. And that's how you describe it. It's just like your church. It's a family.

First-time visitors. It's almost impossible to see our own churches with a fresh eye. Can you imagine what it would be like to be a first-time visitor? Think about a first visit from beginning to end. If you were new in town, how would you learn about the existence of the church? Worship times? Get the yellow pages and look up the ad. Drive by your church, pretending you don't know it's there. What does it look like? Can you read the sign?

Call the church phone. How's the phone answering machine message? Does it give directions and worship times? Is the secretary friendly? Pretend you're a fly on the wall this Sunday. Watch and see how any visitors are greeted. Look at their expressions. Are they lost? Looking intimidated? Do people talk with them and invite them into their pew? Are close parking spots and back pews available two minutes before the service starts, the time when visitors often arrive? Are bathrooms and coat racks clearly labeled? Is the building entrance accessible? Well-kept? ***IS THE NURSERY SPOTLESS? and Easy to Find?*** How many people talk with new visitors? Show them around? Invite them for lunch afterwards?

Many fears accompany first-time visitors (remember chapter 6). How are you working to calm those fears? Do you have social events to which your members can invite visitors? One congregation has an annual women's Christmas lunch. Two members set a table for eight of their unchurched friends with their most beautiful china and silver and flowers from home. They invite their friends, act as hostesses and have a program on a faith theme. People with no connection to a church may be scared of going to a worship service, but it's rare to find someone scared of lunch!

Is your worship service inspiring and meaningful? Is it overwhelming or tedious? Do the music and language feel comfortable or foreign to the bandwidth of people God is calling you to reach?

Most mainline Christians have a fading fear of Hell, but a vivid horror of being embarrassed or looking obnoxious!

Do you spell out the Lord's prayer and when to stand or sit? Many churches print the words worshipers say or sing in the bulletin or on projection screens. We can no longer count on people knowing the structure of a worship service, the doxology or even the Lord's prayer. Is there welcoming follow-up (a gift, a call, an invitation, a visit)? It is such a challenge to think about first impressions!

Returning visitors. Next comes another set of questions. How easy it is for second- or third-time visitors to find a place or small group in the church so that they make real friends in the congregation? How many opportunities do they have to learn more about the faith? To have opportunities to serve others?

After joining. Think further down the road. How easy is it for new members to ease into positions of leadership and responsibility? Do you support new leaders and train them, or ask them to do a job and let them figure it out on their own? Does it take a decade to be welcomed into central places of service and commitment?

Feedback. Think about these things yourselves. Then check out your thinking. Give feedback cards to all visitors. Provide feedback cards in each pew. People will write things they would **never** have the courage to say to your face. Always remember the key point—***ask the people who know***. You can ask the elders how well you're doing with first impressions, or the ease of integration of new members into the congregation's life. They will have a few good ideas. But if we want to know for real, we have to ask the visitors and the new members themselves! It's like the family reunion. The new son-in-law will have insights now that he'll have forgotten in three years. After three years, he ***still*** knows more about what it's like to be new in the family than the grandmother knows.

Many books and many articles on the Internet can give you wonderful ideas to try in your church. Once you begin to see the barriers you have up, as individuals and as a church, you can begin to take steps to dismantle them. Like Sally's congregation, ask the Spirit to help you see where you're stuck in old habits or how you could be more open. Ask for help from a consultant, from a denominational minister, from visitors, or from pastors and laypeople from churches that are doing a good job of evangelism.

Bridges can be built, bit by bit. Those first forays toward faith sharing often feel like swinging over quicksand on a Tarzan rope. They have none of the secure sense of standing on the bedrock of

We understand anything better when we try to say it out loud. Could this be one reason Christ asks us to share our faith? Is the Great Commission (Mt. 28:18–20) a cosmic "Help *me* help **you**" from God?

habit! But don't worry! Soon, with many people helping, you could be tiptoeing gingerly on a sturdy rope ladder over a waterfall. Next you'll be rambling across a covered bridge. One day you may open the door of your church and see the Golden Gate Bridge leading straight into your sanctuary.

DISCUSSION QUESTIONS

1. *How is your individual prayer going? Spend the first 15-20 minutes of your group time talking about the highlights: What was the most wonderful prayer day? What happened? What did you learn? What challenged you? What are you wondering about? Go around the circle and everyone say something!*

2. Have you ever tried to share your faith? What happened? What felt right in the experience? What might you do differently next time? Does anything stop you from talking with others about faith? What could help change that?

3. Think about the bandwidths of evangelism. Who is your church already reaching? Discuss what God is doing to connect people with your church now. What would be the logical next step to expand your church's evangelism? Do you have any inklings, any promptings from the Spirit about whom you might be called to reach? Does the "logical next step" you identified fit with the way the promptings of the Spirit feel? Talk about ***that***!

4. Is your church like the Lincoln Memorial for visitors and new members, with its wide, easy entrance steps? Or is it like a medieval castle complete with turrets and moat? Name any barriers to visitors or new members that you can think of. What are the top three barriers you would dismantle? How do the barriers change when you switch stations to a different bandwidth? Are these barriers different, depending on which bandwidth of evangelism you're tuned to? Which are the first three bridges you'd build if you could wave a magic wand?

5. So what arc you going to do?

6. Did any Bible passage come to mind when you read this chapter? Does one occur to you now? Discuss how it connects with what you have read. (If no passages come to mind, you might want to look at: 2 Timothy 1:6–8; Hebrews 13:1–3; Colossians 4:3–4; Colossians 3:12–17.)

EXERCISE _____

Divide into groups of three or four. Sit quietly with a notebook and pen in your lap. Pray in silence for a couple of minutes. Ask God to show you what you need to know about what your church looks like/feels like to people who have:

1. never heard of it
2. never been inside
3. not joined a small group yet
4. not been members long
5. never served as board chair

Take notes as words, images or ideas occur to you.

The leader will close the silent time with a prayer. Open your eyes. Divide into small groups. Let each group make a large drawing of your church on newsprint. Label the barriers and bridges you thought about during the prayer time, or that occur to you as you talk. Pay particular attention to the insights of people who have not been in your church long. You are an evangelistic architect. What would you do to redesign this "building?"

As a full group, talk about the small groups' drawings and see if the groups came up with similar barriers and bridges. What are possible next steps? Pray in silence for two or three minutes and ask Christ to show you what one or two changes he would like you to make. Talk about it.

Exercise during the week: Now it's time to test out your perceptions. Half of you invite a new member out to lunch and ask him or her about the church. What do they perceive as the welcoming strengths of the church? Its barriers to newcomers? What works beautifully? What could the church do better?

The other half of your group could each ask a good friend to visit your church and pretend to be shy. Invite someone you know will be able to be honest with you. Ask them to call the church to get worship times and directions. Give them a list of questions you will find on the Hospitality Inventory on our Web site at www.GraceNet. info. Ask them to keep track of how many people spoke with them, what was welcoming, what was off-putting. Would they come back? What could you do better? Don't forget to thank them exuberantly and to invite them back for real! If you make changes later based on their help, let them know about it. (And ask them to visit again!)

---

[1]We do not have exact statistics for these categories. The Mainline Evangelism Project did collect recent statistics on adult baptisms, which help us measure how churches are doing in evangelism with unchurched people—Bandwidths 101.8 and 101.9. What we know for sure is that only half of 1% of 30,000 congregations performed what we considered a significant number of adult baptisms (chapter 3). Compare that to the fact that almost all of those 30,000 congregations would be working in some way to help their young people have a relationship with Christ.

[2]The Mainline Evangelism Project survey showed that there are inner barriers to evangelism even in pastors and members of churches who are doing some of the most effective evangelism with unchurched adults in the country: 38.3% of these pastors report that they have hesitations because they don't want to risk a friendship, 70.8% of the pastors don't want to pressure others. Meanwhile, 39.5% of laypeople don't want to risk a friendship, 83.5% don't want to pressure others. Yet, they have figured out ways to acknowledge their hesitations and do evangelism anyway!

[3]An overwhelming majority of 73.3% of laity say that not knowing how to talk about their faith is a great barrier to doing evangelism. Meanwhile, 24.5% of pastors and evangelism leaders cite this as somewhat of a barrier or a great barrier. Finally, 19.3% of pastors/leaders and 63.8% of laity say that not knowing how to talk about their faith is at least somewhat a barrier.

[4]Martha Grace Reese, *Unbinding Your Heart* (St. Louis: Chalice Press, 2008).

[5]Martha Grace Reese, *Unbinding Your Soul* (St. Louis: Chalice Press, 2009).

[6]*Jerry Maguire,* Sony Pictures, 1996.

CHAPTER 8

The Holy and the Practical

Who Does What?

Life with Christ is reality. It is joy. It is hope. It is salvation. It matters more than anything in the world. It is life that infuses and subsumes the world. In despair, we have hope in God. In fear, the shattering surrender of Christ on the cross shines live glory on us. This is the heart of faith. This is the good news.

Some moments of faith sink so deep they can't be described. They happen in the recesses of your soul. You may have felt some of them—being prayed for before surgery; sitting in candle-lit quiet in the Christmas Eve service; hearing the one phrase that unlocks your heart in a sermon written for you. Words cannot express the feelings of forgiveness, overwhelming love, resting in God in silent prayer. This is mystery and depth and holiness. This is what God has made known to us, and this is what Christ has asked us to show others.

Think. A soul is linked to a body. Evangelism is the same way. Sharing the mystery of God is a sacred gift contained in the practical structures of sermons and small groups, newcomer's dinner parties and signs for the parking lots. The holy is encased in the pragmatic.

Some churches are disconnected from the power and mystery of the holy. They live with details of yellow pages ads, but have nothing to share but muted friendliness and pale assurance. Other churches, in the old African-American saying, are "so heavenly minded they're no earthly good." If you lose the mystery, you have

A soul is linked to a body. Evangelism is the same way. Sharing the mystery of God is a sacred gift contained in the practical structures of sermons and small groups, newcomer's dinner parties and signs for the parking lots. The holy is encased in the pragmatic.

Some churches are disconnected from the power and mystery of the holy. They live with details of Yellow Pages ads, but have nothing to share but muted friendliness and pale assurance. Other churches, in the old African-American saying, are "so heavenly-minded they're no earthly good." If you lose the mystery, you have nothing to share. If you don't focus and organize the sharing, the church turns inward.

nothing to share. If you don't focus and organize the sharing, the church turns inward.

So should we strike some nice average? A little mystery with a little detail and organization? Add the two extremes together, divide by two and live in the middle? I want to hear you shouting the words of Paul, "God forbid!" We'll end up lukewarm centrists like the church in Laodicea (Rev. 3:14–16), and Jesus will want to throw up. No! We have plenty of *those* churches already. Let's do something real instead.

Faith has to be real. Faith has to go as deeply into the holy mystery of life with God as we can stand. We are invited into give-it-all-away, bet-the-farm, choreographed-by-the-Spirit, life-walking-by-Christ's-side in minute-by-minute miraculous glory.

AND we've been given gifts of minds and hearts and computers and bread pans and nine irons and magic markers and QuickBooks® and singing voices and digital cameras. We've been given enthusiasm, relationships, minds, compassion, money and abilities to organize. All these joys and gifts and graces can live in and be utilized in a choreographed-by-the-Spirit life. *We have to hold the opposites together. It's All Mystery. It's All Practicality. All the time.*

Keys to Doing Evangelism

Practically, how do you do evangelism? Here are the keys:

FIRST: Everyone—pastors, laypeople, conference ministers, the whole congregation together—must have a live, current, attended-to spiritual life. We have to know God in our lives today to share the good news, or, as Peter Marshall said, the Good News will be "diluted into good advice."[1]

SECOND: Everyone—pastors, laypeople, bishops, the whole congregation together—must be focused, minds engaged and open to see patterns, details, opportunities, changes and miracles. We have to think. We have to read and research. We have to plan. We have to be ready to see, evaluate and change what we are doing.

Evangelism is holiness borne in details.

Who Does What?

What does evangelism look like in a great congregation? Who does what to help evangelism flourish? We'll just touch highlights of the human part. Keep in mind that all faith, all reality, all love and any real movement come from God. In our study we did find a "most typical" pattern for the human part of evangelism:

- *pastors* see, promote and guard a vision of evangelism as a congregational priority; they oversee practical implementation of the vision
- *church members* learn to articulate their faith and figure out specific ways to share it; they develop congregational programs and patterns for faith sharing
- *bishops* (regional and classis ministers, presbytery executives) raise up evangelism as a regional priority and encourage a vision of evangelism and experimentation in this new time.

Let's look at these three groups of people. Evangelistic churches are all different, but the best ones, with sustained vibrancy over time, hold mystery and details together. They work from the strengths of the areas listed above. I want to speak directly to pastors, laypeople and bishops in the sections below. You others may listen in when I'm not talking to you directly. Think about how you can support the people addressed! *Baseline assumption: Everyone prays for everyone.*

Pastors

Great pastors listen for God's whispers, find God's vision, and prophetically speak God's words. They try to see people, situations, programs and the church with Christ's eyes. When the experience with God is real, a pastor is holding up God's vision in the congregation's sight. The pastor and people then have a better chance of being effective.

The development of faith and faith sharing doesn't exist in a vacuum. God gives us faith as a gift. But we, as humans, can impede faith's growth. If we fail to work with God, we can quench the Spirit's urgings to help people toward faith and into faith maturity. Pastors have to live it, preach it, and help develop the classes, the programs, the initiatives that can serve as vehicles for Christ's request that we carry the gospel to people who don't know it.

1. Set the priorities. See the big picture. What is the pastor's hardest task? Almost every evangelistic pastor we interviewed had the same answer. They agreed that keeping their own focus outward, on evangelism, is the most important and the hardest thing they do. Leaky roofs, grumpy trustees, and rounds of hospital visits threaten the evangelistic priority. The pastor must start by practicing spiritual discernment and time management. A pastor, like each of us, can do only a few things well. If the pastor doesn't cling to evangelism as a highest priority, daily, the church will turn inward. Period. To

Faith has to be real. Faith has to go as deeply into the holy mystery of life with God as we can stand. We are invited into give-it-all-away, bet-the-farm, choreographed-by-the-Spirit, life-walking-by-Christ's-side in minute-by-minute miraculous glory.

focus on evangelism means handing off other important things or deciding not to do them.

One pastor said, "I always have to pull back and take a new look at the big picture to keep evangelism in focus. Every time I settle in and just "do my job," or do what everybody wants me to do, within a week or two the tide rises above eye level. I've turned into a chaplain. I catch myself thinking only about what we're already doing and about these incredible people who are already here. For me, keeping a tight focus outside these church walls is like guarding my middle-aged waistline. If I forget the exercise for a week, I'm reaching for the loose-fit cargo pants! Then I have to shake it off. I have to remember that Jesus wants us pointed out into the world. It helps that I have three guys in the church I talk and pray with every week. They hold my feet to the fire so I don't shut my eyes, don't drift into maintenance!"

See the crucial elements here? (a) Evangelism is a priority and (b) corrective accountability structures are in place.

2. Preaching and worship are crucial. The pastor must be in communion with God. The pastor must see the big picture. And the pastor must live it out vividly in worship. Powerful worship is crucial, both to current members and to new people. The importance of the sermon *cannot* be overrated. The sermon, in its worship setting, has the potential to reflect the Gospel, convey key Christian content, and to clinch worshipers' connections with the pastor and the congregation. The sermon can hold out a vision of next steps for the community. Where evangelism is a priority, its themes are woven into sermons, prayers, and/or communion meditations weekly.

A centered, spiritually healthy pastor has a priestly role in worship. S/he is iconic in a way we don't understand, but praying through the letter to the Hebrews nudges us toward this truth. Pastors, in the rush of Sunday morning, please do not forget for whom you pray and speak and to whom you guide worship.

3. "Outer" evangelism: dissolving barriers, building bridges. The pastor needs to be sure that identifying and removing barriers and building bridges into the congregation are both happening (chapter 7). Many mainline churches look at these barriers and bridges issues of hospitality as the real stuff of evangelism. This "outer evangelism" is only half the picture. Hospitality is an important part of evangelism, but without a core of deep relationship with God, hospitality is just niceness. Hospitality must always be integrated into a well-developed congregational structure of teaching the practices of the faith and

We have to hold the opposites together. It's All Mystery. It's All Practicality. All the Time.

teaching faith sharing. The pastor can help hold these two areas in healthy balance.

4. "Inner" evangelism: teach faith practices and faith sharing. We must have live faith to share faith at all. You must attend to your own spiritual life and make sure that every member has opportunities to learn, experience and live the faith God is offering us. You and the people you serve won't do much (except incidentally) to help new people toward a relationship with Christ unless the stream of your relationship with Christ has some current to it. When our lives with God are stagnant, we are much more likely to impose rules, smother others with sentimentality, or spout arid concepts. A vivid faith has power and moves. It carries the freight of the gospel.

As we saw in chapters 2 and 7, the biggest personal barrier to doing evangelism exists when people don't know **why** to do evangelism, why it matters that we are Christians. Teaching faith practices and helping people grow into more mature spiritual lives changes this picture. If we know why to do evangelism, we get to move on to the second and third internal barriers to sharing the gospel! ("I don't want to pressure people" and "I don't know **how** to do evangelism" [Chapter 7].) Learning how to share our faith helps dissolve these barriers.

Many congregations discover that a key piece of their new member integration is a four- or six-week new members' class, taught by the senior pastor. The most effective of these classes are small group experiences in which new members get to know each other well as they learn basic concepts of the faith, spirituality, relationship with God and Christian community.

5. Practice relational leadership. How do the best pastors lead? It always looks different. Some great pastors are introverts, others are extroverts. Few pastors of healthy evangelistic churches are dictatorial. Few view consensus as more important than the discernment of leadings from the Spirit. The best pastors have deep, authentic faith. They tend to be optimistic. They love the people they serve. They have clear priorities and do not drift. They are smart. They shift easily between big picture and details. The best pastors do a beautiful job of working relationally with staff and key leaders. They delegate, empower, and express appreciation. Seeing what people are doing and thanking them matters.

6. You are God's beloved, too. No one of us can do or be all these things. Leading a church is a hard and occasionally heartbreaking

Keys to Evangelism

1. BE: live vibrant spiritual lives
2. DO: think, research, plan, try, evaluate, change

business. Every church has members who don't like what you're doing. Living at the heart of people's lives comes with inherent anguish. The burdens, the stresses, the joys of ministry are unimaginable to someone who has not borne them. Please, pastor, remember these crucial elements. They need to be in place if your ministry is to be effective and sustainable:

- spiritual disciplines
- days off
- exercise
- friends outside the church *(besides your spouse!)* with whom you are completely honest and accountable

Please value yourself as God values you. (Church members—negotiate an agreement to hold your pastor's feet to the fire on this one!)

> Without a core of deep relationship with God, hospitality is just niceness.

Remember, pastors, your job is to be responsive enough to the Spirit to see when you and the church wobble off course. It will happen! You must be healthy enough to help God correct the trajectory. Your call is to preach in a way that reminds people of the mystical holiness of faith, the profound logic and truth of the Gospel. Limits on time, energy and gifts have practical ramifications. You won't be able to meet some of your favorite parishioners' expectations. You won't be able to meet some of your *own* favorite expectations! That's fine. Your "Stop Doing" list is as important as your "To Do" list!

7. Keep your eyes on the Lord, not the status quo. If you slip out of sync with God, if you skip retreats with other pastors or meetings with your accountability partners, if you get frazzled and overworked, if you stop exercising and overeat, if you sense your joy evaporating and yourself acting cranky, you'll soon be reaching for the pastoral equivalent to loose-fit cargo pants. You'll slide into chaplaincy. You'll maintain the "what is." Have your fail-safe backup plans and corrective spiritual disciplines in place. Make sure that your life contains people who love you and who will be honest with you. Your only job is to let Jesus love you, do the best you can, pretty much of the time, and be willing to listen to the Spirit so that you can be used by Christ. God can work unimaginable miracles with that!

Church Members

A wonderful old Billy Graham pamphlet suggests thinking of the Bible as a love letter that God has sent to you, specifically to *you*. Don't let the Bible become a confusing, chaotic bundle of weird history, strange names and bizarre rules. Treasure it as a love letter God has written to you.

Let's do something similar with our lives. See the faces of the people around you—at work, at the shoe store, at your son's Boy Scout meeting. Think:

"These are people Christ wants me to care for."

"I am God's love letter to them."

"And they are God's love letters to me."

What if your mailman; your mother-in-law; your neighbor with the incessantly-barking sheltie; and every mink-clad, nonblinking, disastrously face-lifted shopper at the fancy mall were **exactly** the person Christ wants you to pray for right now? And maybe that person is the one God wants to use to teach you what **you** need to learn next.

If we live deeply with God, we will start to see fragmentary glimpses of people through Christ's eyes. A pastor told me, "The more I pray, the more I just **love** people with tattoos!" Once we have these glimmers of how God must see us, we want to help God care for those people; we want to learn from them. Could life be different for the frazzled mother dragging her shrieking two-year-old away from the Twinkies™ display? Could God use you to bring a life-changing experience to the married businessman hitting on the flight attendant? To the lonely, brilliant physics student? How about the frazzled chef who snorts cocaine? What might be different for each of these people if they were living with Christ with the support of a church? Envision the difference Jesus could make in these people's lives. This "envisioning" is prayer. The prayer may open opportunities for you to listen or speak a word. The love, the prayer and the word are pure evangelism.

How can you support sustainable faith sharing in your life? In your church? Here are some ways:

1. The bedrock of sustainable Christian action is a spiritual life. Prayer, accountability, the study of Scripture, history and theology matter. Commit yourself to a small group of Christians who study and pray together. Your individual prayer life is also crucial. You can start ministry without a prayer life, but soon it will be some combination of shallow, misdirected and burned out! *Please* don't try to skip this step.

2. Do what you love. Have you ever been arm-twisted into teaching the junior high Sunday School class out of duty? That hardly *ever* works out well. Don't get dragged into some slotted, pigeonholed

When our lives with God are stagnant, we are much more likely to impose rules, smother with sentimentality, or spout arid concepts. A vivid faith has power and moves. It carries the freight of the Gospel.

job "doing evangelism." Reread the first story in chapter 4, about the group of women who formed an evangelism team at Benton Street Church. This story combines steps 1 and 2 here. First, pray. Second, don't do it if it's not fun! Do what you love. If you like baking bread, for heaven's sake don't head up the evangelism team. Bake bread! If you are a computer geek, volunteer to write software and keep systems going. Researchers should research things. People who love to teach should teach. Intercessors should intercede! Natural leaders should head up teams. Get the picture? Does a scripture occur to you here? (Hint: Ephesians 4 might be good!)

3. Learn to talk about your faith. All of us in churches have some sort of faith life. Will you join a class (or start a class) for people to learn and practice talking about their faith? Remember, evangelism isn't handing some pamphlet to a stranger. It's seeing who needs to be prayed for. It's waiting for an opening in a conversation with that friend to mention church or your faith. It can be as simple as, "You know, going to my church really helps me. Do you want to come to church with me on Sunday?" It can be more self-revealing, like, "I know you feel guilty. I wish I didn't know so much about **that!** When I was…" Like anything else, practice makes it easier to do the next time.

4. Members of congregations do much more direct evangelism than pastors. Pastors preach and work with church members. They don't spend the day at IBM, the hardware store, the gym, the grade school or the golf course. People see **you**, not your pastor, as the person with the "real" faith life. You have credibility. You are the one with friends in the neighborhood. You are the one with a job in town, friends in classes. And no one sees you as the hired gun, paid to talk about God. Think of people in your life who have no one to pray for them. People you know, people you run into every day need different types of help. Many have no church to turn to. Could you start by praying for them? Then see what ideas the Spirit gives you.

5. Evangelists are all kinds of people. At the beginning of the Mainline Evangelism Project, I assumed that most of the people who helped non-Christians move into a faith life were like Bob Hope. No, not "Bing and Bob" Bob Hope, but a smiling, retired mechanic who was the heart of the Indianapolis-area church I served as pastor. Bob was one of the most loving, outgoing men I have ever known. Bob knew the name of every visitor who had ever set foot in the church. He had invited a third of them.

Typical pattern for the human part of evangelism:

- pastors hold up vision of evangelism, oversee implementation
- church members learn to talk about faith, find ways to share it
- bishops make evangelism a priority, encourage experimentation

Bob drafted a bucket brigade out of the choir one Sunday morning between services. They filled the baptistry to hip height with tepid water from the kitchen sink and water heated on the stove. A junior high school student had the flu when she should have been baptized the week before. She had shown up for Sunday School and wanted to be baptized! I don't remember if the choir practiced the anthem. I do remember that we baptized Heather!

One afternoon, the church secretary walked into my office, laughing. She told me she had just seen Bob Hope at the grocery store loading 17 paper bags bulging with Pampers,™ formula, and hotdog buns into the trunk of a young woman's car. The woman grinned feebly at Bob as she juggled a fractious four-year-old and a crying baby. The whole family appeared in church the next Sunday. Bob was a magnet for Christ and for our church. I don't know who he's evangelizing in heaven, but I want to hear *those* stories!

I have thought of Bob Hope as the "real" kind of evangelist ever since. Then along came the Mainline Evangelism Project, which gave me a surprise. I asked hundreds of people to describe the great evangelists in their congregation. People usually mentioned the pastor, then a person like Bob Hope first. But then I often heard, "Well, this is sort of strange, but there's this very shy woman […quiet man, … little kid, …awkward high school student, …science librarian who barely talks above a whisper]…"

> You won't be able to meet some of your favorite parishioners' expectations. You won't be able to meet some of your **own** favorite expectations! That's fine. Your "Stop Doing" list is as important as your "To Do" list!

The stories are amazing. Often the pastor or evangelism team leaders didn't know that these shy ladies, gawky kids, nonverbal librarians had anything to *do* with the visitors arriving on the doorstep. Sometimes the people "in charge" heard the stories years later. Occasionally, churches asked new members for feedback and found out that way.

When finally asked what they were doing, these quiet people described praying for friends, neighbors and coworkers. God often showed the shy evangelists situations of a kid getting beaten up in school, a coworker going through a divorce, a neighbor's daughter needing a pastor to perform her wedding. The quiet evangelists placed phone calls and wrote little notes. They invited these people to church. And the beaten-up kid, the divorced husband, and the neighbor, her daughter and new son-in-law become Christians and begin their own adventures with Christ.

6. New Christians as evangelists. We learned that new Christians' first desire is to learn the faith. They fall in love with God. They absorb the way Christianity makes the world make sense. They try to become more Christlike. They tell their friends—Microsoft executives, rock band guitarists, nursing home residents, Chinese historians, tenth graders and soccer coaches. Mainly, they're learning. Evangelistic churches nurture this growth and understand how tender it is.

Typical churches say that new members do most of their evangelism. I am sure that is true. But that may say more about typical churches' lack of focus on evangelism than about who does the most inviting and faith sharing in a healthy church! Our study demonstrated that in the high adult baptism churches, it's the longer-term members who are doing most of the inviting and faith sharing.

Our newest members, our newest Christians, should be able to share their faith. They are usually very enthusiastic about their new faith/new church. Many of their friends are not Christians. But we must let them grow up. We must not burden them with responsibilities until they are ready. We must be sensitive to their needs and their stages of spiritual growth.

> Your only job is to let Jesus love you, do the best you can pretty much of the time, and be willing to listen to the Spirit so that you can be used by Christ. God can work unimaginable miracles with that!

If your evangelism team is a loving, praying small group, in which new members and new Christians can learn and grow, it's a wonderful idea to include them. If you ask them, they'll help you identify and dismantle the church's barriers and build bridges. Even the most statistically successful evangelistic church pastors in six denominations aren't doing a good job anticipating what unchurched people think—at least they are making very different guesses about it than new Christians.[2] (See Wenger report, www.GraceNet.info.)

So, let's incorporate our newest Christians and newest members into our evangelism teams, perhaps as "consultants," or on a one-time basis. If you ask them, they'll have ideas for how to reach people that wouldn't occur to long-time church members. Their enthusiasm will encourage everyone. Just go gently. Don't create a "New Members as Prey" scenario! New Christians' first priority is learning the faith and connecting with the church.

7. Your evangelism team is a prayer group. We long-time members aren't prey, either! Please don't let your evangelism team turn into a group of exhausted task-doers. Devote the first half of your meeting time to prayer and sharing about your own lives. It can be your small group, your prayer group. If we talk about our own lives, study Scripture and pray together, God can work through us more directly. If we're open to God and in spiritual agreement, we don't block out the Spirit as much!

Review the stories in chapter 4. Learn how to discern and pray with people who know how. It would be great to invite a friend from a fast-growing evangelical or charismatic church to be on your team and pray with you for a year. Cross-pollination can work wonders! Being part of your evangelism team can be life-changing for you!

8. Pray for the people who have no one to pray for them. Dwight Ozard, a young, brilliant, evangelical music lover; dark chocolate fanatic; author; church consultant and wild, free spirit was a friend. He died too soon after a long struggle with cancer. He ended every e-mail, "Thanks for praying for Sheri and me, but please also pray for all the unnamed people with no one to pray for them."

Remember, Christian sisters and brothers: You are the only person whose life touches all of the people you know, work with and meet every day. You may be the only one praying for them. You may be the person Christ has put in their lives to help. We can pray for the ones we don't know yet who God could use us to help. Evangelism is about relationships. All relationships are in God's hands. So are all people. Prayer and awareness can lead us into amazing places.

Envision the difference Jesus could make in these people's lives. This "envisioning" is prayer. The prayer may open opportunities for you to listen or speak a word. The love, the prayer and the word are pure evangelism.

Bishops and Denominational Ministers

Bishops, synod executives, regional and classis ministers, presbytery executives, district superintendents—thank you.[3] You spend your lives on the road and on the phone. You may deal with more painful emotions, shrinking budgets and explosive meetings in a year than most of us will have to face in a lifetime. The confidentiality must lie very heavily some weeks. Thank you for what you are doing for all of us.

I have worked closely with a number of you for the last decade. Those bishops asked if I would include some suggestions for how you can help support pastors and congregations who are trying to do evangelism. Here are a few thoughts I have gleaned from my travels with the Mainline Evangelism Project:

1. Read a good book by a bishop. Bishop Claude Payne of the Episcopal Diocese of Texas co-wrote a book called *Reclaiming the Great Commission.*[4] He described the process of changing the major focus of the Episcopal Diocese of Texas (the Houston area) to evangelism. They started five new congregations during a ten-year period. They held large worship services, they reorganized the diocese's financial priorities, hired consultants and held the focus on evangelism for a decade. Membership in the diocese grew by 5% a year for a period of four or five years. Bishop Payne's book is incisive, thoughtful, informative and inspiring.

2. The church changes when evangelism is a true conference priority. Making evangelism a high priority encourages evangelism across the range of the conference's churches. A bishop's prominent emphasis on evangelism in sermons, newsletters, assemblies, and funding makes a huge difference. Emphasis on youth programming is a great support to congregations that are trying to attract and work with young families. Pastors of all types of churches have volunteered how important it was to them when their bishop asked evangelistic speakers to keynote large assemblies rather than asking the evangelism types to lead smaller-attendance workshops.

One regional minister told me that he hadn't been excited about evangelism initially. (He was one of the "evangelism cautious!") However, many pastors in the region were "passionate" about it ("evangelism lovers"). Together, they've moved evangelism higher and higher up the regional priorities list. As he gave me details, the regional minister laughed, "Okay, St. Matthew is right. We're putting our treasure in evangelism. I don't just mean money—I'm spending some real time and attention on evangelism these days. And my heart and mind are following.[5] I have moments when I feel like a convert myself!"

3. Ask the "annual question." One of the most heartening examples of judicatory support of evangelism came from a Midwestern presbytery. At a big annual gathering of the presbytery's pastors and lay leaders, the presbytery executive asked, "How many of your congregations have baptized adults this year?" After a moment of frozen silence, a few hands rose cautiously. Despite initial reaction from some, which the presbytery executive characterized as "reserved at best," she asked the question again the next year. More hands hit the air. The third year, pastors stood up and made announcements like, "We hadn't done any adult baptisms in eight years, but this year we did three!" The room exploded with applause.

The fifth year, just before the presbytery executive gave her address, someone told her that one of her dearest pastor friends had been diagnosed with cancer that week. She autopiloted through her talk, finished and turned away from the podium. Multiple voices shouted after her, "YOU FORGOT ADULT BAPTISMS!!!"

Churches baptized more adults because she asked the question. Repeatedly. More evangelism, more faith sharing happened in the presbytery because she asked that question. Repeatedly. She thinks

---

Pastors' Advice for Bishops:

"Make evangelism a *real* priority!"

that the most important change was a shift in the presbytery's culture. That presbytery witnessed a huge change because one minister asked one question, once a year. That change cost no money.

4. Ask successful evangelists for help. Pastors told me lots of stories about their bishops pulling together small groups (three to five) of the most effective evangelistic pastors. The bishops asked the pastors to talk about what they were learning. Often, the bishop asked the pastors to lead an initiative to help other pastors interested in evangelism.

Pastors loved the fact that the bishop came to them for advice. Pastors loved the freedom to negotiate with the other pastors about what would be helpful to them. Evangelistic pastors also praised bishops who could give support without controlling the outcome. Frequently, the bishop worked one-on-one with a leader of the pastors' group, and the group met on their own. The bishops provided support, but from behind the scenes. Since evangelistic pastors often have strong personalities, working with them can feel like herding cats. I suspect that the bishops involved had great self-confidence, healthy lives in Christ and good senses of humor!

The programmatic outcomes of these meetings differed significantly. Some groups developed mentoring programs. Others brought in consultants to do workshops and congregational evaluations. Some conferences created accountability/study/prayer groups for pastors. In many cases, a personal request to a small group of highly successful pastors, with supportive backup that the pastors didn't perceive as controlling, did two things. First, it provided a helpful, useful program for the conference that got some evangelism and esprit de corps going. Second, it turned pastors who had felt distanced from the diocese or critical of it into allies.

5. Urge Experimentation. I asked pastors what advice they would give their bishops. "Make evangelism a real priority!" was almost always the first answer. Then I asked them what great advice their bishops had given them. Many pastors praised their bishops to the skies for encouraging radical experimentation. Some bishops are telling congregations and groups of pastors that we're living in a new world. Pastors report what sound like half-time locker room pep talks: "All right, you all, get out there and try stuff. Nobody knows exactly what is going to work. A lot of things will fail, but we'll all learn from that. Come back and let us know what's helping and what isn't. We're working together. The only sin is sitting there waiting for the perfect plan."

A Bishop's Locker Room Pep Talk:

"All right! Get out there and try stuff! A lot of things will fail, but we'll learn from that! Come back and let us know what's working! The only sin is sitting there waiting for the perfect plan!"

6. *Great evangelism is possible in mainline denominations.*
Mainline churches are discovering the power and joy of trying to be faithful to God by sharing the faith with new people. At one time, mainline church leaders viewed evangelism as antithetical to social justice ministries. Remnants of this myth persist. Our research showed solidly that healthy evangelism flourishes alongside substantial and creative service to the poor and disenfranchised. These ministries are as varied as the theologies of the churches who perform them. The African-American church has stood on a bedrock of evangelism linked with social justice ministries for years.

Great evangelism exists along the entire theological spectrum. At one time, we excused ourselves from sharing the Gospel by saying that evangelism is "not authentically Lutheran," "not in the Disciples ethos," "not how real Methodists talk." Those days are gone. Bishops and heads of communions are involved in evangelism in personal, prayerful, prophetic ways.

Cliff Kirkpatrick, Stated Clerk for the Presbyterian Church USA,[6] wrote a beautiful letter interpreting 2003 statistics for all Presbyterians. He entitled the letter, "Hear what the Spirit says to the churches!" The letter opens: "We know that coming to faith is only possible through the power of the Holy Spirit. We as Presbyterians will only become a growing church if we begin on our knees, praying for forgiveness for our timidity in evangelism and seeking God's renewal, so that we and our churches lose our image as 'God's frozen chosen' and become joyful evangelists, actively sharing the Good News and inviting others into the fellowship of our churches."[7] I wouldn't call that timid!

Some pastors are not yet aware of the shift that is going on in the mainline churches. They aren't clear that it is loyal and faithful for us to share our faith. Our evangelism can provide a conduit for a compelling call to relationship with God and love for other people. Middle judicatory ministers can support, encourage and pray for this growth. Your opinions matter to the pastors you serve. Your approval and support, your disapproval or silence are noted and followed. Your leadership can galvanize the fainthearted, encourage the meek, bless the strong. Your opinions can bind or unbind, both on earth and in heaven. Your blessing matters more than you know.

Conclusion

Every church is different. People's gift mixes, skills and calls are different. The suggestions in this chapter are general. If God nudges you and your church in a different direction, talk about it, pray more

Healthy evangelism flourishes alongside service to the poor and disenfranchised. The African-American church has stood on a bedrock of evangelism linked with social justice for years.

and try doing *that* for a while. Then evaluate it. Talk about the strengths and weaknesses of the new plan. Ask God what to change, what to keep. The gospel is permanent. We must be ready to change any nonessential.

The main point is to recognize that each of us responds to a call from God to share the gospel of Christ. We can allow the Spirit to choreograph those calls so we don't bump into each other. Bishops and regional ministers serve pastors and congregations. Pastors serve other pastors through denominational and geographical ties. The perceptions and gifts of laypeople—all ministers through the priesthood of all—have been vastly underrated. New Christians bring new gifts and fresh perceptions that are critically important to the church. We must think, talk, pray and work together.

In 1922, after decades of archeological toil in Egypt, excavator Howard Carter struggled to take the first candle-lit look into King Tut's tomb. His patron, Lord Carnarvon, asked, "Can you see anything?" Carter, squinting at the first unlooted royal tomb ever discovered, could only gasp out, "Yes, wonderful things!"

I really don't want to compare churches to tombs here! But I challenge you to work together with each other and with God to share the gospel. If we do, we will see wonderful things, great treasures, and treasures in heaven, too.

DISCUSSION QUESTIONS _____

1. *How is your individual prayer going? Spend the first 15-20 minutes of your group time talking about the highlights: What was the most wonderful prayer day? What happened? What did you learn? What challenged you? What are you wondering about? Go around the circle and everyone say something!*

2. Who do you know who has done amazing evangelism? What did it look like?

3. How do the descriptions of who does what strike you? Take a few minutes to think about the words addressed to each group of people. To which group do you belong? Evaluate yourself, personally, as an evangelist. Discuss how you are doing. What is going well? What one step will you take in the next month to do better?

4. Now, talk together about how you are functioning as a church and how your area/region/presbytery/classis/synod is doing. What is working well? What could you do better? What one step will you take during the next three months to change as a church?

5. Did any Bible passage come to mind when you read this chapter? Does one occur to you now? Discuss how it connects with what you have read. (If no passages come to mind, you might want to look at: Romans 12:3–8; Matthew 7:7–12; 24-27; Hebrews 7:22–25.)

EXERCISE

Set aside a day this week to focus on viewing people differently. At the beginning of the day, or in the group studying this book together, pray for the people with whom you come into contact during your daily routine. Think about family, friends, and people at work, at the store, people you "talk" with on the Internet. What about the customer service people when you have to call *again* to complain about the mistake on your cell phone bill? At the end of the prayer, ask God to help you think of each person you come into contact with for the next 24 hours as a messenger from God, either someone you can help or pray for, or someone who God can use to teach you something. Keep meticulous notes throughout the day. At the end of the day, ask the Spirit if there is anyone you should be praying for intentionally, or whom you should get to know better.

Talk with a prayer partner about your day, or discuss it together when your group reconvenes. What happened? How did your way of seeing people change? How did your way of thinking of yourself change? How did you pray for people? Discuss your insights with the group. How has this exercise changed the way you think about evangelism?

---

[1]Peter Marshall, *The Best of Peter Marshall,* ed. Catherine Marshall (Old Tappan, N.J.: Fleming H. Revell Co., 1983), 15.

[2]For example, new Christians think that the most pressing spiritual questions non-Christians have are, "How can a good and powerful God allow so much evil to happen?" (71%) and "Is there a God?" (42%) Only half of the most effective evangelistic pastors in our study thought the evil question was important to unchurched people! Only 18% of these pastors thought the "Is there a God?" question mattered to unchurched people. These great pastors thought unchurched people were concerned with why to choose Christianity rather than another religion, or how to have a better life! ***We have to talk with unchurched people and new Christians! We have to continue to ask what they think! We can't presume!***

[3]I will use "bishop" language from here on for simplicity. It's hard to choose which horn of ***that*** dilemma upon which to impale myself!

[4]Claude Payne and Hamilton Beazley, *Reclaiming the Great Commission: A Practical Model for Transforming Denominations and Congregations* (New York: Jossey-Bass, 2000).

[5]"For where your treasure is, there your heart will be also" (Mt. 6:21).

[6]"Stated Clerk" is a title similar to Presiding Bishop or General Minister and President (or Pope).

[7]The letter is available through www.pcusa.org at www.pcusa.org/oga/newsstories/statsarticle04.pdf

CHAPTER 9

Smart Sailing

Navigating through Growing Pains, Conflict and Distractions

Imagine floating on a big raft in the lake. The sun is warm. Close your eyes. Feel the drift and swell of little waves. Life is easy. Life is good. If you fall asleep and bump into the edge of the dock, it's just a little jolt as you float lazily in the sun.

Were you ever a 12-year-old at the lake? Did you hitch up a sail to that old raft? If there was a decent breeze, you could really get that thing going. "Alright, ye swabs, haul in those sheets and belay the mizzenmast!" (or is it "take a belaying pin to those scurvy black-guards on the f'oc's'l"?); well, "hand me me grog." *Ahhhhhrrrrrrrrr, Pirrrrattes.* The thing is, when a pirate raft gets going, if the breeze is good and if the cap'n is 12 and paying more attention to the mutinous knaves aboard than to the rudder, you can take that dock at quite a clip…with impressive effect upon both ship and crew. The dock's usually fine.

It's the same with churches. Most of our congregations are floating along, drifting luxuriously in the warm sun, drowsy with the gentle rise and fall of the waves. Life is easy. Life is good. So long as no hotshots in motorboats cut too close, we're fine. But every once in a while somebody gets the idea to hitch up a sail and try to catch the Spirit. Then the old ship starts to move. Sails billow in gusting winds, the ship is heeling, spray flying, life is joyous, alive, free. And dangerous.

Did you know that one of the most ancient pictures of the church was a ship? It's drawn in the Roman Catacombs and in our earliest Christian art. As in the gospel of John, the Spirit is the wind, moving the church through dangerous waters.

A decision to let God use us to share real faith pries us loose from old habits, perceptions and moorings. We always thought of our church as First Church, on the corner of Broadway and Main Street. Now First Church is a clipper ship, canvas spread, filled with treasures, bound for the Indies. You may feel a little seasick. Change is hard. God is trustworthy.

121

I began ministry like a 12-year-old pirate, hoisting a sail on the raft, whooping, "Whoa, this is so *cool!*" We got going at quite a clip. The dear old raft could have hit that deck hard or wound up on rocks. Thank heavens there were some great sailors in the boat. Captains of frigates, the admiral on his flagship, radioed instructions in response to my S.O.S. signals. I didn't have a clue about the type of ministry I had slipped into by hoisting that sail. Sometimes I felt scared. Other times I was blissfully ignorant of skimming past underwater rocks. Experienced sailors read rocks by wave patterns. I was looking at the sunrise and the flying fish. That church did well only by the grace of God, not by Martha Grace.

After hearing similar stories from other pastors, it's clear to me I wasn't alone in my blithe, sailing ignorance. Everyone who has tried to put a sail on a raft has their shuddering-into-the-dock moments! Some of what I'll say here may sound simple. I will be grateful if it gives you one or two thoughts that help you watch more closely, see rocks earlier, or sail through shoals.

The key point is that life with the Spirit, or a decision to let God use us to share real faith, pries us loose from old habits, perceptions and moorings. We always thought of our church as First Church, on the corner of Broadway and Main Streets. Now First Church is a clipper ship, canvas spread, filled with treasures, bound for the Indies. You may feel a little seasick. Change is hard. God is trustworthy.

Waves and Weather Conditions Changing Churches Meet

If you take one point from this chapter, let it be this: safety lies in God, not in our habits. If you feel unsafe, talk with each other and pray. Hand God your feelings and ask what you should do next. Do that individually and together. Our safety always lies in God, as dangerous-feeling, seasick-swirling, lee-shore-looming as life with God may feel! Our safety, as well as our joy, lies in our glimpses of the Lord, in letting the Spirit play through our sails and move us forward. When wild stuff happens, don't panic. Talk with each other, run it past someone wise, and pray.

Let's examine sample wave and weather conditions many evangelistic churches meet.

1. Growing pains ("outer" waves)

2. Conflict ("inner" waves)

3. Distractions

Christ is the calmer of waves, the master of the storm. God holds the untamable chaos of our lives in God's hands and can calm it. Don't stop. Keep going. Step up communication with your team members. Step up communication with God. Your instinct will be that this slows the pace. Your instinct is probably wrong.

1. Growing Pains ("Outer" Waves)

Growing pains are the natural result of change. Children can grow so quickly that they have pain in their joints. Wrists shoot out of sleeves, ankles extrude from pants that were let down last week. It's exhausting to watch! Churches can be the same way.

Example: Grandville Church began praying. Faith deepened. Members felt a call to share their blossoming faith with others. Within three years, the church grew from 110 adults in worship to 215. They have 60 children and youth instead of 8. Grandville hired a young associate pastor. Worship is exciting. The pastor is working 80 hours a week to keep up with all the new people and to orient the associate and a second church secretary.

All the old ways of doing things aren't working in this changing environment. Growth requires new software, a new Web site, new accounting and record-keeping systems, new ways of integrating members and training teachers. Some of these learning curves are steep! The church has only four classrooms for 28 small groups. Three groups need the one big common space at the same time. The sanctuary is 90% full. A second service is in the works. For now, last-minute visitors have trouble parking and finding seats.

Diagnosis: Waves are beginning to roll around Grandville. The wind has picked up. I call these "outer" waves because most people can see that the upsets are the result of the objective situation of the church growing. Most members don't feel as if other people are causing the frustrations. They see that it's the situation. People's feelings don't tend to get hurt. Members fumbling through new systems of reserving a classroom may feel frustrated, but not mad. Their instinct is to laugh or shrug, rather than swear or go tell a friend about what just happened.

The danger comes in Grandville's situation if they ignore the stresses of change. Leaders can lighten loads and change pacing in churches. One thing is sure: pastors cannot work 80-hour weeks for long without damage to their spiritual lives, families, health or abilities to perceive situations and deal with them in the Spirit. I predict that if Grandville's pastor doesn't attend to his spiritual, psychological, physical and family health, by the end of this fourth year, he will be emotionally brittle and making "people" mistakes. He is probably making them now. The same holds true of every leader in the church. We can all put on a big push in a good cause. But an adrenaline rush that lasts for years corrodes physical and spiritual health.

Sailing Conditions

1. Growing pains ("outer" waves)
2. Conflict ("inner" waves)
3. Distractions

One of the hardest things about change in churches is that people think of church as the one fixed point in an otherwise spinning universe. Our relationships with God have to be Mother Teresa-mature before we see God as our stability—our North Star—instead of the church. God *is* the North Star, the fixed point by which we can navigate while the church sails, while the world swirls and buffets us.

See the situation early. The key to dealing with outer waves is to see them coming so you can make adjustments. Spot those "outer waves" early and talk about them. Who will see these types of waves first and most accurately? Individuals who are sensitive to people and to what's happening in the church. Ask the assistant in charge of scheduling or the pastor's spouse. Ask the quiet, wise deacon who prays and is in the church office a lot. These people can tell you things others don't see. They usually will not volunteer the information.

Don't count on the people leading the change to monitor the pacing accurately. Leaders tend to speed up under pressure and think they can handle "one more thing." They lose perspective as they lose sleep and get into addictive patterns of coping. Don't ask them what's going on. Ask their spouses!

Don't count on the people who are upset by changes to see whether the church is moving too quickly. Some people have very faithful and constant personalities. They are the salt of the earth. But they have a hard time making changes. Some people can make adjustments in other areas of their lives, but need the church to stay put at Main and Broadway. Switching classrooms can rattle these people for months. Sometimes those switches have to be made, even though it is hard on some people. Understanding and tact in making changes go a long way in helping folks adapt, but their feelings shouldn't be used to plan the church's pace of change.

Who can help? You can do very specific, practical things to deal with growing pains—the outer waves. Ask someone outside the church to help you monitor and deal with the changes you are navigating. It is best to ask someone to help you early on—before the wind picks up and the waves get choppy.

- ***A coach***. Many churches in the study have said that hiring an experienced coach to work with their pastor was the wisest money they ever spent. A coach can help pastors budget time, pay attention to what matters and see patterns. Coaches can help the pastors hold themselves accountable for the health of their bodies, their spiritual lives and their marriages.
- ***Denominational pastors*** can be tremendously helpful with growth management techniques, when to expand building facilities, how to work with stewardship and capital campaigns.
- ***Other growing churches*** have sailed through these waves before. Don't think you're the only one! Don't isolate yourself. Bring together a group of churches to try evangelism together

(see chapter 10). TALK! Attend workshops and conferences that deal with specific issues of growing churches. Large congregations host great conferences to help others learn from their successes and mistakes. The presentations can be very helpful. You may meet another participant who gives you the exact insight or piece of encouragement you need.

- ■ **God** is there to help. God will not lead you out of Egypt, into the desert and dump you there. You are God's messenger. You're trying to serve God, and you are not alone. Pray by yourself. Jesus loves you and will spend time with you. He will care for your soul, body and family. Pray with others in the church. The Spirit will help you when you don't even know how to pray. The Spirit will give you glimmers of understanding and subtle leadings for where to turn next.

Christ is the calmer of waves, the master of the storm. God holds the untamable chaos of our lives in God's hands and can calm it. Don't stop. Keep going. Step up communication with your team members. Step up communication with God. Your instinct will be that this slows the pace. Your instinct is probably wrong. Talk, pray, attend to your judicatory people, your coaches. Don't do everything yourself. Ask for help. Don't panic. Sail smart. You are, now and forever, in God's hands.

2. Conflict ("Inner" Waves)

God is our North Star; the church is the moving ship. Remember, growing churches are changing. After a while, we will have to sacrifice things we love to help new people move into faith. We all have different tolerances for change, but it is hard for each of us to let go of dear old things we love. In some ways, our lives are a continual process of surrendering the old and adjusting to the new. Sometimes we make a natural transition (we graduate from fourth grade and move into fifth). Sometimes a change is exciting and wonderful (we get married). Sometimes a change is traumatic or dreaded (an accident or a death). But we consistently face something new.

God is always in the new place.

One of the hardest things about change in churches is that people think of church as the one fixed point in an otherwise spinning universe. Our relationships with God have to be Mother Teresa-mature before we see God as our stability—our North Star—instead of the church. The reality is that God *is* the North Star, the fixed point by

The best way is to help each other navigate the change and look for God, our North Star, in each new place our church sails. God will always be with us, but we can get scared, shut our eyes and forget to look. The result can be conflict, or "inner" waves.

which we can navigate while the church sails, while the world swirls and buffets us.

Most of us, most of the time, only see God through a particular chapel window, from the viewpoint of the end of the fourth pew on the left, through the lens of a particular pastor's sermons. We live in the particulars of our lives. Because God and church are so important to us, any fussing with those particulars can threaten us.

A decision to follow the leadings of the Spirit and enter into intentional evangelism will bring slightly different responses from everyone in your church. Some will whoop with excitement as they clamber up the rigging. Others will be seasick. Some will feel as if they have been impressed (kidnapped from a seaside tavern, waking up aboard a ship heading out on a three-year tour of the South Seas). We must be gentle with each other. We each have a different focus, a different tolerance for change.

> Be open to mid-course corrections. Leading a congregation, like sailing, calls for tiny adjustments of sails and pinpoint responsiveness to new conditions. Just keep the ship pointed in the same direction.

The best way is to help each other navigate the change and look for God, our North Star, in each new place our church sails. God will always be with us, but we can get scared, shut our eyes and forget to look. The result can be conflict, or "inner" waves.

Example: Rocky Springs Church has exactly the same situation as Grandville Church, but with these additional elements: They have the same type of growth, but the pastor is running on empty. One Sunday School class and some of the elders are upset over the children's program using their space. The Senior High room had to be sprayed for roaches because the kids keep grinding Doritos™ and chocolate chip cookies into the carpet. People are grumpy. The pastor's daughter's impressive ship tattoo is causing significant talk. (And why do they let her wear her jeans that low ***anyway***?) Tension in board meetings causes headaches. People are talking about "the new people." The elder who caused so much trouble for the last two pastors is getting upset and starting to make phone calls. Groups are forming. Stomachs are nervous. Teeth are on edge.

Diagnosis: Growing pains or conflict? Do you see the difference between "outer" waves (simple growing pains), and these "inner" waves (conflict)? Growing pains are about "things," a situation. Conflict feels different. Some people are angry. Some are avoidant. Some have hurt feelings. Some are suspicious and taking sides. The church's forward movement is starting to bog down. Water is sloshing into the hold. The difference between growing pains and conflict is like the phrase from the guy in *The Godfather* who just shot someone's father "Look, kid, this isn't personal. It's business."[1] Growing pains aren't personal. They're business. Conflict is personal.

Identify conflict early. Just as with growing pains, the earlier you see and start to deal with conflict, the more easily it can be resolved. Here are some ways of seeing the situation quickly, before it progresses too far:

- ■ *Listen to your sensitive people.* Who are they? Your intercessors, key leaders, pastors' spouses, spiritually mature elders tend to be good candidates. People with strong leadership gifts, the driving initiators of change, are usually not the ones who see conflict early. (One of these great leaders told me, "No, *I* don't feel stress. I'm a carrier!")

- ■ *Canaries in the mineshaft.* Have you heard stories of the old days of coal mining when miners took canaries down into the mineshaft with them? Then, if they cut into a pocket of poisonous gas, the canaries would be affected first. A canary drooping on its perch was the miners' first warning of trouble. Some people are like those canaries. Some smell the first whiff of conflict, recognize what's going on, and can articulate it clearly. Others can be quite unconscious about why they're edgy. (These are often great people you love.) These "canaries" go off like bottle rockets in meetings, snap out some nasty comment on the way out of worship, launch into a tirade over a spoon filed away in the wrong drawer. They are your canaries in the mineshaft. They are more sensitive than most to the gasses of conflict. *What* they're saying is probably exaggerated. *The fact* that they're exploding is what matters. The explosions themselves constitute your early warning system. Thank them! Pay attention! Those canaries are singing an important song.

Disagreements can be healthy. Conflict can reach dangerous levels. As in good marriages and close friendships, churches engaged in vibrant ministry always have differences of opinion and some friction. Differences and a certain degree of friction are part of human relationships. Without some change and some challenge, relationships and churches stagnate. Their souls grow numb. They die of boredom.

However, at some point differences and friction can move to a level of destructive conflict. The Rocky Springs Church is starting down this path. Their mild to middling conflict could elevate to the

The difference between growing pains and conflict is like the phrase from the guy in *The Godfather* who just shot someone's father: "Look, kid, this isn't personal. It's business." Growing pains aren't personal. They're business. Conflict is personal.

point where it tears down ministries and leaves streams of wounded people in its wake. The healthiest way of dealing with differences of opinion and friction is to listen carefully, talk kindly and honestly, get some outside help, and pray together.

Be open to mid-course corrections. Flexibility counts at this point! Pay attention to your advisors, your coach, your denominational ministers. Sometimes the sails need to be let out a little bit. Let the ship slow down a trifle while people adjust to the new movement. Leading a congregation, like sailing, asks for tiny adjustments of sails and pinpoint responsiveness to new conditions. Just keep the ship pointed in the same direction.

Keep an eagle eye on the weather. You're safer if you see situations soon!

Antagonists. Most conflict in churches is the result of normal people reacting to extraordinary situations. Sometimes, however, conflict is due to people who thrive on conflict and chaos, who willfully attack others. Kenneth Haugk, founder of Stephen Ministries, calls them *antagonists* and describes them in detail: "Antagonists are individuals who, on the basis of non-substantive evidence, go out of their way to make insatiable demands, usually attacking the person or performance of others. These attacks are selfish in nature, tearing down rather than building up, and are frequently directed against those in a leadership capacity."[2] The Rocky Springs elder who has a history of difficulties with pastors and is currently making phone calls and stirring up trouble might well be an antagonist.

Churches are peculiarly vulnerable to antagonists because most people, from church leaders to members in the pews, are trying to live together kindly and lovingly. We can be confused and baffled by someone who is launching a blatant, destructive attack. We don't intuitively know how to respond. Dr. Haugk's book gives clear, practical, specific suggestions for recognizing and dealing with people who stir up destructive, unhealthy conflict.

Who can help with conflict? The same people and resources who can help with growing pains/outer waves: coaches, denominational ministers, conferences, great books, colleagues and God. Everything said in the growing pains section applies here, but it is particularly important to ask an outside person to help you navigate through conflict. It's hard to see and trust each other fully once feelings are riled up. When a situation has gotten to be "personal, not business," none of our perceptions are completely accurate. We see through the haze of our own emotions. An independent outsider can help us navigate the situation.

Summary: It is normal for churches to experience some degree of conflict if they are growing. Some conflict is part of creativity and change. But conflict can move to destructive levels. If your church is experiencing conflict,

a. identify it early
b. work with your outside advisors
c. ask God for healing, protection and leadings of the Spirit
d. be open to mid-course corrections and changes of pace
e. remember that the call to share the Gospel is Christ's. Keep going.

Do you remember the end of the movie *Star Wars*?[3] The hero, Luke Skywalker, is leading a small band of heroic pilots into the very center of the world-destroying Death Star. If they can drop a bomb into a narrow shaft that leads to the core of the Death Star, they can destroy it. Bad guys are shooting at them. Good guys are catching on fire and exploding. It's terrifying. It's hard to concentrate on the pinpoint precision drop they're trying to make at such speed, in so much confusion. The voice you hear through the scene says, "Stay on target....stay on target."

That's what we need to do in conflict. Stay on target.

3. Distractions

John Peterman, founder and president of the brilliantly quirky retail company (www.jpeterman.com) once told me that organizations are like rubber bands. You can stretch them, and they adapt. You keep stretching, they keep getting longer. But if you stretch too quickly, or too far, the rubber band flips out of your fingers and snaps back to its original size.

This is a dynamic of institutional change that applies to churches. We stretch the rubber band until we get to a point of having a new, larger, rubber band to put in its place. Then we can stretch the new rubber band and retire the old one. In churches, you stretch the rubber band as the sanctuary begins to fill to over-flowing. The new worship service you put in place is like a new rubber band. It's flexible and stretches. It relieves the pressure and you can fill it (stretch the new rubber band) again. At times when a church is changing, the rubber band is stretched thin. The Grandville Church is stretching. The Rocky Springs Church is in danger of snapping back.

People and churches that are stretched are vulnerable to distractions. The further the rubber band is stretched, the more vulnerable.

Distractions can look like anything, wear any kind of clothes. The hallmark of a distraction is that it tends to drag our attention away from our focus.

I don't want to give just one scenario here, as in Rocky Springs and Grandville. There isn't just one scenario for distractions. Distractions can look like anything, wear any kind of clothes. However, the hallmark of a distraction is that it tends to drag your attention away from your focus. Let's look at some typical types of distractions, so you can begin to see the patterns.

Other good things. Can you hear the voices in the board meeting? "Let's have everybody take a course in Christian money management this year." "Let's start a ministry to children in the neighborhood." "But there are people who we are really *helping* with the thrift shop." Which do you do? All of them? Any of them?

The frustration with following a charted course in a church is that churches can do *many* important ministries. If we try to decide to do a ministry based on whether it is a *good* ministry, we can start to drift off God's course or end up on rocks. Most ministries are important. How do we decide what to do?

> If we try to decide to do a ministry based on whether it is a good ministry, we can start to drift off God's course or end up on rocks. Most ministries are important. How do we decide what to do? We have to discern which ministries to do based on what God is calling us, specifically, to do.

We have to discern which ministries to do based on what God is calling *us, specifically,* to do. If God has called your church, and you as a person, to found a homeless shelter, you must *do* it! If God wants you to lobby in the state legislature for environmental issues, *that's* your job. If God asks you to do evangelism, that's **your** call. Stay on target.

Once you know your call, you can make decisions about which ministries to do. The question is: Will this ministry support the call? If you have five ideas of ministries that would support the call, you look at them, pray about them and discern which one or which combination best fit the gifts of your people, your time and money, and the people you're called to serve.

God is the one with perspective, the only coach who can call this play. We can't be rigid. God can change plans. But stay on target. Follow your call. Ask first: "What is our call?" Ask second: "Will this ministry serve our call? Is this the way God is calling us to spend our limited time and limited resources?" That is the framework with which to make decisions. Remember: the "Don't Go There" list and the "Stop Doing" list are as important as the "To Do" list!

Alluring distractions. A banker friend described giving a major presentation at the bank's annual board meeting. They were running late. It was past time for lunch. Down the table, one of the board members pulled a Hershey™ bar with almonds out of her purse and slipped a bite into her mouth. Herb, my friend, said, "What was the deal? Okay, I was sort of hungry, but I was *captivated* by the thought of that candy bar. The almonds were calling to me. I must have been staring at that chocolate like a lost soul. I fumbled a sentence, got lost in my presentation and felt as if I ought to stop my talk, sit down, take a sip of my coffee and say, "Hi, I'm Herb. I'm a chocoholic.'"

Is there anything in your life so alluring it makes you fumble your presentation?

Oh, these alluring distractions are brutal! They can be *anything*, although food, praise and recognition, an attraction to a person, television, checking your e-mail constantly, Internet sexual searches, spending money, living through children and drinking too much are top contenders! An alluring distraction distorts, captivates, ensorcells. It pulls us away from our focus on what God is calling us to do.

How can you tell if you are dealing with an alluring distraction? Perhaps the best clue is if you feel like tucking it away out of other people's sight. If you feel like hiding something you're doing or thinking, tell someone about it. If you feel hesitant to be open with some trusted person, you may be dealing with an alluring distraction. What do you do then? Tell someone about it!! Light and air work wonders on anaerobic infections and alluring distractions.

The further the rubber band is stretched, the more vulnerable we can be to this type of distraction. A fascinating person, a mind-numbing book, a bag of Oreos start to shimmer like a mirage in the desert when we're tired, emotionally isolated, stretched too thin, or not in good spiritual shape. Alluring distractions can act as canaries in the mineshaft! They show us when we're stretched too thin and need to take better care of ourselves. The best ways of coping are to talk with someone you trust; pray; get some sleep; go for a walk; play with the dog; work with a counselor, your accountability group or a 12 step group.

Do you see the effect of an alluring distraction? It's just like any other distraction. Its tendency is to deflect your attention from what God is calling you to do. What do you do about it? Drag your eyes away from the Hershey™ bar *and* the almonds. Fix the fumbled sentence. Finish your presentation. Stay on target!

Tragic distractions. One of the sweetest-spirited pastors with whom I spoke in the Mainline Evangelism Project was a young pastor of a new church. He and the founding members prayed that God would send them people to love who were really different from them. God sent them a couple of bikers who were on drugs and dealing with arrests and prison. That presented a challenge!

But this remarkable group of people rose to the occasion. Those first "different" people have transformed lives today. They are drug-free, have brought many friends to the church and are now congregational leaders. About 850 people worshiped together only eight

> How can you tell if you are dealing with an alluring distraction? Perhaps the best clue is if you feel like tucking it away out of other people's sight. If you feel like hiding something you're doing or thinking, tell someone about it!

years after the church began. At the end of the eighth year, the wife of the associate pastor, a social worker who was part of the ministry team from the beginning, was killed in a car accident. The driver at fault was a stranger to the church. He was on drugs.

This is agonizing irony.

After a tragedy of this sort, the church must care for its soul, deal with its grief. The distraction in a situation like this would be if the pastor and key leaders started muttering, "Stay on Target…Stay on Target…Stay on Target," like a mantra. At a time like this, frantic recitation of "stay on target" can act as a defense against dealing with the leaders' own feelings. Leaders would be falling for the distraction if they acted as if nothing had happened or if they tried to get the shell-shocked congregation psyched up for some cheery new evangelism program.

A tragedy shatters the target. But beneath the evangelism target you saw before is *another* evangelism target, a deeper one.

The point of evangelism is sharing the life with God you know. A tragedy opens up a much deeper life with God. Whatever we learn, we can share with others later. What new things about faith can you learn during a time of tragedy? Tragedy lets us see how fragile life can be. It presents Job-like questions. "How could a loving God let such evil happen?" "What possible meaning could such tragedy have?" "Why did this happen to us, now, when we're working so hard and things are going so well?" It helps us see how deeply we can trust God.

It is frightening even to *think* these questions, let alone say them to another person or whisper them in God's direction. But asking these questions is the beginning of a new layer of spiritual growth. The more we can ask the questions—of the Bible, of our theologians, of each other—the better. It also helps to allow ourselves to acknowledge some bit of our pain, our confusion, our anger. God is more real, more powerful, more loving than we ever know from easy times. We can learn this through tragedy, if we will.

If church members can hang in there with each other during the hard times, new growth will begin. It will be inner, soul growth. Don't worry about the evangelism target for this season. The target is the *deeper* evangelism target—to see life and people, yourself and God, more clearly. God is alive and working throughout our most painful times. If we allow ourselves to feel the hardest feelings, ask the most painful questions, God will be able to reveal Godself to us in more powerful ways than before. You will know when it is time to share

---

A tragedy shatters the target.

But beneath the evangelism target you saw before is *another* target, a deeper one.

that even more profound good news. Soon, God will bring you new people who need *exactly* what you are learning now.

Confusing distractions. Let's end this distractions talk on an easier note! Sometimes quirky distractions, "coincidental" distractions, can swirl up around us like a sudden sand storm. The result is confusion, feeling rattled or off center. Like all the other distractions, confusing distractions tend to pull us away from a peaceful focus on Christ and our calls. Here are some examples:

Scenario A: It's Maundy Thursday. A tree falls on the power line and the electricity goes out. The bulletins haven't been run. The church secretary receives a phone call from her child's school to let her know that she bounced a check for the first time in her life. She is mortified. The pastor is felled by a migraine.

Scenario B: Dense fog has socked the preacher for your Weekend Worship Extravaganza in at the Seattle-Tacoma Airport. The hospitality committee has forgotten the paper plates. They're frantic. As you leave the house to go meet with the group trying to figure out a new plan, your spouse asks sharply, "So, *why* did you let Johnny take your car when you knew you were going to be needing it? All right," in martyred tones, "you can use *my* car, but I wish you'd cleared it with me in advance." On your way to the meeting, you get a call that dear, 17-year-old, responsible Johnny had a fender bender in *your* new car. Aaaaaaahhhhhhhhhhh!!!

Confusing distractions rattle us because they come in a rush and in a flurry. You could handle one thing, but at a critical moment, six odd, annoying little tests of your spiritual stability start swimming around you. As a pastor friend said, "I feel like I'm being minnowed to death." So, what do you do when you feel the nibbling begin?

Recognize what's going on. Knowing that you're dealing with a distraction gives you a handle on the situation. If you can, *say it out loud* to somebody, "Oh…, I think these are confusing distractions! I know this crazy feeling!" Then *pray* with someone. Ask God for peace and protection from getting rattled and off center. You might want to memorize Philippians 4:6–7 and use it as your prayer, "Do not worry about anything, but in everything by prayer and supplication with thanksgiving let your requests be made known to God. And the peace of God, which surpasses all understanding, will guard your hearts and your minds in Christ Jesus."

Confusion tends to drag us out of Christ's peace and into anxiety. We need to remind ourselves that we are in this situation because

How to Cope with Distractions

1. *Recognize it* as a distraction as quickly as you can.
2. *Name it* and get it out in the open with the people with whom you're in ministry.
3. *Pray* that God will take care of it, protect everyone and show you the path to tread through the difficulty.
4. *Stay on target.* Go to your board meeting or prayer retreat or meeting with your friend as planned.

God has called us here. God will *never* desert us during a crazy time. If we train ourselves to turn to Christ and ask for help, distractions will dissolve.

Stay on target. Once we have recognized that we're just dealing with distractions, talked with a person or two, prayed for peace and protection against getting all frazzled, we can get on with it! We figure out backup plans. The electricity may go back on. If not, somebody runs the bulletin copies somewhere else. We pray that the fog lifts in Seattle and we arrange for a backup preacher. Once we're calmed down, the details aren't a problem.

Safety lies in God, not in our habits.

Conclusion

Growing pains and conflict, distractions and difficulties will crop up whenever God entrusts us with work that matters. Growing pains will stretch us. Conflict can hook our emotions. Sometimes conflict will enrage or scare us. Distractions can confuse, entice, terrify. Some distractions are tragic, others merely unsettling.

There is one way to deal with any of these bits of waves and weather: recognize it for what it is, talk about it with someone, pray for peace and protection, then get on with it! Stay on target.

Waves and weather are part of any ministry that matters to God. They are part of all rich, real lives. If we commit our lives to God to be used, we will set off on adventures unimaginable. We'll run into challenges, growing pains, conflict, and distractions. But God called us into it and will not desert us. Other great sailors are in the ship with us. We aren't alone. We will endure wild rides, but if life with God weren't hard, it wouldn't be great!

DISCUSSION QUESTIONS _____

1. *How is your individual prayer going? Spend the first 15-20 minutes of your group time talking about the highlights: What was the most wonderful prayer day? What happened? What did you learn? What challenged you? What are you wondering about? Go around the circle and everyone say something!*

2. Describe a time in your faith life (or your church's life) when it felt like sunbathing on a raft. Have you felt a wind-in-the-sails faith life (or church life)? Describe that. Discuss how floating times and sailing times are the same. How are they different?

3. Think of a time when a disagreement has turned out to be helpful in the long run. How did your first thoughts about the situation

change? Did you talk honestly with the other person? Pray about it? Describe how your impression of other people involved in the situation shifted.

4. Have you experienced destructive conflict? Would you do anything differently given what you know now?

5. What is your reaction to the distractions discussion? Have you ever experienced distractions? What happened? How did you deal with the situation? Are there any distractions in your life now? In your church?

6. Is there any Bible passage that came to mind when you read this chapter, or that occurs to you now? Discuss how it connects with what you have read. (If no passages come to mind, you might want to look at: Philippians 4:6–7; Isaiah 30:19–21; 1 Corinthians 9:24–27; Mark 4:35–41.)

EXERCISE

Sit quietly and think. Ask God to show you anything that is operating in your life as a distraction. Sit quietly and listen. Then ask God to show you anything that is acting as a distraction in your church. Sit quietly and listen.

Are there any distractions going on in your life, or in your church now? Discuss them with your group. These are the first two steps of dealing with a distraction—recognizing it and naming it. Next, pray as outlined in the "confusing distractions" section. If a particular person is feeling especially affected by the distraction, s/he might want to sit in a chair or stand. The rest of the group can gently lay a hand on the person's shoulder, head, or back as you pray together. Ask God for protection and relief from anxiety. If there is a distraction in the church, you each sit in your chairs and imagine that you are holding the church in your hands. Close your eyes and ask God to heal the church you are holding. Then pray as a group for healing for the church and for protection from the distractions. Ask for discernment of what it means in your situation to Stay on Target. Thank God for the discernment, the healing, the protection, and the Target!

---

[1] *The Godfather*, Paramount, 1972.

[2] Kenneth C. Haugk, *Antagonists in the Church: How to Identify and Deal with Destructive Conflict* (Minneapolis: Augsburg, 1988), 25–26.

[3] *Star Wars: Episode IV–A New Hope*, 20th Century Fox, 1977.

CHAPTER 10

Getting Started

You've read this book now. From Part 1, I hope you have a clearer idea of why it matters to be a Christian, why evangelism is important, and how the church is doing. In Part 2, we focused on the real relationships and spiritual life that is at the heart of true evangelism, for both mature and new Christians. Part 3 is more practical. We analyzed different types of evangelism in congregations, the organization of congregational efforts and ways of recognizing and navigating through typical challenges.

Do you remember the questions with which we started this book? Why *do* evangelism? What's motivating *you*? What difference does being a Christian make in *your* life? How could it matter in someone else's life?

How do you get started? You already have! You have lots of ideas now. You may already be testing some of them. This chapter contains a plan you might start with. Feel free to ignore the entire chapter. The only indispensable element of sharing the Gospel is that you love God and are trying to follow the Spirit's leadings. All else is icing.

We're in This Together

God is a Trinity—one and three. Somehow, relationships and community lie at the very heart of God. We Christians live in relationship: with God, with each other in the church, and with people we've never met. The best way of starting out to do evangelism is with a group of people. Jesus sent the disciples out in pairs, not alone (Lk. 10:1–12). The foundation for evangelism efforts will be much more stable if your church is not alone. I recommend that the pastor invite three other pastors and that the four churches they serve commit to spend a year together in prayer and helping each other begin to do evangelism.

The Pastors' Group

The pastor is the only one with a vote on the composition of this group! The key elements are: (1) the pastors in the group like and trust each other, (2) the pastors have a genuine desire to reach people with the Gospel, (3) the churches are physically close enough to have meetings, and (4) a desire to try an evangelism experiment.

Pastors, pray about this. You will need to ask people who can get along, but who bring something interesting to the mix. You might ask another pastor and then you two talk and pray about which other two to invite. It is helpful to have some background differences, people with different theological frameworks. It's great if someone has had experience with successful evangelism and growing churches. It's great if someone has real prayer background. We always need to compensate for the partial nature of our understandings.

The Meetings. Covenant to meet for four hours once a month, for an entire year. Set your schedule for at least the first six months during your first meeting. Select a private place where there will be no interruptions. It is great if the time and place of meetings are consistent. Covenant that cell phones and pagers will be off. Start meetings on time and honor the end time. Rotate serving as time-keeper. The agenda of each meeting is to spend the first half of your time talking about your personal lives and praying for each other. The second half is spent discussing church and evangelism issues.

In the first two hour block of time, opening with worship, silent prayer or singing. Then the first person takes ten minutes to share the most important thing God is doing in his/her life. Then take five minutes for prayer. Pray for the person who has just shared or pray in silence. Each person should have a turn. Please honor the time.

The second half of your time together is to talk about your churches, evangelism, what you are learning, how it is going. You decide how to use this time. You could read books together and discuss them, discuss a theme, or talk about what is going on in your specific churches as you move into the year of working with your evangelism teams (the "E-Teams"). Close with prayer and intercession for the churches and for the people whom God would like to bring to your church. Early in your time together, review the stories in chapter 4.

Try this format for at least three meetings, then renegotiate how you work with your time after that. My experience has been that if worship, prayer and personal time are first, you will have enough

---

Pastors' groups

4 pastor friends
- prayer
- accountability
- vision
- support for E-Teams

time to talk about church issues. The issues conversation also tends to be more centered and substantial. Change anything you need to at the three-month point.

Plan for the Year

Months 1–3: Let the pastors' group meet for at least three months before E-Teams are assembled. During this three-month period, schedule an overnight retreat, either by yourselves, or with a retreat leader/coach.

Month 3: After the pastors have met and prayed for two months, begin to assemble the evangelism team. Pray about which members to ask. Ask them to pray about it. Do not strong-arm anyone to be part of this group. Reread chapter 4, in particular the Benton Street Church story. The E-Team should spend its first three months together praying, reading, researching. This book would be a good study guide during that time.

Months 3–12: The pastors' primary job in relation to evangelism is outlined best in chapters 8 and 9. Your key role as pastor is to discern the vision for your congregation, hold it before the church and help the church navigate the changes. Preach well. Pray for the church and the E-Team. You pastors will lead or be responsible for coordinating monthly joint meetings of all four E-Teams. I do not suggest that you meet with your own church's E-Team after the beginning. Generally, the more self-directed the E-Teams can be, the better. Pray for them. It's great if you can act as a coach and resource person for the team leader. You will be the best one to gauge the extent of your involvement.

The E-Teams

Composition of the E-Teams: Each congregation will select an evangelism team (an E-Team) with the following specific spiritual gifts distribution:

1. outgoing, artistic, loving, "people" persons
2. intercessors who pray as a natural part of life
3. research, computer, investigative types

It would be best to have six people on the E-Team, but it may be a few more or less. Do try to keep the balance of the personality/gifts mix. Discern the person with the gifts to serve as leader for the group and ask them to serve as leader/convener for the year.

The E-Teams

2 outgoing, artistic, "people" people

2 research, computer types

2 intercessors

Work of the E-Teams. E-Teams will decide how they will work together, but it should be in accordance with their gifts and interests. The extroverted, artistic people will plan and carry out the outgoing relational parts of whatever you come up with. Intercessors will pray for the group, new people and the church. Researchers can dig through evangelism books, work on the Internet for ideas, research demographics for your neighborhood and design whatever systems you need.

E-Team meetings. E-Teams will meet at least twice a month for two hours. One meeting will serve as a time for each church's E-Team to meet by itself. E-Teams will spend time the same way as pastors' groups: the first half in real sharing and prayer, the second half studying together or sharing what you have been learning. The pastor may or may not be part of this meeting. Discern this in prayer.

Alternate meetings during the month will be with all four E-Teams together. The first half of the meeting will be life-sharing and prayer, as always. Assemble sharing and prayer groups so that the outgoing, "people" people from each church are together, the intercessors are together and the researchers are together. Pastors will plan some joint discussion or presentation or facilitate a group exercise for the second half of each meeting. Use these times to share what you are learning, to brainstorm about challenges and insights you are having.

E-Team road trips. Several times during the year, and at least once during the first three months after the E-Teams are formed, plan a road trip! Go to an evangelism conference together. Check out conferences at large churches near you, or weekend evangelism events. Visit successful churches. Take along other friends and family on some of these expeditions! These trips will help you get to know each other, have fun, see ways other churches are choosing to worship and greet visitors. You will meet other people passionate about sharing the Gospel. You will be more open to new ideas if you see them for yourself outside your own, normal, comfortable sphere. A great pastor who read this book before publication told me to make the print for this paragraph huge, bold and to have a border of shiny gold stars all around it! GET OUT THERE AND SEE NEW THINGS!!! Do it now! Do it together! Bring friends!

Be Each Other's Eyes

Besides the encouragement and momentum provided by pastors and E-Teams working together, you will be able to help each other gain

What do E-Teams do?

Be each other's eyes

Enlist an outside coach

Evaluate

Celebrate!

new perspective on your own churches. Two or three times during the year, ask members of Church A's E-Team to visit Church B's Sunday worship service. (Church B sends a team to Church C, etc.)

Your job is to figure out what it would be like for a visitor to visit that church. Come up with a list of areas (use questions in Chapter 7 in the "Barriers" section, or go to www.GraceNet.info for a sample evaluation form). Go to churches where you aren't known. Go as singles or family groups and let people know you are just "looking around at churches."

See what the church is doing that might be attractive to visitors. What works? What could be improved? Is the church physically welcoming? Is the church well set up for visitors (can you understand the service?)? Are people warm, friendly? How is the worship service? Would you want to come back? You might want to do these visits just before your monthly joint E-Teams meeting so that impressions will be fresh in your minds. Perhaps visitors to each church could meet for lunch after worship to compare impressions. Then all the teams could meet together to discuss how it went. As you report to each other, use the format:

The bumper sticker of the decade gleamed from the stopped car's rear bumper. "***Jesus is the Answer***." My friend muttered under his breath, "So ***what*** was the question?"

(1) These things were great: _____.
(2) You might want to think about improving these:_____

_____.

Give specific examples, and be kind as well as incisive! Pastors will help you structure a sharing format.

As you help each other figure out what each church is doing well and what can be improved in their welcoming, you will almost certainly get insights for things your own church might do better! Send visitors to each other's worship services again in the middle and at the end of the year. Change churches you visit so that you get to see a different congregation. Add questions to your questionnaire if you want. Have fun with this!

Enlist an Outside Voice

In addition to being each other's eyes and ears, it helps to have some outside person coach the pastors during this time. I strongly suggest that you contract with a consultant/coach/outside pastor with evangelism and spirituality understanding to lead a retreat for the pastors at the beginning of the year and to hold phone conversations with each pastor throughout the year. You will have an intense year if you are praying and making shifts in your church's evangelism efforts. This could be a pivot point in your church's life, therefore a prime time to utilize the help of an outside accountability partner.

The most frequent objections to hiring an outside consultant are: (1) it costs too much money, and (2) that's what our regional minister/ presbytery minister/district superintendent is for.

1. Does an outside coach really cost too much? I saw hundreds of examples of congregations moving into evangelism efforts as I directed the Mainline Evangelism Study. Pastors who used outside consultants or coaches during key transition times reported that they did better: (a) in numbers of people who joined the church, (b) the ease of the new members' entry into full church life, (c) the healthy management of change and conflict, and (d) the pastor's spiritual health and emotional resiliency. Congregational leaders in churches that hired good coaches/consultants frequently pointed out that the consultant/coach saved the church untold costs in terms of conflict, stress, burnout and wasted energy poured into nonproductive efforts. Coaches increase pastors' tenure in the congregation. It can cost tens of thousands of dollars and great disruption in the congregation to search for a new pastor. A coach is a good investment.

2. Why can't we use our judicatory minister as our coach? Judicatory ministers have important functions in relation to evangelism among the churches they serve. Your bishop or regional staff person will undoubtedly be an important part of your evangelism plans. Their support, vision for the region's churches, programmatic support and sage advice can be invaluable. Invite them into your planning and ask for their help! They want to be involved. They should be involved.

However, bishops, conference ministers and their associates are some of the most overloaded ministers in our churches today. They are stretched very thin because of funding cuts. They do not have time for monthly, in-depth phone calls with the pastor of each church they serve. They can help pastors and churches in many important ways, but please do not load more rocks into their backpacks!

Many church consultants will work with churches to arrange support that will fit your budget. I have discovered that paying a fee for services helps individuals and churches pay attention to advice and to get serious about making changes! Please do not skip this step.

Keep Records and Evaluate

Pastors and E-Teams: keep prayer journals and notes of what you think, talk about and do. Keep records of what God does and what

What's the problem a life with Jesus solves? We need to know. The church has asked this question for 2000 years. The answer is, "Jesus saves us." The question is, "*From **what*** does Jesus save us?"

happens with evangelism and in people's lives this year. Review your notes every three or four months and discuss them. What are you learning about prayer? about your own faith? about the way the Spirit moves? about evangelism? about God's Kingdom and the growth of souls? about church and community? What is working amazingly well? What flopped? What could be changed, shifted or discontinued? Keep records, keep thinking, keep talking, keep praying.

The End of the Year

How about ending the year with a joint evaluation session to review what you have learned and all God has done during the year? You may choose to continue for another year. You may want to help some other churches in your diocese start E-Teams. Ask God and see. After you evaluate, celebrate with a huge, exciting worship service for all the congregations with a great big party afterward! You deserve it! You've worked hard this year! Thank you from all of us for what you have opened yourself up to do.

Jesus Is the Answer. So What Is the Question?

You've finished this book. And you're ready for a new beginning. I'm trying to think of a final word, a final paragraph that might help launch each of us into this next year of our lives with God. Do you remember the questions with which we started this book? Why **do** evangelism? What's motivating **you**? What difference does being a Christian make in **your** life? How could it matter in someone else's life? Do you have clearer answers to those questions than when you started reading this book? I hope so.

A bumper sticker in the '70s and '80s proclaimed, "Jesus Is the Answer." I have a vivid memory of getting a ride home from law school with a couple of friends. We had just finished five hours of grilling by law school professors. The day had been a mix of exhaustion and boredom, punctuated with random moments of terror. Professors had a nasty tendency to fire sudden salvos at the jokers in the back row of the classroom. "Ms. Reese, what is the critical point upon which Justice Brandeis' argument for the dissent turns?" I usually maneuvered for time to think by rising slowly to my feet, saying, "Excuse me, sir, would you mind rephrasing the question?" Eventually, I had to stand in front of 90 classmates and try to bumble out a coherent answer, at the expense of my entire nervous system.

It had been a long day. Now we were cruising home. A traffic light turned yellow. The rattletrap car in front of us gunned the accelerator, then screeched to a stop. My law school friend slammed on the brakes,

Sin, death, demonic social conditions—they're pivotal human questions. They are questions rooted deeply in scripture. Jesus can save us from each of them. Jesus is the answer to all of these human problems—in scripture, in theology, in human experience.

Whatever our individual or communal presenting problems—sin, confusion, illness, loneliness, isolation, poverty, violence, drugs, death—God can save us through Christ. No space in the human psyche is too small for God's healing through Christ. No far point of the universe is beyond the Spirit's whisper of forgiveness, the creative life of God's touch.

swearing. The bumper sticker gleamed from the stopped car's rear bumper: "*Jesus is the Answer*." My friend muttered under his breath, "So **what** was the question?"

I realized at the time, after a day of being pummeled by scary questions, that my friend was right. It **matters** which question is asked. I realize more clearly today, decades later, that knowing the question to which Jesus is the answer unlocks the universe. What's the question Jesus answers? What's the problem a life with Jesus solves? We need to know. The church has asked this question for 2000 years. We say, "Jesus saves us." The question is, "*From **what** does Jesus save us?*"

What is the biggest problem of human existence? From what does Jesus save us? Sin? Yes. Jesus saves us from sin. Some parts of the church focus strongly on sin as the main problem. Other churches see death as the biggest human problem. Jesus saves us from death, too. Some parts of the church look at the biggest human problem as distorted human community that draws us away from God and truth. They know that Jesus can heal community, miraculously transform isolated individuals and sick societies.

Sin, death, demonic social conditions—they're all pivotal human questions. They are questions rooted deeply in scripture. Clearly, Jesus can save us from each of them. Jesus is the answer to all of these human problems—in scripture, in theology, in human experience. Jesus saves us from sin. Salvation is forgiveness, healing and union with God. Jesus saves us from death. Salvation is life forever with God. Jesus saves and heals human communities: families, churches, neighborhoods, countries. Whatever our individual or communal presenting problems—sin, confusion, illness, loneliness, isolation, poverty, violence, drugs, death—God can save us through Christ. No space in the human psyche is too small for God's healing through Christ. No far point of the universe is beyond the Spirit's whisper of forgiveness, the creative life of God's touch.

The deeper our lives, the more we dwell in scripture, the more alive our prayer, the more thoughtful our reflections, the more conscious our relationship with God, the richer our community experience, the more clearly we will see the questions. And the more we can see that Jesus is the answer. We can live shallow lives. God is there, luring us deeper. When we move into more complex lives, God is there, enticing us further in, higher up. Don't worry. A life of faith has no glass ceiling. The waters that flow into the well of life with God are infinite.

We can never outgrow God or outgrow faith. We can test the limits, ask the questions of Job, challenge each other, wrestle with God. What is the deepest place in your soul? Open your inner eye—you will see Christ there. We can never reach beyond the limits of God or of God's love for us. What question wracks your being? Jesus is the answer. What questions are other people asking? Are they lonely? Are they guilty? Are they afraid? Are they angry? Jesus is the answer. The path to loving community, to forgiveness, to peace, to rest, to healing, to resolution, to justice lies in a growing relationship with God. Jesus is the answer. This is the Good News.

Are you going to tell someone?

We can never outgrow God or outgrow faith. We can test the limits, ask the questions of Job, challenge each other, wrestle with God. Step into the deepest place in your soul. Open your inner eye—you will see Christ there.

Unbinding the Gospel

PART FOUR

■ **PART ONE** looks at evangelism in churches today. What is evangelism? Why <u>do</u> it? How is the church doing?

■ **PART TWO** shows examples of great churches sharing their faith. You can see and analyze what is possible.

■ **PART THREE** will help you move into the possibilities God has in mind for you.

■ **PART FOUR** is your 40-day personal prayer journal. Move closer to God through your individual prayer, then discuss it with your *Unbinding the Gospel* group.

Then I heard every creature in heaven and on earth and under the earth and in the sea, and all that is in them, singing, "To the one seated on the throne and to the Lamb be blessing and honor and glory and might, forever and ever!" (Rev. 5:13)

Your 40-Day Prayer Journal

Start your prayer journal tomorrow.

Welcome to your own time with God, a page for each day for six weeks. Let's start with a confession—mine! I talk *such* a good game about prayer, but doing it isn't always so easy! I swoop eagle-like on currents of glorious inspiration—every once in a while. But many days I'd rather talk than pray, read than pray, sleep than pray. Gosh, I'd rather alphabetize the garage than pray! I possess impressive avoidance mechanisms to shield myself from going face-to-Face with God. And yet, I *have* developed a daily prayer discipline.

I've learned not to wait to brush my teeth until I am moved by a spontaneous burst of creativity. I don't wait to exercise until I am smitten with a wild desire to lift the dreaded weights! It's pretty much the same with prayer. I've learned that my life is better if I pray every day. Other people's lives are better if I pray every day. So at 5:30 almost every morning, we're up praying at our house. On the other days, I pray when I take long walks or paddle my kayak. So if you have tendencies to think, "I'll pray in an hour...I'll pray after I finish changing the oil in the car...I'll pray tomorrow—at Tara," here are daily prayer exercises from a kindred spirit! They may help you get into the habit of praying. I promise—it's worth the effort!

Why Pray?

Good prayer habits act like an incubator for our relationships with God. If we pray, if we show up, God has a much better chance of getting through to us. Over time, we know ourselves better.

I have great news: prayer affects more than you! Our research demonstrates that when people pray, talk with a prayer partner, and

> "Pray as though everything depended on God. Work as though everything depended on you."
>
> *St. Augustine, Bishop of Hippo (North Africa) (354–430)*

talk about faith with others at church, something exciting happens. Relationships improve. Families tend to get happier. People who pray mysteriously "have the words" when the Holy Spirit arranges situations for them to talk with people who don't have a conscious faith life. Prayer helps us *listen* to other people for real.

Prayer changes things—within us and for others.

We're probably not going to slip one day and fall into Christian maturity. Prayer is about developing a relationship with God, not just "believing in God." God is consistent with us. Could we learn to be consistent with God? Are you ready to get started? Leaf through this section of *Unbinding the Gospel* and see if it looks inviting to you. Take a moment in the quiet (or several days) to ask yourself if the Spirit is nudging you to commit to this prayer habit.

Are you ready to try—for yourself, and for what God can do for others through *you*?

Will you try to pray consistently for six weeks? If you agree to try, sign here:

Signature:_____Date:_____

How Do I Use This Prayer Journal?

Use Part Four of *Unbinding the Gospel* as you study the rest of the book with a small group of people. You can certainly read *Unbinding the Gospel* on your own. You can pray through the prayer journal (Part Four) and never mention it to a soul. However, the book and the exercises are most effective if you study the chapters with a small group of people, and if you talk about your individual prayer insights with your small group or with a prayer partner. The best way is to combine all three elements:

- Pray through the journal by yourself
- Talk and pray with a prayer partner on Day Five each week
- Study the ideas in the book with your small group

<u>When</u> Should Your Group Start Praying through These Exercises?

Your group will probably study *Unbinding the Gospel* for eight weeks. This prayer journal lasts for 40 days. When should you begin praying? Begin the exercises when it makes most sense for your group. *If I were leading an eight-week study, I would <u>complete</u> the first week of exercises in time for the group's discussion of* *chapter 4.* This timing allows your group to form before you add the prayers. It also gives everyone in the group a week of common prayer experience at the same time you discuss chapter 4, the prayer chapter in *Unbinding the Gospel.*

I have labeled the exercises with numbered days rather than days of the week. Your study group meets on Day 7. Start Day 1 right after your group meeting. You will each have completed a full week of prayer exercises by the time you meet together again. You'll have lots to talk about!

Prayer Partner

Talking about your reaction to these exercises with someone else from your small group at church, a neighborhood friend, someone in your retirement community or your family will maximize the benefit of your six weeks of prayer. A mother told me, "We are praying together in the morning and talking about what God's showing us at dinner [two parents, a very active second grader and two junior high school kids]. We all love the prayers, scriptures and exercises for different reasons. Doing this together is awesome—it's helping us understand each other better and love each other even more." Whatever your living situation, please talk about your response to these exercises with at least one other person, once a week, in person or by phone. Budget at least a "check-in" time about your prayer when your *Unbinding the Gospel* study group meets each week. Half the fun is getting to see how everyone's individual prayer is progressing.

"It is true that we cannot be free from sin, but at least let our sins not be always the same."

St. Teresa of Avila, Spanish mystic, theologian & reformer of the Discalced Carmelites, (1515–1582)

Prayers for Can't-Sit-Still *and* Artistic Types!

Not everyone thinks, works, learns or prays the same way. Some people are highly creative and learn best when they use their hands, voices, bodies. Do what you works for you—do what you love. Draw, act out parts, sculpt a model of the scripture! Some of us pray best while moving or talking. My ADHD (attention deficit hyperactivity disorder) friends have fits when they even *think* about sitting in one place in silence. *Our motto is: give new ways to pray a chance, but pray in the ways that work for you!* This prayer journal offers you 40 days of varied prayer exercise suggestions. I could never list all the options, but here are a few:

■ Walk around the room while you read the scripture, timing the words with your steps or your breath

- Read the scripture out loud
- "Act out" the Bible story
- DRAW or form a Play-doh™ figure of the scripture
- Read the scripture sitting, then pray walking. Return to your chair to sketch or write notes.

I include a "Notes, Lists, Drawings, Thoughts, Insights" section for each day. Write a list, sketch a drawing, do whatever makes the day's exercise most effective and memorable to you. Experiment. Have fun with it. If you don't know what you want to do, ask God. You may be surprised at some of the nudges you get from the Spirit!

Same Time, Same Place

William Law, a wise eighteenth-century English theologian and writer, influenced generations of pastors, including the Wesleys, from whose work the Methodist churches began. Law suggested that we have one special chair in which to pray each day. Choose a (not too) comfortable, straight-backed chair in a room away from family traffic patterns. Only pray and do your devotions in this chair during these six weeks—no mystery novels, no TV, no phones, no iPods,™ no directing kids' homework! Keep your supplies right next to your chair so you don't have to interrupt your prayer time to go get something.

Choose a specific time to try to pray each day. Although I have written as if you are praying early in the morning, you may be drawn to a time after breakfast, when everyone else has left the house; lunch time in your office; or evening (instead of TV or before bed). If in doubt, ask God what time you should choose. Don't drive yourself crazy about exact adherence to A Rigid Plan, but consistency will help you develop the habit of prayer! Light a candle each day as you sit down if you wish, to remind yourself that Christ is right there with you. You can develop simple habits that will help grow your relationship with God.

Supplies

- Bible
- Pens, pencils, art supplies, clay
- Reading glasses
- This book
- Prayer candle and matches
- Journal or extra writing paper
- 3" X 5" cards

Plan Ahead

You will need to make a few, simple preparations for the prayer days listed below.

1. **Prayer partner days** are Day 5 of each week. You'll want to look at that day's reading before you arrange to meet with your prayer partner, whether in person or by phone. It may be more convenient to meet on a different day. That's great – just try to do the other days in order.

2. **Extra supply days**, when a household object will help your prayer:

   ▲ *Week 1, Day 3:* Your newspaper or a news magazine (*Time, Newsweek,* etc.)

   ▲ *Week 2, Day 2:* A scarf, a blindfold or a sleeping eye-cover (anything to cover your eyes), and a cup or mug

   ▲ *Week 2, Day 3:* Your church's latest newsletter (or website printout of your church's mission projects)

   ▲ *Week 5, Day 4:* A string of pearls or beads, prayer beads, or Mardi Gras beads

> "Prayer is as natural an expression of faith as breathing is of life."
>
> *Jonathan Edwards, American Congregationalist pastor & theologian (1703–1758)*

Pattern of the Exercises

You will have a scripture, a prayer exercise, note-taking space and a closing prayer for each day of the next six weeks. Some days suggest an exercise to be carried out during the day, but you will always have your scripture and prayer time first. If you pray in the evening, pray the night before. Do the exercise the next day. The weeks' prayers follow a pattern:

Days 1–4: a new prayer exercise
Day 5: an exercise that works best with a prayer partner
Day 6: a review/reflection day when you:
  (A) Review this introduction, and answer two key questions:
    (1) What are the most important things I've learned this week?
    (2) What one thing am I going to tell my study group tomorrow?
Day 7: group day. Take notes or jot down ideas in your journal.

Bible Readings

Each prayer day starts with a scripture. Scripture means "writing." In this case I'm referring to a passage from the Christian Bible. The

Bible contains two main parts, the "Old Testament," sometimes called the "Hebrew Scriptures." They were originally written in the Hebrew language. These scriptures were all written before Jesus was born. We date our years as starting with Jesus' birth at time point zero and his death in year 33. The second part of the Christian Bible is called the "New Testament" or the "Greek Scriptures." This part was written (in Greek) about Jesus' life, death and resurrection, between the years 55 and 125 A.D. (Anno Domini), or C.E. (Common Era).

You may have studied the Bible for years and feel very comfortable with biblical literature and history. You may not own a Bible. If you don't have a Bible, could you ask your pastor or the person leading your group where to get one and which translation they'd suggest? I would suggest a study Bible, because they explain things. I list a scripture for each day by the name of the "book" of the Bible (often the name of the person who wrote it). The first number after the name of the book is the number of the chapter. Then there's a colon (:). The next number is the number of the verse in the chapter. Most Bibles include a list of the books of the Bible somewhere near the front. The books consist of different types of writings—histories, letters of advice, poetry, writings from prophets and "Gospels," which are stories about Jesus' life. Your Bible may have tabs on the side so you can get to different books quickly.

Don't be a hero! Don't gut this out alone. **Loads** of people have questions about the Bible, and lots of them have been sitting in church for 20 years. Ask for help **before** you get frustrated or feel awkward! If you aren't sure how to locate the scripture readings, ask your group leader or best friend in the class to mark the next week's passages in your Bible with Post-it^R notes—no fuss, no muss and no lost time! (Read the notes in your study Bible—they're fascinating.) You'll learn a bit about the Bible, and get right on to the fun part—actually *reading* the scriptures and praying! Enjoy!

As You Pray Each Day

Sit in your chair. Light a candle if you wish. Breathe deeply and slowly. Close your eyes and ask Christ (or God, or the Spirit) to help you pray. Ask God to help you understand whatever you need to see next. Then, when you feel centered, read the entire day's exercise to familiarize yourself with it. Finally, take a deep breath, exhale, read the scripture and begin!

Keep the Main Thing the Main Thing!

The point of these prayer exercises is to help you pray with scripture, move closer to God and grow as a Christian. If you are drawn into a certain phrase of scripture, if you feel a sense of God's presence one day, tarry with it (stay there)! Our increasing awareness of the presence of God is what matters in our spiritual lives. The exercises are only a tool to help you try new ways of being more receptive to the Spirit. If you and God are drawn into a "side conversation," it's probably the main thing. Stay with God, not the program!

Christ loves us. He loves it when we try to mature in our relationship with him. Our prayers help us. Our prayers help others more than we will know. Ready to move into this faith adventure? All right, let's go!

"It was love that led God to create. There could be nothing lacking in God, nothing wanting to his goodness or his joy. It was out of love alone that he willed creation, that there might be beings, apart from himself, who would partake of his infinite goodness and joy."

St. Birgitta of Sweden (1303–1373)

Steadfast Love, from Everlasting to Everlasting

Scripture: Psalm 103

Light a candle to remind you of God's presence. Take some slow, deep breaths and relax. Sit quietly for a few moments and ask God to bless this six-week prayer adventure and your group's study of *Unbinding the Gospel*.

Let's start with Psalm 103.

Will you read the Psalm slowly? Which lines speak to you most powerfully? Write them down. Sit quietly for a moment. Now read the Psalm again, slowly. What words or phrases shine out at you this time? Mark them in your Bible or jot them down here.

What in this Psalm do you ___know___ to be true? Have you experienced any of this yourself? Can you remember a specific time in your life when you blessed the Lord with all that is in you? When you experienced forgiveness? Healing? Redemption? Love? Renewal of your youth? Mercy? Graciousness? Steadfast love? Compassion? Your own mortality? God's majesty? Everyone's moments with God are different. Ask God to show you yours. Write down what feels most important.

Notes, lists, drawings, ideas:

Prayer: God, you are the Holy One of Israel. Your steadfast love endures forever, from everlasting to everlasting. I bless your holy name with everything that's in me. Thank you for my life, for my family, for my friends and the people you can reach through me. Please let me know you better as I go through these next six weeks. I will meet you here tomorrow. Amen.

Leave It?

Scripture: Matthew 4:17–22

The Bible has four gospels, books that tell the story of Jesus' life: Matthew, Mark, Luke and John. This story tells about the beginning of Jesus' ministry. Jesus starts with two things: (1) he asks people to repent (the word means "turn around") because the kingdom of heaven is getting close, and (2) he starts calling disciples. Peter, Andrew, James and John leave their whole lives behind—boats, jobs, families—to go with Jesus. Immediately.

We only have so much time, so much energy and so much focus in our lives. If we want to follow Jesus, we have to create some space and time. You've started. You're connected with a church. You are praying right now. That's a big deal. But it might be only the beginning of starting a richer life with God.

Close your eyes. Ask Jesus if he'd like you to follow him. Does he want you to leave anything behind? An opinion? A sin? TV? A habit? Something you want? Money? Being a couch potato? A relationship? Some old, moldy bitterness? Ask Jesus directly if there is anything you are using to keep him at a "safe" distance!

Hold your hands in front of you, palms up, little fingers touching. Imagine the idea or habit or activity or grudge rests in your hands. Now, with a prayer, with great love in your heart, even if it's a little scary, hand it to the Lord.

Notes, lists, drawings, ideas:

Prayer: Oh, Lord. Here is what I think you'd like me to leave behind to follow you. I'm handing it to you now. Help me not to pick it up again! Help me see you and myself with better focus in these 40 days. Please let me begin to understand how much you love me. Amen.

Seeing with Jesus' Eyes

Scriptures: Mark 1:39–45; 6:30–44; 8:2

Read these stories slowly. Picture what was going on. How did Jesus feel toward the people? Write down a few words in the space below. Jesus was moved with pity toward the leper in Mark 1. He had compassion for the crowd that had gathered in Mark 6. This is how Jesus looks at us—with love, with pity, with compassion. Then he cares for us and gives us what we need: healing, teaching, encouragement and physical help like food.

Last week, I read on CNN.com about a 15-year-old girl in Atlanta who saw a Mercedes parked next to a homeless man. She was overwhelmed by the sight and thought, "if that guy had a smaller car, the homeless man could have something to eat." Her idea started a family discussion. Her family decided to sell their large house and downsize to a smaller one so they could send the extra money to feed families in Africa. We can *feel compassion _and_ take action* if we see people and situations with Christ's eyes.

Will you try an experiment? Pick up your newspaper or news magazine, or go to your Internet news site. Ask God to let you see with Christ's eyes. Now pray for someone you have read about. Is the Spirit is moving you to do anything?

Notes, lists, drawings, ideas:

Realization: "In Louisville, at the corner of Fourth and Walnut, in the center of the shopping district, I was suddenly overwhelmed with the realization that I loved all these people, that they were mine and I theirs, that we could not be alien to one another even though we were total strangers. It was like waking from a dream of separateness...I have the immense joy of being human, a member of a race in which God Himself became incarnate..."
Thomas Merton, Trappist monk and American Catholic writer (1915–1968)

A Prayer Exercise—Literally!

Scripture: Mark 7:24, 31; 8:22, 27; 9:2, 30, 33

Jesus and the disciples sure walked a lot! If we want to be Christlike, this may be part of it. Walking slows you down. It clears your mind and gets the kinks out of your body. Walking gives you time to think about bigger things than grocery lists, shrieking toddlers and when-can-I-run-the-to-the-post office? Walking gives you time to pray. Walking can become prayer. So let's try a literal prayer *exercise* today. Marathoners, cane-walkers, swimmers, dancers, weight lifters, wheelchair athletes, basketball players—pick your sport!

Get to your exercise place, outside or in. Drink some water. Feel it filling you up. Ask God to "baptize" the time. Then start moving slowly. As you move, think about your breath. Breathe in and feel as if you're breathing in new air that will expand you, that will clear you out, get the buildup out of your system. Exhale and imagine the old ideas, obsessive thinking, stale opinions, frustrations leaving your body and soul.

After a while you may want to pick up the pace to fit what your body needs. Inhale and ask the Spirit of Christ to come into you and to heal you. Exhale and let go of more gunk!

Later in your exercise time, you could ask God to give you images of people or situations that you could pray for. They could be the other people in your gym, or in the park where you're walking. Stay attuned to how *you* pray with *your* body. One way you might pray is to imagine surrounding the person or situation with the same Spirit that is cleansing you. When you're done, walk slowly. Look at everything around you, notice the sounds and smells, the people. Bless them all. Do some stretches as you thank God.

Notes, lists, drawings, ideas:

Prayer: Oh God, renew my strength. Let me run and not be weary, walk and not faint. Amen.

Encouragement in Christ

Genesis 2:18; Mark 6:7; Philippians 2:1–4

What do these scriptures have in common? Read them again — do you see a common thread? God says it isn't good for Adam to be alone and makes Eve, Adam's partner. Jesus sends the 12 disciples out into ministry — in pairs. Paul tells the Philippians that because they are Christians, that they should be like Christ. They should be of the same mind, be humble, serve each other, and look to each other's interests. Have you ever heard anyone say that you can't be a Christian alone, that being a Christian has to do with relationships, both with God and with other people? These readings are a few of the places where the Bible says it!

There are times when we need to be alone with God, alone with our souls. Other times, we need to be able to talk with a trusted friend about our faith.

In ancient Irish monasteries (during the sixth, seventh, and eighth centuries), the brothers and sisters each had a "soul friend." Soul friends, in the deep and mysterious love of Christ, listened, held confidences, prayed together and talked about the deepest spiritual matters. Would you be willing to invite someone to be your prayer partner for this 40-day prayer journey? You could ask your spouse, your best friend, your dad, or someone at church whose faith you respect. Your *Unbinding the Gospel* group could choose prayer partners at your next meeting. Will you sit quietly and reread the scriptures? In the silence, think about serving someone else by being their prayer partner. Think what it would be like to have someone with whom you could talk for real, in absolute confidence. Ask God to show you anything you need to see.

Notes, lists, drawings, ideas:

Inspiration: "Our method of proclaiming salvation is this: to point out to every heart the loving Lamb, who died for us, and although He was the Son of God, offered Himself for our sins .... to name no virtue except in Him, and from Him and on His account, to preach no commandment except faith in Him; no other justification but that He atoned for us; no other sanctification but the privilege to sin no more; no other happiness but to be near Him, to think of Him and do His pleasure; no other self denial but to be deprived of Him and His blessings; no other calamity but to displease Him; no other life but in Him."
Count Nicholas von Zinzendorf, founder of the Moravians (1700–1760). Early Moravians sold themselves into slavery to evangelize the West Indies.

Reflection Day

REVIEW. Think back over your week of prayer. Reread your favorite scripture from the week. Review your notes, lists, insights. How is your prayer going? Review the introduction to Part Four, beginning on page 149. Which ideas from the Introduction do you need to pay attention to this week? Take some notes.

Then, answer two questions:

Question 1: What are the most important things I've learned/discovered/remembered this week?

Question 2: God, what one insight would you like me to share with my study group when we meet?

Insight: "But not only faith, perfect and in every way complete,

But all right knowledge of God is born of obedience."

John Calvin, French/Swiss theologian, founder of Presbyterian and Reformed churches (1509–1564)

Group Meeting Day

Enjoy your time together! Tell each other what you've learned. Talk about your *Unbinding the Gospel chapter.* Pray together.

Notes & insights from your group time:

Hymn

REFRAIN: It's me, it's me, it's me, oh Lord, standing in the need of prayer.
            It's me, it's me, it's me, oh Lord, standing in the need of prayer.
VERSES:
Not my brother, not my sister, but it's me, oh Lord
Standing in the need of prayer. *(sing twice, then refrain)*

Not the preacher, not the sinner, but it's me oh Lord
Standing in the need of prayer. *(sing twice, then refrain)*

Not my mother, not my father, but it's me oh Lord
Standing in the need of prayer. *(sing twice, then refrain)*

Traditional African-American Spiritual

Holy Reading

Scripture: Isaiah 40:10–17; 28–31

Will you read these words as a love letter from God?

Sit quietly for a minute, breathing slowly, letting go of thoughts and feelings. Just be with God for a few minutes. As you inhale, then exhale, feel as if you are living in the very center of your body, where you breathe.

Now read the prophet Isaiah's words slowly. Which lines speak to you most powerfully? What does Isaiah teach you about God? About yourself?

Sit in the silence with God for several more minutes. Now read the scripture again, slowly. What words and ideas strike you as most important? Gleam out at you? Offer God several more minutes of silence. Just be with God. What do you notice?

Notes, drawings, memories, insights:

Prayer: Holy God of Israel, thank you. I can't begin to understand how great you are. Whole countries are like drops of water to you. Please help me to understand that even though you are that majestic, the creator of all, you love me so much that you gather and carry me like a lamb, that you lead me gently through my life, that you will give me power and strength to mount up with wings like an eagle. Thank you, God. Amen.

Blind? *What* Don't I See?

Scripture: Mark 10:46–52

Supplies: blindfold, cup/mug

Sit quietly, breathe deeply. Exhale slowly. Then slowly read this story about Jesus and the blind man named Bartimaeus. Read it again and pay close attention to the details. What feels important in this story? Make some notes. Do you see that Bartimaeus won't stop badgering Jesus for healing? Jesus asks him a direct question, "What do you want me to do for you?" Bartimaeus answers and he regains his sight.

We all have blind spots in our lives. What are yours? What can't you see clearly? What do you do over and over because you can't re-envision anything new? What's keeping you from seeing? What *don't* you want to see?

Will you try an experiment? Sit quietly. Read the story again. Now, sit in your prayer chair and put on your blindfold and hold your begging cup and pretend to be Bartimaeus for a while. What do you notice around you? Do you *want* to be healed, or is it more comfortable to stay the way you are? Do you have the courage to call out to Jesus? Loudly? What's your blind spot?

If you dare, answer Jesus' question: "What do you want me to do for you?"

Alternate version: You could take a field trip and be Bartimaeus on a bench at the mall, at a museum, at church, at a bus stop. It might be a bit more subtle if you skipped the blindfold and cup in public! But you could shut your eyes and pretend! Listen to the people rushing past you, living their lives, seeing clearly. Do you want to join them, or do you want to keep sitting? Will you ask Jesus to heal you?

Notes, drawings, thoughts:

Singing Prayer: Amazing grace, how sweet the sound that saved a wretch like me.
I once was lost, but now am found, was blind, but now I see.
John Newton, English hymn, 18th century

Prayer for a Ministry

Scripture: 1 Thessalonians 1:1–5; Ephesians 6:18–20

Supplies: printout of ministry opportunities from your church's website

Did you know that these first words of Paul to the Thessalonians are the earliest writing in the New Testament (the Greek Scriptures)? First Thessalonians is even older than the Gospels. What are these very first words from a Christian leader? He sends a loving greeting, then tells them, "we're always praying for you, and for your ministry." Later, he instructs the Ephesians to pray always in the Spirit and to "always persevere in supplication for all the saints. Pray also for me…"

Are we praying this seriously for each other today? Not most of us. Not most of our churches. Most of us don't know that prayer is a lifeline to God, not a flowery speech. Let's start with the kind of prayer that Paul is talking about—prayer for the saints and for ministries. Read about your church's ministries in your newsletter or on the website. Ask God which ministry you should pray for: the Habitat project, the kids' mission trip to Tennessee, the women's group's collection of school kits, the medical trip to Honduras.

The Quakers have a deep understanding of the mystery and subtle power of Christ's Spirit. Quakers do not demand. They don't "storm the gates of Heaven." They wait upon the Spirit to work in the Spirit's own time and ways. Quakers describe intercessory prayer for people as, "holding them in the light."

Try it now. "Hold" the ministry and the people in your hands as you pray, feeling that you are surrounding them with God's love and blessings. Let God put different people into your hands, into the light of the Spirit. Perhaps you hold the youth group for a while. Next the chaperones, then the people they will be serving. Ask God if there is anything else you could do, beyond today's prayer—volunteer? Recruit more people to go on the trip? A money contribution? Notes of encouragement? More prayer tomorrow?

Notes, drawings, thoughts:

Prayer: Oh God, hold me in the light as your Spirit teaches me to pray for others. Amen.

Joy

Scripture: Psalm 66

Joy! Deep, abiding joy in God and in being God's child—that's what this psalm is about. What a concept!

Is joy something you think about when you think about being a Christian? (Or do you usually think about stuff like ordering the communion supplies and racing off to the next committee meeting?) What is this joy about? Joy probably isn't the giddy happiness of the hippity-hoppity, smiling, giggly Christian. Joy probably isn't the cartoonish "fear of the Lord" of the dour, frock-coated, rigidly upright Christian with an overbearing sense of the majesty of God. Yet both excitement and awe at the majesty of God would be part of our response to the Creator of the Universe, our Father which art in Heaven.

Is the joy this psalm talks about our response to a glimpse of God's glory and love? How do you perceive God's awesome deeds and great power? Do you know the joy of answered prayer? Have you ever felt joy to see Christ's presence in some person? Do you respond with joy when you sense that the Spirit is at work? Write about it here. Speak the psalm's words out loud.

Carry some 3" x 5" cards in your pocket today. As you go through the day, look for signs of God's work, God's actions, God's power, God's glory. Look for signs of joy—outside you and inside you. Every time you think you may be seeing something that reflects God, write it down. Paperclip or copy your notes here.

Notes, drawings, thoughts:

Prayer: Beloved God, I ***want*** to praise you. I ***want*** to sing the glory of your name. But I know I don't see you clearly enough. Please give me glimpses of your mighty deeds, your power, your glory, your mysterious presence in my life today. Let me be a little more conscious of you in my life. Thank you. Amen.

Praying for Each Other

Scripture: James 5:13–18

Prayer for each other has always been a crucial part of being Christians together. Read this scripture to see what James thought about it. (James was Jesus' actual brother and one of the most respected leaders of the Jerusalem church, along with the apostles.) Are you willing to pray for another person and to allow that person to pray for you? Here is an exercise to do, first alone, then with your prayer partner:

Sit quietly for about two minutes. Breathe deeply and get quiet inside. Ask God one thing God wants you to ask your prayer partner to pray about for you. It may be forgiveness, strength to go through each day without satisfying an addiction. The Spirit may prompt you to ask for prayer for healing, for a healing of anger, for boundaries, for a growth in understanding, patience, love, or for discernment of a specific situation or relationship.

There's only one rule: the prayer must be for *you*—not your mother-in-law, not your child, not for people at work. Ask God what you need prayer for.

Arrange to meet with your prayer partner sometime today. You can meet for lunch, for a walk, at church, or even on the phone if it's not possible to get together in person. Talk with each other about what you're learning through these prayer days. Then go somewhere private and pray for each other. You could choose to pray in lots of ways. Do what's comfortable for you. Some of you will want to talk in person or on the phone, then pray for each other at home, during your prayer time. Some people sit in comfortable chairs in the same room, or on the phone, and pray silently for the other person for five or ten minutes. (You could do the "hold them in the Light" Quaker prayer from two days ago.) Others pray out loud. Some people hold hands, or place a hand gently on the other person's shoulder or forearm. Talk about it first, and do what's comfortable. Praying at ALL is hard for most of us, so you don't need to do things that make you squirm in embarrassment! (But I'm not letting you totally off the hook—no cell phone prayer while driving! Pray for real!) Agree to pray for each other each day until you meet again next week.

Notes, drawings, thoughts:

Prayer: Lord Jesus, please bless my prayer partner in this way:

_____

_____Amen.

Reflection Day

REVIEW. Think back over your week of prayer. Reread your favorite scripture from the week. Review your notes, lists, insights. How is your prayer going? Review the introduction to Part Four, beginning on page149. Which ideas from the introduction do you need to pay attention to this week? Take some notes.

Then, answer two questions:

Question 1: What are the most important things I've learned/discovered/remembered this week?

Question 2: God, what one insight would you like me to share with my study group when we meet?

Prayer: Pardon, O gracious Jesus, what we have been; with your holy discipline correct what we are. Order by your providence what we shall be; and in the end crown your own gifts.
John Wesley, Anglican priest and preacher, founder of the Methodist churches (1703–1791)

Group Meeting Day

Enjoy your time to talk, laugh and pray together! Tell each other what you've learned. Pray together.

Notes, thoughts & insights:

Prayer:

The cross is the hope of Christians
The cross is the resurrection of the dead
The cross is the way of the lost
The cross is the savior of the lost
The cross is the staff of the lame
The cross is the guide of the blind
The cross is the strength of the weak
The cross is the doctor of the sick
The cross is the aim of the priests
The cross is the hope of the hopeless
The cross is the freedom of the slaves
The cross is the power of the kings
The cross is the water of the seeds
The cross is the consolation of the bondmen
The cross is the source of those who seek water
The cross is the cloth of the naked.
We thank you, Father, for the cross.
African prayer, 10th century

The High Priest Sympathizes with Our Weaknesses

Scripture: Hebrews 4:14–16

The writer of the letter to the Hebrews loved and understood the Jews' worship of God in the temple in Jerusalem. (The Western Wall, sometimes called the Wailing Wall, is the only part of the temple that remained after the Romans destroyed it in 70 A.D./C.E.) Priests in the temple offered sacrifices to God. The letter of the Hebrews is beautiful. It explains who Jesus is, and the unique sacrifice he made for us—not goats or cattle, but himself. The writer of the letter to the Hebrews calls Jesus the "great High Priest," Because Jesus made the ultimate sacrifice—because he poured out his own life for our sakes, once for all—we can approach the very throne of God and receive mercy and forgiveness.

Light your candle, close your eyes and take a minute or so to get centered. Then read today's passage slowly. Close your eyes and think about it. What phrases felt important to you? Write them down. Then pray for a minute and ask God to show you more. Read the passage again, slowly. Did anything else seem important? Go back and ask God why those parts of the passage are more real for you. What in you needs sympathy from Jesus? What are your weaknesses? What in you needs mercy? Which parts of your life ask God for grace?

Read the passage one more time. Close your eyes. Ask God for the mercy, grace, sympathy or forgiveness you need. Be as specific as you can be.

Notes, drawings, thoughts:

Prayer: Beloved God, you understand me—every part of me, every action of my life. You've been human and know what it is. Thank you for your love for me, for your understanding of my imperfection. I love you for your sacrifice for every human being throughout time. Thank you for your sacrifice for me. I ask for mercy and grace, as you stand beside me before God's throne. Amen.

Blessing

Scripture Numbers 6:22–27

Light your candle. Take a few deep breaths. Now read Numbers 6:22–27. Do you recognize this blessing? Have you ever heard a minister say it? Did your choir sing it at the end of your worship service on Sunday? God gave this blessing to Moses. Moses was to give it to the priests to bless the Israelites. (Moses' brother Aaron was the priest, and Aaron's sons inherited the priestly role.) Blessings in ancient times were very tangible things. They were a spoken word that stayed with the people and places that were blessed. Blessings today are very real, in mysterious ways we can't fathom.

Read the blessing again and let it bless *you*. Think about the times you have felt blessed. Read the blessing again. Ask God to bless you right now, as you sit in your chair. Ask God to bless the whole room. Ask that God keep the room in safety, make his face shine upon you, your family and the whole house. Ask God to lift his countenance upon you (to see you, to look with grace and kindness upon you, your family, your house, and to give you peace). Say "Amen."

"Field trip" option: Thank God for the blessing and ask if you are to bless somewhere else today. You could write the words of the blessing on a 3" x 5" card, then take them to the office, the coffee shop, your neighborhood, and do this same, prayerful blessing. Walk and think the words, pray the blessing silently, wherever God asks you to go. Will God ask you to walk around the block at your neighborhood school, blessing all the children and teachers? Walk the streets of your neighborhood, blessing the homes and your neighbors? Walk through your office, blessing your coworkers and the work that you do together? Walk through the grocery store, silently blessing the shoppers, the salespeople and the food being offered?

Notes, drawings, thoughts:

Prayer:

The Sacred Three, my fortress be encircling me,
Come and be round my hearth, my home.
Fend Thou my kin and every sleeping thing within from scathe, from sin.
Thy care our peace, through mid of night to light's release.
Ancient Celtic blessing on a home, 6th–8th century

Pass It on!

Scripture: 2 Timothy 1:1–5

Timothy was a young Greek man that Paul took under his wing. Timothy helped Paul with letters, he learned from him, prayed with him, acted as Paul's surrogate to churches when Paul was busy. Paul thought of Timothy as his son. Listen to this sentence: "I am reminded of your sincere faith, a faith that lived first in your grandmother Lois and your mother Eunice and now, I am sure, lives in you."

Lois and Eunice had a living faith. That's how Paul talked about Timothy's faith; it was a *faith that lived in him.* And it was a faith that lived first in Timothy's grandmother and mother. This way of talking about faith sounds like some 2,000- years-ago way of talking about DNA! The faith was transmitted through the generations. This mysterious connection with the living God comes to us through the living faith of other people.

Who passed faith to you? How did they do it?

Could you thank them? Call or write a letter? If they are not still alive, you can still whisper "thank you" to them in prayer. You might tell their children. You can always thank God for them.

To whom are you passing your faith? The passing of the faith may take years of praying and loving and caring for someone. This is a precious, living gift that lives within us. Are you willing to ask God to give you spiritual children? They may be young or old. Will you care for them?

Notes, drawings, thoughts:

Prayer: Lord God, thank you for _____, _____ and _____, my spiritual fathers and mothers. I will never forget them. Bless them and let them know of my gratitude. Blessed Holy Spirit, please show me anyone you would like me to take under my wing to care for, so that this burning, living faith will not flicker out with me. Amen.

Pick Your Favorite Scripture

Scripture: ??? You choose!

This is a fun day. You get to pick your ***own*** scripture. Nobody's going to tell you what to do! So go ahead— choose.

Now pick out one sentence or phrase from that scripture. Say it out loud often enough to memorize it.

Decide to do something repetitive today. You could hammer nails, knead bread dough, hand wash delicate clothes, saw boards, beat egg whites, pedal a bike, go for a run, or sit right there and be conscious of your breath. Do something rhythmic, and when you do, repeat your scripture phrase in time to your steps or your canoe paddling, or your hammering. Do it for a long time.

Now go back and read the whole scripture again. Do you understand it differently? Is it more a part of you?

Notes, drawings, thoughts, insights:

Prayer: Thank you, God! Here's what I've learned_____
_____. Will you show me more as the day goes on? Amen!

Praying in Spiritual Agreement

Scripture: Matthew 18:15–20

Prepare to meet your prayer partner: Sit quietly for a bit. Read the scripture carefully. I have written a bit about my understanding of this passage on pages 54 and 55. Will you turn to those pages and reread it? How does this passage strike you? Think about it—write a bit.

Close your eyes and take several minutes to pray silently. Empty your mind; breathe slowly and deeply. After you feel centered, ask if there is any person or situation God would like you to pray for with your prayer partner. Write them down.

Time with your prayer partner: Meet with your prayer partner (face-to-face is best, but if necessary, make an appointment to talk on the phone at a time when you won't be disturbed.) Review how your prayer for each other has gone. How are those situations? Would it help to pray the same prayer, or differently for each other in the coming week?

Discuss today's preparation prayer and the idea of "spiritual agreement." Talk about the situations you discerned you should pray about. Discuss what the real issues are in the situations—and ***how*** to pray. ***What's the situation?*** …A teenager who's getting a bit wild? ***How should you pray for him/her?*** It's best to try to figure out the heart of what's going on. Might it be better to pray that he'll find a deeper relationship with Christ and be drawn to healthier friends? Would it be good to pray for patience and a sense of detachment for his parents? Talk about it with your partner. You may have an "aha!" moment.

When you're in agreement about ***how*** to pray, pray together for these people/situations. You may pray silently, you may pray out loud. Then keep praying during the coming week.

Notes, drawings, thoughts:

Prayer: "Almighty God, you have given us grace at this time with one accord to make our common supplication to you; and you have promised through your well-loved Son that when two or three are gathered together in his Name you will be in the midst of them. Fulfill now, O Lord, our desires and petitions as may be best for us; granting us in this world knowledge of your truth, and in the age to come life everlasting. Amen."

St. John Chrysostom, Archbishop of Constantinople (347–407 A.D./C.E.)

Reflection Day

REVIEW. Think back over your week of prayer. Reread your favorite scripture from the week. Review your notes, lists, insights. How is your prayer going? Review the introduction to Part Four, beginning on page 149. Which ideas from the introduction do you need to pay attention to this week? Take some notes.

Then, answer two questions:

Question 1: What are the most important things I've learned/discovered/remembered this week?

Question 2: God, what one insight would you like me to share with my study group when we meet?

Insight: "The miracle of Communion means the rich bowing down with the poor, the learned with the unlearned, the clean with the filthy, the master with the slave, the privileged with the deprived, the white with the black, and the black with the white."
Rosa Page Welch, Disciples of Christ gospel singer and missionary, 20th century

Group Meeting Day

Enjoy your time to talk, laugh and pray together! Tell each other what you've learned. Pray together.

Notes & insights:

Hymn:

A mighty fortress is our God, a bulwark never failing,
Our present help amid the flood of mortal ills prevailing.
For still our ancient foe doth seek to work us woe,
With craft and power great, and armed with cruel hate, on earth without an equal.

Did we in our own strength confide, our striving would be losing,
But there is one who takes our side, the one of God's own choosing.
You ask who that may be? Christ Jesus, it is he, with mighty pow'r to save,
Victorious o'er the grave, Christ will prevail triumphant!

God's word above all earthly powers, not thanks to them, abideth.
The spirit and the gifts are ours, through Christ, who with us sideth.
Let goods and kindred go, this mortal life also.
The body they may kill, God's truth abideth still, God's reign endures forever.

Martin Luther, founder of the Lutheran churches (1483–1546)
Translated by Frederick H. Hedge, 1852

An Hour for the Spirit

Scripture: John 14:16–26

When you think of God, do you think first of the HUGE God who created the universe, the God on the ceiling of the Sistine Chapel, the God "Out There?" I think many people think first of the God of majesty and mystery, of awe and power, the "transcendent" God. But we also talk about the "immanent" God who's right here with us, in the middle of groups of us, inside each one of us. That's "God *with* us." Jesus in the manger, Jesus who walked on earth, Jesus who is risen and walks beside us, and also the Holy Spirit

Read John 14:16–26. Jesus was preparing his disciples for his death and resurrection. He told them he would be with them in a different way after his death. God would send the Spirit. The Holy Spirit is available to *us,* because *we're* Jesus' disciples too. Jesus offers us guidance, power, minute-by-minute connection with God. This isn't some nice little metaphor. Life in the Spirit is more like plugging into an electric current!

Powerful Christians, mystics, prophets and missionaries have sensed the power and subtle leading of the Holy Spirit for thousands of years now. Too many of us leave God at arm's length, "up in the sky," a vaguely comforting idea, but not too real. Would you be willing to try an experiment? The intent of this isn't to minimize the majesty of God, but to help us see that we can turn to God every moment of the day. The Spirit is with us.

Experiment: Choose an hour of your day today when you're going to offer every choice to God. Each minute of this hour, ask God what you're supposed to be seeing, what you're supposed to do next. It could be an hour at the office—should you talk with someone? Make a phone call? Sort those papers? Bless the lunch room? Ask the Spirit to guide your decisions. If it's the first hour of the day, which side of the bed should you get out of? Should you wash your face or brush your teeth first? Ask which child you should kiss first. Before you open your mouth to speak, ask the Spirit to give you the words to say. Oatmeal or Raisin Bran? This isn't about the cosmic importance of cereal. It's about the cosmic importance of what God can do with us if we learn to offer the daily stuff to God.

Ask. Then do it. What happened?

Notes, drawings, thoughts:

Prayer: Come, Holy Spirit! Please show me how you can be with me every day, every minute, in every decision and action. Come into my life. Be with me, help me grow into holiness. Direct my thoughts and steps. Make me completely your servant. Amen.

Get Ready to Take a Break

Scripture: Luke 4:1–13

Light your candle, relax, breathe slowly and ask God to bless this prayer time.

What a scripture! Think what it must have been like for Jesus when the Spirit led him to be away from other people, food, the safety of town—and straight into the dangers of the desert.

What was the point? Why do people fast and do retreats? Christian spiritual teachers over the centuries have prescribed fasts and retreats. The idea is that if we give up a normal routine, we destabilize ourselves and allow ourselves to find a new stability with God more at the center of our lives. It seems strange that giving up beer or desserts, or not using our computer, iPod,™ cell phone, television, radio, or electric lights could bring us closer to God. But it can.

Pray now. Ask God if there is a day-long fast God would like you to make day after tomorrow. Sit quietly and ask Jesus if there is one specific thing he'd like you to give up so that you can follow him more closely.

We'll do the fast in two days.

Notes, drawings, thoughts:

Prayer: "Grant, Almighty God, that as you shine on us by your word, we may not be blind at midnight, nor willfully seek darkness, and thus lull our minds to sleep. Rouse us with your words every day. May we stir up ourselves more and more to fear your name and thus present ourselves and everything we do as a sacrifice to you, so that you may peaceably rule, and perpetually dwell in us, until you gather us to your celestial home, where you have prepared eternal rest and glory for us, through Jesus Christ our Lord. Amen."

John Calvin, French/Swiss founder of the Presbyterian and Reformed churches (1509–1564)

Feeding Hungry People

Scripture: John 6:1–14

Sit quietly for a few minutes. Read John's story about Jesus feeding 5000 hungry people—hungry for food, hungry for healing of their illnesses, hungry for help from Jesus. Imagine what they felt like.

There was a boy with five barley loaves and two fish. Jesus took the loaves, blessed them, broke them, and the disciples fed 5000 people with the boy's food. Those are the words we use for the Lord's Supper. That meal was like communion. Two thousand years later, a little bit of bread is blessed, broken, and we are filled.

Christian faith satisfies many kinds of hunger: mystical hunger, spiritual hunger, relational hunger, intellectual hunger and physical hunger. We can understand scripture on many levels—from the most abstract to the most literal. We've just thought about this story in an almost literary, poetic way—as a forerunner of communion. Would you like to pray this scripture into reality on another level today? Do you want to *be* one of the disciples in the story? Will you distribute real food to some hungry people?

Pray now, and ask Christ *which* hungry people he'd like you to feed. (Think about it—he's already taken, blessed, broken the food and handed it to you to share. It's in your kitchen. It's in your checking account.) Which of Jesus' people are sitting on the grass in your row? Is it the people at the Salvation Army? At the homeless shelter? Your food pantry? The food donation baskets at your grocery store? Might Jesus want you to buy a goat for the Heifer Project (www.heifer.org)? Pray. Ask Jesus to point out the row of people sitting patiently on the grass, waiting for you.

Notes, drawings, thoughts, insights:

Prayer: Lord Jesus, I want to be your disciple. I want to help you. Will you point out the people in the row I'm supposed to be serving? I will help them. Please bless them, heal them of their pains and illnesses. Let them somehow know that this food is from your hands. Amen.

Make room for God. Make room for joy.

Scripture: Matthew 6:1–18

It's fast day. You asked God two days ago what you could let go of today to make space for God. Be a little hungry so that you can feel your hunger for God. Offer God the space inside yourself so that the Spirit can move in. You joyously served others yesterday. Enter into the joy of offering yourself to God.

Sit silently for several minutes. Read these beautiful words from Matthew's sermon on the mount, particularly Matthew 6:16–18 (you may want to skip the oil on your head part!). This is a day for joy, a secret day for you and God to have an ongoing conversation, between dearest friends. Your faith will grow today.

When you're ready, tell Jesus that you are ready to give up _____ today so that you can learn to rely on God rather than on _____. Each time you want to use the thing from which you're fasting, you might say this prayer: "God, I'm leaving this space open for you to come into. I have gotten used to relying on _____ to fill my emptiness. Fill me with your Spirit, instead."

May your fast for the Lord be a blessing to you. May your day be filled with joy.

Notes, drawings, thoughts:

Insight: "Joy is prayer—Joy is strength—Joy is love—Joy is a net of love by which you can catch souls."
Mother Teresa of Calcutta, Albanian-born Roman Catholic missionary (1910–1997)

Just *Talk* with Your Prayer Partner!

You're great! Congratulations! What an intense four weeks of prayer you've finished. How has this week been? Would you like a day to thank God, to relax a bit? Why don't you meet with your prayer partner and talk about everything. How did this week of fasting and feeding the hungry people affect you? What happened? What did you do? How did you fast? What thoughts did you have? What did you learn? How did you grow close to God?

How is your prayer for each other going? How are those situations in your lives? Talk about what it has been like to pray together for others. Do you need to refocus those prayers? Pray together and thank God for this time. Pray for your church and its leaders.

Notes, drawings, lists, thoughts:

Prayer:

Peace between neighbours,
Peace between kindred,
Peace between lovers,
In love of the King of life.

Peace between person and person,
Peace between wife and husband,
Peace between woman and children,
The peace of Christ above all peace.

Bless, O Christ, my face,
Let my face bless everything;
Bless, O Christ, mine eye,
Let mine eye bless all it sees.

Traditional Celtic Prayer, translation by Alexander Carmichael

Reflection Day

REVIEW. Think back over your week of prayer. Reread your favorite scripture from the week. Review your notes, lists, insights. How is your prayer going? Review the introduction to Part Four, beginning on page 149. Which ideas from the introduction do you need to pay attention to this week? Take some notes.

Then, answer two questions:

Question 1: What are the most important things I've learned/discovered/remembered this week?

Question 2: God, what one insight would you like me to share with my study group when we meet?

Prayer: "My Lord God, I have no idea where I am going. I do not see the road ahead of me. I cannot know for certain where it will end. Nor do I really know myself, and that I think I am following your will does not mean I am actually doing so.

But I believe the desire to please you does in fact please you. And I hope I have that desire in all I am doing. I hope I will never do anything apart from that desire. And I know if I do this, you will lead me by the right road though I may know nothing about it. I will trust you always though I may seem to be lost and in the shadow of death. I will not fear, for you will never leave me to face my perils alone."

Thomas Merton, Trappist monk and American Catholic writer, United States (1915–1968)

Group Meeting Day

Enjoy your time to talk, laugh and pray together! Tell each other what you've learned. Pray together.

Notes & insights:

Hymn:

When peace, like a river, attendeth my way, when sorrows like sea billows roll;
Whatever my lot, thou has taught me to say, it is well, it is well with my soul
    Refrain: It is well (it is well) with my soul (with my soul)
     It is well, it is well, with my soul.
Though Satan should buffet, though trials should come, let this blest assurance control,
That Christ has regarded my helpless estate, and hath shed his own blood for my soul
    (ref)
My sin, oh, the bliss of this glorious thought! My sin, not in part, but the whole,
Is nailed to the cross, and I bear it no more, praise the Lord, praise the Lord, O my soul!
    (ref)
May God haste the day when my faith shall be sight, the clouds be rolled back as a scroll;
The trump shall resound, and the Lord shall descend, even so, it is well with my soul.
    (ref)
Horatio G. Spafford, 1873

Light of the World

Scripture: John 8:12

Jesus is the light of the world. You may dwell in one verse of scripture today. Jesus says, "I am the light of the world. Whoever follows me will never walk in darkness but will have the light of life." Pray it, over and over, synchronizing the phrases with your breathing, or with your walking. Write it on a 3" X 5" card and carry it with you throughout the day. Memorize it.

What do you think about when you hear these words? How can Jesus be the light of the world? What does that mean? What does that mean in your life? Have you ever had dark moments into which Jesus brought light? Has a person brought you the light of Christ?

Close your eyes and ask Jesus to be your light, to help you be aware of how he can enlighten your life. As thoughts occur to you today, write them down on the back of your 3" X 5" card.

Notes, drawings, thoughts:

Prayer:

Soul of Christ, sanctify me
Body of Christ, save me
Blood of Christ, refresh me
Water from Christ's side, wash me
Passion of Christ, strengthen me
O good Jesus, hear me
Within thy wounds hide me
Suffer me not to be separated from thee
From the malicious enemy defend me
In the hour of my death call me
And bid me come unto thee
That I may praise thee with thy saints
and with thy angels
Forever and ever
Amen
The Anima Christi, early 14th century, possibly written by Pope John XXII & a favorite prayer of St. Ignatius Loyola

Surrender

Scripture: Chapter 1 of 1st Samuel

The first chapter of 1 Samuel is the story of the great prophet Samuel's mother, Hannah. In the ancient world, having children was crucially important. Hannah despaired of having children. She offered sacrifices at the place of worship at Shiloh (vv. 9–16). She begged for a boy, promising that she would give him back to God to be a nazirite, a consecrated one. (Numbers 6:1–20 describes nazirites.) Hannah had a son. When he was about two, she gave him to the priest at Shiloh. She gave him back to God forever.

Think about two things: (1) Hannah's desperate longing for a child; and (2) her complete relinquishment to God of the child for whom she had yearned for years. Read the story again.

How could she do it? Surrender of your dearest dream is a thread that runs through the Bible. Think of Hannah and Samuel, of Abraham being willing to sacrifice his son Isaac (Genesis 22), of the death of Jesus on the cross. These are heartbreaking stories of surrender. And of trust in God. These stories twist, midway, into a new story that turns out God's way, a way you'd never expect. Samuel becomes one of the greatest prophets in Israel. God supplies Abraham with a ram to sacrifice instead of Isaac, and Isaac is the ancestor of all the Jews. Jesus' agonizing, unfair death is the foundation of life for the world.

Surrender is giving up your greatest hope, letting go of control, handing over what you'd most love to hang on to. Surrender is one of the deepest ways God works. Have you ever experienced it? Talk with God about surrender. Listen.

Notes, drawings, thoughts:

Prayer: Lord Jesus, thank you. All I have is yours. All I am is yours. Help me hand it to you. Amen.

They Will Know We Are Christians by Our Love, by Our Love.... Oops! Maybe Not!

Scripture: Acts 8:26–40

Did you grow up singing the song, "They will know we are Christians by our love (by our love). They will know we are Christians by our love?" You may have heard St. Francis of Assisi's saying, "Preach the gospel at all times. If necessary, use words." I **hate** to have to say this, but we're surrounded by people who won't have a **clue** that we're Christians by our love. They'll just think we're really nice. They'll never connect the dots! Today in the United States, we have to use words. Most people are like the Ethiopian eunuch. They won't know about Jesus. They won't know the church. We, like Philip, are going to have to explain.

Make a list. Who do you know who isn't connected with a church or consciously connected to God? (You don't need to know them well—your children's friends, new neighbors, new people at the AA meetings, residents of the nursing home or the prison.) Don't say anything to them. Just make your list. Now pray for them. Pray that if it's right, you'll have an opportunity to invite them to lunch, to write them a note. At your **Unbinding the Gospel** group meeting, pray for each others' lists. Pray for a chance to be with them. Pray that they will ask a question or start talking about deep things in their lives. Pray and keep your eyes open. The Spirit may nudge you, just like Philip, and tell you to go over to some chariot and join it!

Lists, notes, drawings, thoughts:

Prayer: Oh, God, please give me a list of people. Help me to pray for them. Let me feel your love for these people. Please give our group ideas about how we can gently and lovingly help the people on our lists to know you. I'm open to nudges of your Spirit. Well, ***help*** me to be open to nudges of your Spirit!! Amen.

The Jesus Prayer—Praying without Ceasing

Scripture: 1 Thessalonians 5:16–22

Supplies: a string of pearls, beads, Mardi Gras beads, prayer beads—anything to hold in your hands, to pass from one hand to the other.

What did Paul mean when he said to "pray without ceasing"? Many Eastern Orthodox monks believe that if we pray simply and often enough, we begin to pray all the time. Our hearts beat in time with the prayer. Our breath is synchronized with it. They pray the "Jesus Prayer," which is very simple:

Lord Jesus Christ, Son of God, have mercy on me, a sinner.

Some people pray the prayer without the last phrase, "a sinner." You choose, or experiment with both. You can pray this prayer many, many ways. I love to pray holding a string of some kind of beads. Hold the first bead and think "Lord Jesus Christ" and inhale very slowly. As you exhale slowly, think "Son of God." Inhale with "have mercy on me," and exhale with "a sinner." Shift that bead into your right hand (or left, if you are left-handed) and pray the same way on the second bead.

You can pray without the beads, just using your breath to feel the rhythm of the prayer. You can whisper the words. You can walk and take a step for each of the four "steps" of the prayer. Pray the Jesus prayer for a long time. When you are finished, thank God.

Notes, drawings, thoughts:

Prayer:

Lord Jesus Christ
     Son of God
     Have mercy on me
     A sinner.
Jesus Prayer, Russian Orthodox Church

Week 5: Day 5 (a Prayer Partner Day)

A Prayer Walk with Your Partner

Scripture: See scriptures from Week 1, Day 4 and Week 3, Day 5

Do you remember all the walking scriptures from our fourth day of Week 1? Jesus and the disciples walked between all the towns. We prayed "on the move." Then, on our prayer partner day in Week 3, we thought about prayer for people in spiritual agreement. Would you like to combine the two today?

Take a prayer walk. Ask God ahead of time which neighborhood or area needs your prayer. It might be the fancy shopping section, an apartment complex near your church or one of your neighborhoods. If it's a tough neighborhood, you might want to go with more than two of you. Pray for everyone who lives there. Pray for each of the houses and schools, the families and visitors. One of you may pray for the right side of the street, the other for the left. Walk quietly together, and "think" your prayer to God. You might ask Jesus to walk through the neighborhood with you. (He is already doing it, but asking may help you to realize it!) Pray for God's presence, peace and protection to blanket the area. Pray that the neighborhood will be infused with Christ's presence.

If people come out and talk with you, you could mention that you're from _____ Church on ___ Street, and that you're doing a prayer walk around the neighborhood. Ask if there's anything specific they'd like you to pray for. Some may say no. Many may ask for prayer.

When you're done, go to a coffee shop and talk about how you experienced the time and the prayer.

Notes, drawings, thoughts:

Prayer:
> We are walking in the light of God, we are walking in the light of God
>> We are walking in the light of God, we are walking in the light of God
>> We are walking (we are walking), we are walking (we are walking)
>> We are walking in the light of God, we are walking (we are walking)
>> We are walking (we are walking), we are walking in the light of God.
> Siyahamb' ekukhanyen kwenkhos, siyahamb' ekukhanyen kwenkhos…
> Caminando en la luz de Dios, caminando en la luz de Dios…

"Siyahamba," South African hymn, 20th century

Reflection Day

REVIEW. Think back over your week of prayer. Reread your favorite scripture from the week. Review your notes, lists, insights. How is your prayer going? Review the introduction to Part Four, beginning on page 149. Which ideas from the introduction do you need to pay attention to this week? Take some notes.

Then, answer two questions:

Question 1: What are the most important things I've learned/discovered/remembered this week?

Question 2: God, what one insight would you like me to share with my study group when we meet?

Prayer:

"Oh God, early in the morning I cry to you.
Help me to pray and to concentrate my thoughts on you:
I cannot do this alone.
In me there is darkness, but with you there is light.
I am lonely, but you do not leave me;
I am feeble in heart, but in you there is help;
I am restless, but with you there is peace.
In me there is bitterness, but with you there is patience;
I do not understand your ways, but you know the way for me…
Restore me to liberty, and enable me to live now
That I may answer before you and before me.
Lord, whatever this day may bring, your name be praised."
Dietrich Bonhoeffer, martyred German theologian (1906–1945)

Group Meeting Day

Enjoy your time to talk, laugh and pray together! Tell each other what you've learned. Pray together.

Notes & insights:

Hymn:

REFRAIN: Get on board, little children; Get on board, little children
            Get on board, little children; there's room for many-a-more.

I hear the train a comin', I hear her close at hand.
I hear those car wheels rumblin' And rollin' through the land. *(ref)*
The fare is cheap, and all can go. The rich and poor are there.
No second class upon this train; no difference in the fare. *(ref)*

Traditional African-American spiritual

Joy Comes with the Morning

Scripture: Psalm 30

Sit with Psalm 30 for a while. Read it. Pray through it. Relax into it. What images, words and phrases catch your attention? Read the Psalm again. Sit quietly and ask God which parts of the Psalm are important for you to see today.

Have you ever experienced a time of great grief? This is a psalm to turn to in a time of real pain in our lives. Somehow, in the times of greatest pain, God waits with us, with hope for the future.

Memorize the last half of verse 5: "Weeping may linger for the night, but joy comes with the morning." Say it to yourself over and over today. Mark it in your Bible. If you ever find yourself in deep trouble or pain, God will be waiting for you here.

Notes, drawings, thoughts:

Prayer: Oh, Holy One! You are always with me. You protect me always. No matter what happens, you care for me, from the depths of your love for me. Help me know that in my deepest sorrow, at the moments of greatest anguish in my life, you are there. You are my hope. Weeping may endure for the night, but joy will come with the morning. Amen.

The Black Rose

Scripture: Numbers 28

Numbers 28 describes the very best things that the Hebrew people offered to God on all sorts of occasions—daily, on the Sabbath, at the beginning of the month and on Passover. They offered God the first and the best. Somehow it feels right that as the flames ascend, crackling, the offering rises up to God. We know God's all around and not "up," but it still makes gut sense that something you burn goes "up" to God.

I think these burnt offerings are the basis for a practice at many church camps, the "Black Rose." At the last campfire, all the campers and counselors write a prayer of confession on a piece of paper. A counselor collects each person's written confession, arranges them all in a neat stack and nails them in the very center of the huge wooden cross. At the end of the campfire worship service, someone lights the prayers of confession. The pages burn and curl around each other. Written words disappear as sparks fly into the night sky. When the fire burns out, the ashen papers, all prayers of confession offered to God, look like a black rose.

Go through your prayer journal from the last five weeks, looking especially at the second day of each week. Make notes of the things you have offered to God—good and bad. Ask God if there is more to add—good or bad. Thank God for accepting your offerings of yourself, who you are, and who God will help you become. Thank God for loving you so dearly. If you wish, burn the pages. Watch your offerings to God rise into the sky.

Notes, drawings, thoughts:

Prayer:

Take my life and let it be consecrated, Lord, to thee.
Take my moments and my days;
let them flow in ceaseless praise,
let them flow in ceaseless praise.

"Take My Life," by Frances R. Havergal, 1874

Pray for the Church

Scripture: Ezekiel 37:1–14

What a scripture! This is a prophecy of prophesies! Have you heard this before? Sometimes people call it the "Valley of Dry Bones." The Spirit took Ezekiel to a valley filled with dried up bones, and God told Ezekiel to prophesy to the bones and tell them that God would bring them to life (vv. 10–11). God told Ezekiel that these bones were the people Israel, the Jews. And God said, "I will put my spirit within you, and you shall live, and I will place you on your own soil; then you shall know that I, the LORD, have spoken and will act" (v. 14).

Have you ever had a moment when you wondered if the church could make it? There are some dead spots! It's pretty scary after a few of those board meetings, or when you look around the sanctuary and only see gray hair (or hair that owes its auburn glories to art rather than nature).

But look what the LORD promised Israel, and through Christ, promises the church. God can bring our driest, deadest, boniest parts to life.

Read this passage again and think of your church and all the churches. Now let's pray in agreement that the breath will enter the bones and they shall live, that vast multitudes of the faithful will stand before God, and that God will put the Spirit upon us. Pray for the church, oh mortal!

Notes, drawings, thoughts:

Prayer: Most powerful God, we are yours. The church is yours. I pray, in spiritual agreement with the others in my group, with all who are reading and have read this book, that you bring life, spirit, energy, joy, creativity and power to us and to your church. We hand the dry bones of our lives to you. Please use us for your purposes, for the rest of our lives. Amen.

Walk to Emmaus—Jesus' Last Words according to Luke

Scripture: Luke 24:13–52

Hope Tinsley Benko, a wonderful, young Episcopal priest, says that if she could only have one bit of scripture, this would be enough. God could use it to teach her the rest! In a way, everything *is* here. Here's the power and might of God revealed in Christ's death and resurrection. Here, on the road to Emmaus, Jesus shows the disciples a great truth that was invisible before. He teaches them patiently, kindly, as he always taught. Now he offers to teach us. Here is the first communion, not Jesus telling about the Lord's Supper, as he did in the upper room the night before he died, but in one way the *real* first communion, where the disciples recognize that the man they've been talking to all afternoon is the risen Lord. They see him for who he is as they eat together.

Read the Walk to Emmaus story slowly. Be still. Read it again. Be still. Read it again and, in the silence, see the hidden thing the Lord has to show you.

Notes, drawings, thoughts:

Prayer: Risen Jesus, risen Lord, I praise you for your power and majesty. Thank you for your Spirit in my life. Let me be your true disciple. Please, show me the parts of myself I would rather ignore. Let me hear sounds to which I've been deaf. Help me slow down. Help me see people and situations with your eyes, understand them with your wisdom. Help me to follow you every day, moment by moment, starting now. Amen.

To the End of the Age—Jesus' Last Words according to Matthew

Scripture: Matthew 28:16–20

This is the "Great Commission." It's the Bible passage we Christians often use to flog ourselves into enough guilt to pry some evangelism out of us! How have we let this glorious promise, trust and challenge become the blunt instrument of "Oughts" and "Shoulds"?

If we hear the promise of Christ's presence with us forever, into eternity, how can we shrink from these words? We are entrusted with the precious people Jesus leaves as he goes to the Father in heaven. These dear ones are left in our care—confused, not knowing, lonely, afraid, some young, some old, some wealthy, some scrambling for rent money—all made for God and not knowing it yet.

What will you do?

Notes, drawings, thoughts:

Prayer: Lord Jesus, Precious One. Thank you. Thank you that you will be with us until you bring us into your unadulterated, shining presence. Use me. Use what is left of my life here on earth to serve you and to help others come to know you. Please give me the chance to share your gospel, to help make new disciples for you, and to teach others about you. Help me see that these aren't your last words to me, but some of your first! Let me live as if I really understood that I will see you face-to-Face, that I will be with you forever. Amen.

Reflection Day

REVIEW. Think back over your 40 days of prayer. Reread your favorite scripture from these weeks. Review your notes, lists, insights. How is your prayer going? Review the introduction to Part Four, beginning on page 149. Which ideas from the introduction do you need to pay attention to as you go forward? Take some notes.

Then, answer two questions:

Question 1: What are the most important things I've learned/discovered/remembered this week and in the past 40 days?

Question 2: God, what one insight would you like me to share with my study group when we meet?

Prayer:

Lord have mercy / Lord have mercy / Lord have mercy
Christ have mercy / Christ have mercy / Christ have mercy
Lord have mercy / Lord have mercy / Lord have mercy

"Kyrie eleison" (Greek for "Lord have mercy"), ancient Christian prayer, with roots in the gospels of Matthew, Mark & Luke

Afterword

I went to my doctor this morning. It was a routine checkup. I need to see him every quarter to make sure that the medications that are supposed to help my blood pressure and cholesterol aren't damaging my liver. Our visits are usually very brief—you know, blood test results, blood pressure, temperature, pulse, followed by, "How are you feeling? Any problems?" to which I answer, "I feel fantastic. No worries at all," and he tells me to come back in three months.

But today was different. My doctor knows that I am a Christian, because it came up in an earlier conversation, maybe a year ago. So today he comes in and says, right off the bat, "I have a question for you. You know, I'm getting older, and that makes any sane person think about their mortality, their spirit…you know what I mean. But any time I begin to feel closer to God, I hear some wacko on TV say something absolutely outrageous in the name of God or religion, and it just smothers my interest. It pushes me in the totally opposite direction."

He said he had a question, but it was left unexpressed. It didn't matter, because with or without a specific question to get us started, we ended up having a good conversation. Three things are still kind of vibrating inside of me from that conversation.

First, people like my doctor—intelligent people, thoughtful, honest people—really want to talk about God and the spiritual life. In spite of the important statistics Martha Grace Reese presents in chapter 3 (don't skip that chapter!), in spite of the fact that generation by generation, fewer Americans identify themselves as religious, everywhere I go I find people like my doctor who are thinking about life, its meaning, its destiny, their soul, their purpose, God. And they want to talk. They need to talk. And they need a conversation partner.

Second, there are plenty of religious wackos around who talk about God a lot. Whatever the religion, there are people who abuse it and say "absolutely outrageous" things "in the name of God or religion," as my doctor said.

And third, there are plenty of sincere and generous people of faith around too who would be great conversation partners for people like my doctor. But here's the problem: so many of them are so afraid of sounding like the wackos that they keep their faith to themselves.

Their silence, of course, makes the strident and outrageous voices seem all the louder, and so their silence ends up being complicit in smothering the interest of the spiritual seekers.

That's why Martha Grace Reese's book is so important. That's why when you turn the last page, you can't just let this be another book you read. You need to let her message affect you, and your faith community, and through you, people like my doctor.

Her image of the pitcher being filled to overflowing is worth the price of the book. Her insight that there can be many sources of motivation and inspiration for faith sharing—many ways to fill the pitcher to the brim—rings very true to me. The statistics she gives sober me, and they motivate me too. And her stories of vibrant congregations give me hope.

Especially today, after my conversation with my doctor.

On my way home from the doctor's office, I turned on the radio and caught the news. More violence. More bad news about global warming. More political division and rancorous name-calling. More stories of people abusing people sexually, kids with guns, crooked politicians, corrupt business executives.

I thought to myself, "What can change this vicious cycle of viciousness?" I switched the radio off as I drove along in silence. I remembered the famous quote from the nineteenth-century British statesman, Edmund Burke: "All that the forces of evil need to win in this world is for enough good people to do nothing," or something to that effect.

I thought, "Somebody should start an organization that would mobilize people—recruit them, train them, support them—so they could be good people who do something so that the forces of evil don't win in this world. This organization would need to accept people just as they are, infuse them with hope, give them a vision of a better world, give them a vision for themselves becoming agents of making that better world a reality. It would need to both practice and preach. Why hasn't somebody started an organization like that?"

And of course, about a quarter mile down the road I realized that somebody had done just that. In fact, it had cost him everything to do so.

But that organization can become so preoccupied with lesser things—including its own institutional survival—that it forgets why it's really here: to recruit people to switch sides and opt out of the vicious cycle and join a cycle of healing, to infuse them with vision, to send them out as change agents, to help them experience transformation and sustain them so they can be lifelong catalysts of transformation, to give them good news to share to counter the bad news that is being reported every hour on the hour.

When you close the covers of Martha Grace Reese's book, I wonder if you could say a prayer asking God to empower you to help your faith community become the kind of organization that Jesus intended it to be, the kind of organization that helps people like my doctor, the kind of organization that brings good news in a bad-news world.

And if your faith community is hopelessly stuck in the mud—let's face it, some are—then don't let that get you down. You have a kitchen table, right? Then invite some friends over and get them talking. Ask them about their faith stories. Ask them about their beliefs about God. Ask them about what kind of world they see, and what kind they dream of, and what they're doing about it, and how God might fit in. Make it clear there aren't "right answers"—just honest answers—and see what happens. See what God does around your table.

If you don't have a kitchen table, invite a friend out for coffee, or take a walk. Don't preach. Just do what Martha Grace talks about in this book. And pray that God will somehow use you to be a blessing to somebody by being an available conversation partner about the things that matter most in life.

You don't need anyone's permission to do this. You don't need a committee or a budget. You don't need a degree in theology or (God forbid) sales and marketing. You just need a pitcher full of motivation—and Martha Grace has given that to you in this book. Let it overflow. Let it pour.

Brian McLaren (brianmclaren.net)

Works Cited

The following is a short list of the religious books referred to in this work. Please refer to the Web site, www.GraceNet.info, for an extensive annotated bibliography of books, Web sites, sociological studies and other resources that may be helpful to you.

Collins, Jim. *Built to Last: Successful Habits of Visionary Companies.* New York: HarperBusiness Essentials, 2002.

Craddock, Fred. *Craddock Stories.* Edited by Mike Graves and Richard F. Ward. St. Louis: Chalice Press, 2001.

Dillard, Annie. *Teaching a Stone to Talk.* Toronto: HarperCollins Publishers, 1988.

Driskill, Joseph D. *Protestant Spiritual Exercises: Theology, History, and Practice.* Harrisburg, Pa.: Morehouse Publishing, 1999.

Duke University. *Survey of Clergy.* www.pulpitandpew.duke.edu/research.html.

Foster, Richard J. *Prayer: Finding the Heart's True Home.* New York: HarperCollins Publishers, 1992.

Haugk, Kenneth C. *Antagonists in the Church: How to Identify and Deal with Destructive Conflict.* Minneapolis: Augsburg Publishing House, 1988.

Marshall, Peter. *The Best of Peter Marshall.* Compiled and edited by Catherine Marshall. Old Tappan, N.J.: Fleming H. Revell Co., 1983.

Montgomery, Lucy M. *Anne's House of Dreams.* New York: Grossett and Dunlap, 1917.

Osmer, Richard Robert. *A Teachable Spirit.* Louisville: Westminster/John Knox Press, 1990.

Payne, Claude, and Hamilton Beazley. *Reclaiming the Great Commission: A Practical Model for Transforming Denominations and Congregations.* New York: Jossey-Bass, 2000.

Peterson, Eugene. *The Message.* Colorado Springs: NavPress, 1995.

Reese, Martha Grace. *Unbinding Your Heart.* St. Louis: Chalice Press, 2008.

_____. *Unbinding Your Church.* St. Louis: Chalice Press, 2008.

_____. *Unbinding Your Soul.* St. Louis: Chalice Press, 2009.

Schwartz, Christian. *Natural Church Development: A Guide to Eight Essential Qualities of Healthy Churches.* Carol Stream, Ill.: Church Smart Resources, 1996.

Smith, Tom W. "The Vanishing Protestant Majority." *GSS Social Change Report No. 49.* Chicago: NORC/University of Chicago, July 2004. (http://www.norc.uchicago.edu/issues/PROTSG08.pdf).

Tuchman, Barbara. *Practicing History.* New York: Alfred A. Knopf, 1981.

For Best Results
download free "Best Practices" memo
at *www.GraceNet.info*
Before You Start

Before you start the *Unbinding Series* in your church, download the latest updates of our organizational resources. Our 10 years of Lilly Endowment-funded research with 3000 congregations reveals startling findings on the best ways to get started. Maximize your results! Use our easy-to-follow, step-by-step, Best Practices Guide for the most powerful impact.

Also download free *Unbinding* supplementary resources (embedded in the *Best Practices Guide* at *www.GraceNet.info).* Find resources for children and youth, coordinated sermons, music and worship plans, organizational planning guides and checklists, retreat plans, prayer resources, promotional materials and detailed research results.